THE PIRATES'
WHO'S WHO

THE PIRATES' WHO'S WHO

*Giving Particulars of the Lives & Deaths
of the Pirates & Buccaneers*

BY PHILIP GOSSE

ILLUSTRATED

The Rio Grande Press, Inc.

GLORIETA, NEW MEXICO · 87535

Edition from which we made
This copy supplied
by
INTERNATIONAL BOOKFINDERS, Inc.,
P. O. Box 1
Pacific Palisades, California 90272

A 1988 RIO GRANDE CLASSIC
First published in 1924
ISBN 0-87380-165-2

The Rio Grande Press, Inc.
GLORIETA, NEW MEXICO · 87535

LIST OF ILLUSTRATIONS

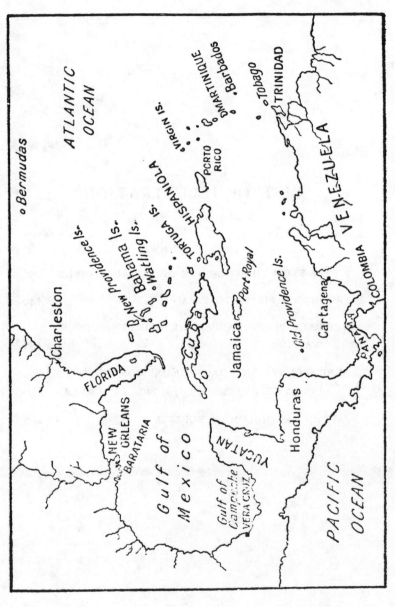

THE DOMAIN OF THE BUCCANEERS

PREFACE

LET it be made clear at the very outset of this Preface that the pages which follow do not pretend to be a history of piracy, but are simply an attempt to gather together, from various sources, particulars of those redoubtable pirates and buccaneers whose names have been handed down to us in a desultory way.

I do not deal here with the children of fancy; I believe that every man, or woman too—since certain of the gentler sex cut no small figure at the game—mentioned in this volume actually existed.

A time has come when every form of learning, however preposterous it may seem, is made as unlaborious as possible for the would-be student. Knowledge, which is after all but a string of facts, is being arranged, sorted, distilled, and set down in compact form, ready for rapid assimilation. There is little fear that the student who may wish in the future to become master of any subject will have to delve into the original sources in his search after facts and dates.

Surely pirates, taking them in their broadest sense, are as much entitled to a biographical dictionary of their own as are clergymen, race-horses, or artists in ferro-concrete, who all, I am assured, have their own "Who's Who"? Have not the medical men their Directory, the lawyers their List, the peers their Peerage? There are books which record the names and the particulars of musicians, schoolmasters, stockbrokers, saints and bookmakers, and I dare say there is an average adjuster's almanac. A peer, a horse, dog, cat, and even a white mouse, if of blood sufficiently blue, has his pedigree recorded somewhere. Above all, there is that astounding and entertaining

7

volume, "Who's Who," found in every club smok-
ing-room, and which grows more bulky year by
year, stuffed with information about the careers, the
hobbies, and the marriages of all the most distinguished persons in every profession, including very
full details about the lives and doings of all our
journalists. But on the club table where these books
of ready reference stand with "Whitaker," "A B C,"
and "Ruff's Guide to the Turf," there is just one gap
that the compiler of this work has for a long while
felt sorely needed filling. There has been until now
no work that gives immediate and trustworthy information about the lives, and—so sadly important in
their cases—the deaths of our pirates and buccaneers.

In delving in the volumes of the "Dictionary of
National Biography," it has been a sad disappointment to the writer to find so little space devoted to
the careers of these picturesque if, I must admit,
often unseemly persons. There are, of course, to be
found a few pirates with household names such as
Kidd, Teach, and Avery. A few, too, of the buccaneers, headed by the great Sir Henry Morgan,
come in for their share. But I compare with indig-
nation the meagre show of pirates in that monumental
work with the rich profusion of divines ! Even during
the years when piracy was at its height—say from
1680 until 1730—the pirates are utterly swamped by
the theologians. Can it be that these two professions
flourished most vigorously side by side, and that when
one began to languish, the other also began to fade?

Even so there can be no excuse for the past and
present neglect of these sea-adventurers. But a
change is beginning to show itself. Increasing
evidence is to be found that the more intelligent
portions of the population of this country, and even
more so the enlightened of the great United States
of America, are beginning to show a proper interest

in the lives of the pirates and buccaneers. That this
should be so amongst the Americans is quite natural,
when it is remembered what a close intimacy existed
between their Puritan forefathers of New England
and the pirates, both by blood relation and by trade,
since the pirates had no more obliging and ready
customers for their spoils of gold dust, stolen slaves,
or church ornaments, than the early settlers of New
York, Massachusetts, and Carolina.

In beginning to compile such a list as is to be found
in this volume, a difficulty is met at once. My original
intention was that only pirates and buccaneers should
be included. To admit privateers, corsairs, and other
sea-rovers would have meant the addition of a vast
number of names, and would have made the work
unwieldy, and the very object of this volume as a
book of ready reference would not have been achieved.
But the difficulty has been to define the exact meaning
of a pirate and of a buccaneer. In the dictionary a
pirate is defined as " a sea-robber, marauder, one who
infringes another's copyright "; while a buccaneer is
described as " a sea-robber, a pirate, especially of the
Spanish-American coasts." This seems explicit, but
a pirate was not a pirate from the cradle to the
gallows. He usually began his life at sea as an
honest mariner in the merchant service. He perhaps
mutinied with other of the ship's crew, killed or
otherwise disposed of the captain, seized the ship,
elected a new commander, and sailed off "on the
account." Many an honest seaman was captured with
the rest of his ship's crew by a pirate, and either
voluntarily joined the freebooters by signing their
articles, or, being a good navigator or "sea-artist,"
was compelled by the pirates to lend them his services.
Others, again, were in privateer ships, which carried
on a legitimate warfare against the shipping of hostile
countries, under a commission or letter of marque,

Often the very commission or letter of marque carried about so jealously by some shady privateer was not worth the paper it was written on, nor the handful of dubloons paid for it. One buccaneer sailed about the South Seas, plundering Spanish ships and sacking churches and burning towns, under a commission issued to him, for a consideration, by the Governor of a Danish West India island, himself an ex-pirate. This precious document, adorned with florid scrolls and a big, impressive seal, was written in Danish. Someone with a knowledge of that language had an opportunity and the curiosity to translate it, when he found that all it entitled the bearer to do was to hunt for goats and pigs on the Island of Hispaniola, and nothing more.

When, at the conclusion of hostilities, peace was declared, the crew of a privateer found it exceedingly irksome to give up the roving life, and were liable to drift into piracy. Often it happened that, after a long naval war, crews were disbanded, ships laid up, and navies reduced, thus flooding the countryside with idle mariners, and filling the roads with begging and starving seamen. These were driven to go to sea if they could find a berth, often half starved and brutally treated, and always underpaid, and so easily yielded to the temptation of joining some vessel bound vaguely for the " South Sea," where no questions were asked and no wages paid, but every hand on board had a share in the adventure.

The buccaneers were a great source of piracy also. When a war was on hand the English Government was only too glad to have the help of these daring and skilful seamen ; but when peace was declared these allies began to lead to international complications, and means had to be taken to abolish them, and to try and turn them into honest settlers in the islands. But when a man has for years lived the free life, sailed out from Jamaica a pauper, to return in six weeks or less with, perhaps, a bag of gold worth two, three, or four thousand pounds, which he has prided himself on spending in the taverns and gambling-hells of Port Royal in a week, how can he settle down to humdrum uneventful toil, with its small profits? Thus he goes back "on the account" and sails to some prearranged rendezvous of the "brethren of the coast."

To write a whole history of piracy would be a great undertaking, but a very interesting one. Piracy must have begun in the far, dim ages, and perhaps when some naked savage, paddling himself across a tropical river, met with another adventurer on a better tree-trunk, or carrying a bigger bunch of bananas, the first act of piracy was committed. Indeed, piracy must surely be the third oldest profession in the world, if we give the honour of the second place to the ancient craft of healing. If such a history were to include the whole of piracy, it would have to refer to the Phœnicians, to the Mediterranean sea-rovers of the days of Rome, who, had they but known it, held the future destiny of the world in their grasp when they, a handful of pirates, took prisoner the young Julius Cæsar, to ransom him and afterwards to be caught and crucified by him. The Arabs in the Red Sea were for many years past-masters of the art of piracy, as were the Barbary corsairs of Algiers and Tunis, who made the Mediterranean a place of danger for many generations of seamen. All this while the Chinese and Malays were active pirates, while the Pirate coast of the Persian Gulf was feared by all mariners. Then arose the great period, beginning in the reign of Henry VIII., advancing with rapid strides during the adventurous years of Queen Elizabeth, when many West of England squires were wont to sell their estates and invest all in a ship in which to go cruising on the Spanish Main, in the hope of taking a rich Spanish galleon homeward bound from Cartagena and Porto Bello, deep laden with the riches of Peru and Mexico.

Out of these semi-pirate adventurers developed the buccaneers, a ruffianly, dare-devil lot, who feared neither God, man, nor death.

By the middle of the eighteenth century piracy was on the wane, and practically had died out by the beginning of the nineteenth, the final thrust that destroyed it being given by the American and English Navies in the North Atlantic and West Indian Seas. But by this time piracy had degenerated to mere sea-robbing, the days of gallant and ruthless sea-battles had passed, and the pirate of those decadent days was generally a Spanish-American half-breed, with no courage, a mere robber and murderer.

The advent of the telegraph and of steam-driven ships settled for ever the account of the pirates, except in China, when even to this day accounts reach us, through the Press, of piratical enterprises; but never again will the black, rakish-looking craft of the pirate, with the Jolly Roger flying, be liable to pounce down upon the unsuspecting and harmless merchantman.

The books devoted to the lives and exploits of buccaneers and pirates are few. Indeed, but two stand out prominently, both masterpieces of their kind. One, "The Bucaniers of America, or a True Account of the Most Remarkable Assaults Committed of Late Years upon the Coasts of the West Indies," etc., was written by a sea-surgeon to the buccaneers, A. O. Exquemelin, a Dutchman, and was published at Amsterdam in 1679.

Many translations were made, the first one in English being published in 1684 by William Crooke, at the Green Dragon, without Temple Bar, in London. The publication of this book was the cause of a libel action brought by Sir Henry Morgan against the publisher; the buccaneer commander won his case and was granted £200 damages and a public apology. In this book Morgan was held up as a perfect monster for his cruel treatment to his prisoners, but although Morgan resented this very much, the statement that annoyed him much more was that which told the reader that Morgan came of very humble stock and was sold by his parents when a boy, to serve as a labourer in Barbadoes.

The greatest work on pirates was written in 1726 by Captain Charles Johnson. The original edition, now exceedingly rare, is called "A General History of the Pyrates, from Their First Rise and Settlement in the Island of Providence, to the Present Time," and is illustrated by interesting engravings.

Another edition, in 1734, is a handsome folio called "A General History of the Lives and Adventures of the Most Famous Highwaymen," etc., "To which is added a Genuine Account of the Voyages and Plunders of the Most Notorious Pyrates," and contains many full-page copperplates by J. Basire and others. The pirates are given only a share in the pages of this book, but it has some very fine engravings of such famous pirates as Avery, Roberts, Low, Lowther, and "Blackbeard."

The third edition of the "History of Pirates," of 1725, has a quaint frontispiece, showing the two women pirates, Anne Bonny and Mary Read, in action with their swords drawn, upon the deck of a ship. While the fourth edition, published in 1726, in two volumes, contains the stories of the less well-known South-Sea Rovers.

After studying the subject of piracy at all closely, one cannot but be struck by the number of pirates who came from Wales. Welshmen figure not only amongst the rank and file, but amongst the leaders.

Morgan, of course, stands head and shoulders above the rest. It is curious how certain races show particular adaptability for certain callings. Up to two hundred years ago the chief pirates were Welshmen; to-day most of our haberdashers hail from the same land of the leek. It would be interesting to try and fathom the reason why these two callings, at first sight so dissimilar, should call forth the qualities in a particular race. Perhaps some of our leading haberdashers and linen drapers will be willing to supply the answer.

I sometimes wonder what happens to the modern pirates; I mean the men who, had they lived 200 years ago, would have been pirates. What do they find to exercise their undoubted, if unsocial, talents and energies to-day? Many, I think, find openings of an adventurous financial kind in the City.

Politics, again, surely has its buccaneers. One can imagine, for example, some leading modern politician —let us say a Welshman—who, like Morgan, being a brilliant public speaker, is able by his eloquence to sway vast crowds of listeners, whether buccaneers or electors, a man of quick and subtle mind, able to recognize and seize upon the main chance, perfectly ruthless in his methods when necessity requires, and one who, having achieved the goal on which he had set his ambition, discards his party or followers, as Morgan did his buccaneers after the sacking of Panama. Nor is Europe to-day without a counterpart to the ruffian crews who arrogantly " defied the world and declared war on all nations."

One great difficulty which the author of this work is met with is to decide who was, and who was not, a pirate.

Certain friends who have taken a kindly, if somewhat frivolous, interest in the compilation of this work have inquired if Sir Francis Drake was to be included; and it must be admitted that the question is not an easy one to answer. The most fervent patriot must admit that the early voyages of Drake were, to put it mildly, of a buccaneering kind, although his late voyages were more nearly akin to privateering cruises than piracy. But if, during the reign of King Philip, a Spaniard had been asked if Drake was a pirate, he would certainly have answered, "Yes," and that without any hesitation whatever. So much depends upon the point of view.

In the 1814 edition of Johnson's "History of Highwaymen and Pirates," the famous Paul Jones holds a prominent place as a pirate, and is described in no half measures as a traitor; yet I doubt if in the schools of America to-day the rising young citizens of "God's Own Country" are told any such thing, but are probably, and quite naturally, taught to look upon Paul Jones as a true patriot and a brave sailor. Again, there is Christopher Columbus, the greatest of all explorers, about whom no breath of scandal in the piratical way was ever breathed, who only escaped being a pirate by the fact that his was the first ship to sail in the Caribbean Sea; for there is little doubt that had the great navigator found an English ship lying at anchor when he first arrived at the Island of San Salvador, an act of piracy would have immediately taken place.

For the student who is interested there are other writers who have dealt with the subject of piracy, such as the buccaneers Ringrose, Cooke, Funnell, Dampier, and Cowley; Woodes Rogers, with his "Voyage to the South Seas"; Wafer, who wrote an amusing little book in 1699 describing his hardships and adventures on the Isthmus of Darien. Of modern writers may be recommended Mr. John Masefield's "Spanish Main," "The Buccaneers in the West Indies," by C. H. Haring, and the latest publication of the Marine Research Society of Massachusetts, entitled "The Pirates of the New England Coast," and last, but far from least, the works of Mr. A. Hyatt Verrill.

The conditions of life on a pirate ship appear to have been much the same in all vessels. On procuring a craft by stealing or by mutiny of the crew, the first thing to do was to elect a commander. This was done by vote amongst the crew, who elected whoever they considered the most daring amongst them, and the best navigator. The next officer chosen was the quartermaster. The captain and quartermaster once elected, the former could appoint any junior officers he chose, and the shares in any plunder they took was divided according to the rank of each pirate. The crew were then searched for a pirate who could write, and, when found, this scholar would be taken down to the great cabin, given pen, ink, and paper, and after the articles had been discussed and decided upon, they were written down, to be signed by each member of the crew. As an example, the articles drawn up by the crew of Captain John Phillips on board the *Revenge* are given below in full :

1.

Every man shall obey civil Command; the Captain shall have one full Share and a half in all Prizes; the Master, Carpenter, Boatswain and Gunner shall have one Share and quarter.

2.

If any Man shall offer to run away, or keep any Secret from the Company, he shall be marroon'd with one Bottle of Powder, one Bottle of Water, one small Arm, and Shot.

3.

If any Man shall steal any Thing in the Company, or game, to the Value of a Piece of Eight, he shall be Marroon'd or shot.

4.

If at any Time we should meet another Marrooner (that is, Pyrate,) that Man that shall sign his Articles without the Consent of our Company, shall suffer such Punishment as the Captain and Company shall think fit.

5.

That Man that shall strike another whilst these Articles are in force, shall receive Moses's Law (that is 40 Stripes lacking one) on the bare Back.

6.

That Man that shall snap his Arms, or smoak Tobacco in the Hold, without a cap to his Pipe, or carry a Candle lighted without a Lanthorn, shall suffer the same Punishment as in the former Article.

7.

That Man that shall not keep his Arms clean, fit for an Engagement, or neglect his Business, shall be cut off from his Share, and suffer such other Punishment as the Captain and the Company shall think fit.

8.

If any Man shall lose a Joint in time of an Engagement, shall have 400 Pieces of Eight; if a limb, 800.

9.

If at any time you meet with a prudent Woman, that Man that offers to meddle with her, without her Consent, shall suffer present Death.

These formalities took time and much argument and the drinking of many bowls of punch, and, when once settled, the next business was to make a flag. The Jolly Roger, consisting of a human skull and two crossed thigh-bones, was generally portrayed in black and white. Some crews preferred a study in red and white. More enterprising captains with imagination and taste, such as Captain Bartholomew Roberts, who was a truly remarkable man and the greatest pirate who ever "declared war upon all the world," aimed at something more elaborate. Roberts flew several flags, all made to his own design.

On one was depicted a "human anatomy," holding a rummer, or glass, of punch in one bony hand, and a flaming sword in the other. Another favourite flag of Roberts had a huge portrait of himself, sword in hand, and two skulls.

Another had a "skellington" standing with either foot firmly placed on a skull, and under one skull were embroidered the letters A. B. H., under the other

A. M. H., which letters stood for a Barbadian's head and a Martinican's head, to warn any inhabitant of either of these islands what to expect if he was so unfortunate as to be taken prisoner by Bartholomew, who never forgot nor forgave two occasions on which he was very roughly handled by ships from Barbadoes and Martinique.

The weak point in all pirate ships was the lack of discipline. Time and again some successful enterprise, almost completed, was thrown away by lack of discipline. No captain could be certain of his command or crew. If he did anything they disapproved of, the crew would throw him in chains into the hold, or as likely overboard, and elect another. It is on record that one ship had elected thirteen different commanders in a few months. Some of the big men retained their commands, Roberts holding the record, for a pirate, of four years, until his death; while Bartholomew Sharp holds the record for a buccaneer.

Having procured a vessel, perhaps little more than a fishing-boat, sometimes only an open row-boat, the embryo pirates would paddle along some coast until they came across an unsuspecting craft, one not too big for the desperadoes to attack. Hiding their arms, they would row alongside, and then suddenly, with shouts and curses, board the vessel, kill any who resisted, and start a cruise in their new ship, their number being increased by volunteers or forced men from amongst the prize's crew. Cruising thus, the pirates would gradually get together a small fleet of the fastest and best sailing vessels among their prizes and increase their crew as they went along.

Both the buccaneers and the pirates had their favourite haunts and places of rendezvous. These had to be within easy sailing distance of one or more regular trade routes, and at the same time had to be in some quiet spot unlikely to be visited by strange craft, and, besides being sheltered from storms, must have a suitable beach on which their vessels could be careened and the hulls scraped of barnacles and weeds. The greatest stronghold of the buccaneers was at Tortuga, or Turtle Island, a small island lying off the west coast of Hispaniola. Here in their most piping days flourished a buccaneer republic, where the seamen made their own laws and cultivated the land for sugar-cane and yams. Occasionally the Spaniards or the French, without any warning, would swoop down on the settlement and break up the small republic, but sooner or later the buccaneers would be back once again in possession.

The favourite and most flourishing headquarters of the West India pirates was at New Providence Island in the Bahama Islands, occupied to-day by the flourishing town of Nassau, now the headquarters of those worthy descendants of the pirates, the boot-leggers, who from the old port carry on their exciting and profitable smuggling of whisky into the United States.

The numerous bays and islands lying off the coast of South Carolina were very popular with the free booters in the late seventeenth and early eighteenth centuries; while Port Royal, in Jamaica, was noted from early days as the port from which the most famous buccaneers sailed for the Spanish Main, and to which they returned with their plunder.

The French filibusters and pirates mostly used the Virgin Islands, while the Dutch patronized their own islands of Curaçao, Saba, and St. Eustatius. But the buccaneers did not allow the chance of nationality to divide them, for Frenchmen, Englishmen, and Dutchmen, all "brethren of the coast," sailed together and plundered the Spaniard in open and equal friendship.

An entirely different group of pirates arose in the South Seas, with their headquarters in Madagascar.

Here the pirates went farther towards forming a permanent society than at any other time during their history, with the exception of the Barbary corsairs, who had their strongly fortified settlements for many years at Algiers, Tunis, and Sallee.

The origin of the buccaneers is interesting, and I cannot do better than quote the opening chapter of Clark Russell's " Life of William Dampier," in the English Men of Action Series, published by Messrs. Macmillan in 1889. He writes :

" In or about the middle of the seventeenth century, the Island of San Domingo, or Hispaniola as it was then called, was haunted and overrun by a singular community of savage, surly, fierce, and filthy men. They were chiefly composed of French colonists, whose ranks had from time to time been enlarged by liberal contributions from the slums and alleys of more than one European city and town. These people went dressed in shirts and pantaloons of coarse linen cloth, which they steeped in the blood of the animals they slaughtered. They wore round caps, boots of hogskin drawn over their naked feet, and belts of raw hide, in which they stuck their sabres and knives. They also armed themselves with firelocks, which threw a couple of balls, each weighing two ounces. The places where they dried and salted their meat were called *boucans,* and from this term they came to be styled bucaniers, or buccaneers, as we spell it. They were hunters by trade, and savages in their habits. They chased and slaughtered horned cattle and trafficked with the flesh, and their favourite food was raw marrow from the bones of the beasts which they shot. They ate and slept on the ground, their table was a stone, their bolster the trunk of a tree, and their roof the hot and sparkling heavens of the Antilles."

The Spaniards, who were jealous of any other nation than their own having a foothold in America.

determined to get rid of these wild but hitherto harm-less buccaneers. This they accomplished, and in time drove the cattle-hunters out of Hispaniola; and to make sure that the unwelcome visitors should not return, they exterminated all the wild cattle. This was the worst mistake the Spaniards could have made, for these wild men had to look for other means of supporting themselves, and they joined the free-booters and thus began the great period of piracy which was the cause of the ultimate breaking-up of the Spanish power in the West Indies.

Of the life on board buccaneer and pirate ships a somewhat hazy and incomplete picture reaches us. The crews were usually large compared with the number of men carried in other ships, and a state of crowded discomfort must have been the result, especially in some crazy old vessel cruising in the tropics or rounding the Horn in winter. Of the relationship between the sea-rovers and the fair sex it would be best, perhaps, to draw a discreet veil. The pirates and the buccaneers looked upon women simply as the spoils of war, and were as profligate with these as with the rest of their plunder. I do not know if I am disclosing a secret when I mention that my friend Mr. Hyatt Verrill, who is an authority on the subject of the lives of the pirates, is about to publish a book devoted to the love affairs of these gentry. I confess to looking forward with pleasure and a certain degree of trepidation to reading his book and to seeing how he will deal with so delicate a subject.

We know that Sir Henry Morgan was married and provided for his widow in his will.

Captain Kidd, wife, and child, resided in New York, in the utmost conjugal happiness and respecta-bility, but then Kidd was a martyr and no pirate.

Captain Rackam, the dashing " Calico Jack," ran away to sea with the woman pirate, Mrs. Anne

Bonny, and they lived together happily on board ship and on land, as did Captain and Mrs. Cobham. The only other pirate I know of who took a "wife" to sea with him was Captain Pease, who flourished in a half-hearted way—half-hearted in the piratical, but not the matrimonial sense—in the middle of the nineteenth century.

A certain settler in New Zealand in the "early days" describes a visit he paid to Captain Pease and his family on board that pirate's handy little schooner, lying at anchor in a quiet cove at that island.

On stepping aboard, the guest was warmly welcomed by a short, red-faced man, bald of head and rotund in figure, of about fifty-five years of age. His appearance suggested a successful grocer rather than a pirate. On the deck were seated two ladies, one nearing middle age, the other young and undoubtedly pretty. At the feet of these ladies sprawled several small children. Captain Pease proceeded to introduce his guest to these as Mrs. Pease No. 1 and Mrs. Pease No. 2. The ladies continued their sewing while a conversation took place on various subjects. Presently, taking out his watch, the pirate turned to the younger lady, observing that it was nearing tea-time. Mrs. Pease No. 2, laying down her sewing, went to the cabin, from which the rattle of teacups and the hiss of a boiling kettle were soon heard. Tea being announced as ready, the party entered the cabin, Mrs. Pease senior taking the place at the head of the table and pouring out the tea while the younger Mrs. Pease very prettily handed round the cups and bread and butter, the guest particularly noticing with what respect and thoughtfulness she looked after the wants of the elder Mrs. Pease.

As a pirate Captain Pease was second or even third rate, confining his daring to seizing small unarmed native craft, or robbing the stores of lonely white traders on out-of-the-way atolls. But as a married man he showed himself to be a master; matrimony was his strong suit, domesticity his trump card. He gave one valuable hint to his guest, which was this : " Never take more than two wives with you on a voyage, *and choose 'em with care."*

One is apt to disassociate serious matrimony, and still less responsible paternity, with the calling of piracy, but with Captain Pease this was far from being the case. Every one of his wives—for he had others on shore—contributed her mite, or two, to the growing family, and the Captain really could not say which of his offspring he was most proud of. It seems at first strange that a man of Captain Pease's appearance, figure, and settled habits, almost hum-drum, should have been such an undoubted success with the ladies; but that he was a success there can be no doubt. Perhaps his calling had a good deal to do with this attraction he had for them.

Before bringing this Preface to a conclusion, there is one other aspect of piracy upon which I will touch.

Death, portrayed by a skeleton, was the device on the flag beneath which they fought; and a skeleton was for ever threatening to emerge from its cupboard aboard every pirate vessel.

The end of most of the pirates and a large pro-portion of the buccaneers was a sudden and violent one, and few of them died in their beds. Many were killed in battle, numbers of them were drowned. Not a few drank themselves to death with strong Jamaica rum, while many of the buccaneers died of malaria and yellow fever contracted in the jungles of Central America, and most of the pirates who survived these perils lived only to be hanged.

It is recorded of a certain ex-prizefighter and pirate, Dennis McCarthy, who was about to be hanged at New Providence Island in 1718, that, as he stood on the gallows, all bedecked with coloured ribbons, as became a boxer, he told his admiring audience that his friends had often, in joke, told him he would die in his shoes; and so, to prove them liars, he kicked off his shoes amongst the crowd, and so died without them.

The trial of a pirate was usually a rough and ready business, and the culprit seldom received the benefit of any doubt that might exist.

If he made any defence at all, it was usually to plead that he had been forced to join the pirates against his wish, and that he had long been waiting for an opportunity to escape.

Once condemned to death, and the date of execution decided, the prisoner, if at Newgate, was handed over to the good offices of the prison Ordinary; or, if in New England, to such vigorous apostles of Christianity as the Rev. Cotton or the Rev. Increase Mather. The former of these two famous theologians was pastor of the North Church in Boston, and the author of a very rare work published in 1695, called " An History of Some Criminals Executed in This Land." Cotton Mather preached many a " hanging " sermon to condemned pirates, a few of which can still be read. One of these, preached in 1704, is called " A Brief Discourse occasioned by a Tragical Spectacle of a Number of Miserables under Sentence of Death for Piracy."

The Reverend Doctor made a speciality of these " hanging " sermons, and was a thorough master of his subject, as is shown by the following passage taken from the above " Brief Discourse " :

" The Privateering Stroke so easily degenerates into the Piratical; and the Privateering Trade is usually carried on with an Unchristian Temper, and proves an Inlet unto so much Debauchery and Iniquity."

On the Sunday previous to an execution the condemned pirates were taken to church to listen to a

sermon while they were "exhibited" to the crowded
and gaping congregation. On the day of the execution a procession was formed, which marched from
the gaol to the gallows.

At the head was carried a silver oar, the emblem
from very early days of a pirate execution. Arrived
at the gibbet, the prisoner, who always dressed himself in his, or someone else's, best clothes, would doff
his hat and make a speech.

Sometimes the bolder spirits would speak in a
defiant and unrepentant way; but most of them pro-
fessed a deep repentance for their sins and warned
their listeners to guard against the temptation of drink
and avarice. After the prisoner's death the bodies of
the more notorious pirates were taken down and
hanged in chains at some prominent spot where ships
passed, in order to be a warning to any mariners who
had piratical leanings.

The number of pirates or buccaneers who died in
their beds must have been very small, particularly
amongst the former; and I have been able to trace
but a single example of a tombstone marking the
burial-place of a pirate. This is, or was until recently,
to be found in the graveyard at Dartmouth, and
records the resting-place of the late Captain Thomas
Goldsmith, who commanded the *Snap Dragon,* of
Dartmouth, in which vessel he amassed much riches
during the reign of Queen Anne, and died, apparently
not regretted, in 1714. Engraved upon his headstone
are the following lines :

> Men that are virtuous serve the Lord;
> And the Devil's by his friends ador'd;
> And as they merit get a place
> Amidst the bless'd or hellish race;
> Pray then ye learned clergy show
> Where can this brute, Tom Goldsmith, go?
> Whose life was one continual evil
> Striving to cheat God, Man and Devil.

THE PIRATES' WHO'S WHO

AISA. Barbary corsair.

A famous Mediterranean pirate, and one of Dragut's admirals in the sixteenth century.

ALCANTRA, CAPTAIN MANSEL.

A Spaniard. Commanded a pirate brig, the *Macrinarian*. Committed many outrages. Took the Liverpool packet *Topaz*, from Calcutta to Boston, in 1829, near St. Helena, murdering the whole crew. In the same year he took the *Candace*, from Marblehead, and plundered her. The supercargo of the *Candace* was an amateur actor, and had on board a priest's black gown and broad brimmed hat. These he put on and sat in his cabin pretending to tell his beads. On the pirates coming to rob him, they all crossed themselves and left him, so that he alone of the whole company was not robbed.

ALEXANDER, JOHN.

A Scotch buccaneer; one of Captain Sharp's crew. Drowned on May 9th, 1681. Captain Sharp, with a party of twenty-four men, had landed on the Island of Chiva, off the coast of Peru, and taken several prisoners, amongst whom was a shipwright and his man, who were actually at work building two great ships for the Spaniards. Sharp, thinking these men would be very useful to him, took them away, with all their tools and a quantity of ironwork, in a dory, to convey them off to his ship. But the dory, being overladen, sank, and Alexander was drowned. On the evening of May 12th his body was found; which they took up, and next day " threw him overboard, giving him three French vollies for his customary ceremony."

ALI BASHA.
Of Algiers.   Barbary corsair.

Conquered the Kingdom of Tunis in the sixteenth century, and captured many Maltese galleys. He brought the development of organized piracy to its greatest perfection.

In 1571 Ali Basha commanded a fleet of no fewer than 250 Moslem galleys in the battle of Lepanto, when he was severely defeated, but escaped with his life.

ALLESTON, Captain.

Commanded a vessel of eighteen tons, no guns, and a crew of twenty-four. In March, 1679, sailed in company with eight other vessels, under command of Captain Harris, to the Coast of Darien, and marched on foot across the isthmus, on his way attacking and sacking Santa Maria.

AMAND or ANNAND, Alexander.
Of Jamaica.

One of Major Stede Bonnet's crew in the *Royal James*. Hanged on November 8th, 1718, at White Point, Charleston, South Carolina, and buried in the marsh below low-water mark.

AMEER, Ibrahim.

An admiral of an Arabian fleet of Red Sea pirates. In 1816 he captured four British merchant vessels on their way to Surat.

ANDRESON, CAPTAIN CORNELIUS.

A Dutch pirate. Sailed from Boston in 1674 with Captain Roderigo to plunder English ships along the coast of Maine, in a vessel called the *Penobscot Shallop*.

Tried at Cambridge, Massachusetts, sentenced to death, but later on pardoned. Afterwards fought very bravely for the English colonists against the Indians.

ANDROEAS, CAPTAIN.

A Chief or Captain of the Darien Indians, who in 1679 conducted the buccaneers under Coxon and Harris across the isthmus to attack Santa Maria and afterwards to make an attempt on Panama.

Captain Androeas had a great esteem for the English, partly because the buccaneers were kind to the Indians, and partly because of the Indians' fear and hatred of the Spaniards. He afterwards led back a party of malcontents under Captain Coxon from the Pacific side of the isthmus.

ANGORA, Sultan of Timor.

Refusing to allow the East India Company to station garrisons on Timor, he was driven out of the whole of his island except the chief town, also called Angora.

Deciding to take revenge, he turned pirate and went to sea in command of a small fleet of five well-armed prows and several galleys. His first prize was a packet brig carrying despatches from Calcutta to the English General before Angora. Captain Hastings, the commander, a near relation of Warren Hastings, and a gallant officer, had thrown the despatches overboard, for which he was hanged, while the crew were

sent to prison at Angora and afterwards poisoned.
His next prize was an East Indian ship, the *Edward,*
Captain Harford, the crew of which were also
poisoned. Cruising off Bombay he defeated a vessel
sent out by the Government to attack him. After
taking other English vessels, Angora met with a
richly laden ship from Burmah, a country whose
sovereign he was on friendly terms with, but the
Sultan-pirate took this ship and drowned every soul
on board except one woman, who, owing to her great
beauty, he kept for himself. His next victim was a
well-armed Malay praam, which he captured after a
severe fight. The crew he shackled and threw overboard, while he burnt the vessel. Paying another
visit to Bombay, he caught the garrison unprepared,
blew up the fort, and sailed off with some sheep, cows,
and pigs. A few days later the pirate seized an English packet, *St. George,* and after he had tortured to
death the captain, the terrified crew joined his service.
Returning to Timor with his plunder, he was surprised by the arrival off the port of H.M.S. *Victorious,*
seventy-four guns, which had been sent to take him.
Slipping out of harbour unobserved in the night in
his fastest sailing praam, he escaped to Trincomalee
in Ceylon, where the East India Company decided to
allow him to remain undisturbed.

ANGRIA.

Brother of a famous pirate, Angora, Sultan of
Timor. When the Sultan retired from practice to the
Island of Ceylon he gave his brother his praam, a fast
vessel armed with thirty-eight guns.

Angria's brother Angora had been dethroned from
the Island of Timor by the English Government, and
this had prevented the former from all hope of succeeding as Sultan. Owing to this, Angria, a very

vindictive man, nursed against the English Government a very real grievance. Declaring himself Sultan of another smaller island, Little Timor, he sailed out to look for spoil. His first victim was the *Elphinston,* which he took some eighty miles off Bombay. Putting the crew of forty-seven men into an open boat, without water, and with scarcely room to move, he left them. It was in the hottest month of the year, and only twenty-eight of them reached Bombay alive.

Angria, being broad-minded on the subject of his new profession, did not limit himself to taking only English vessels, for meeting with two Chinese junks, laden with spices and riches, he plundered them both, and tying the crew back to back threw them into the sea to drown. One of the Chinamen, while watching his companions being drowned, managed to get a hand free from his ropes, and, taking his dagger, stabbed Angria, but, missing his heart, only wounded him in the shoulder. To punish him the pirate had the skin cut off his back and then had him beaten with canes. Then lashing him firmly down to a raft he was thrown overboard. After drifting about for three days and nights he was picked up, still alive, by a fishing-boat and carried to Bombay, where, fully recovered, he lived the rest of his days.

Angria continued his activities for three years, during which space he was said to have murdered in cold blood over 500 Englishmen. He was eventually chased by Commander Jones in H.M.S. *Asia,* sixty-four guns, into Timor, and after a close siege of the town for twelve months, Angria was shot by one of the mob while haranguing them from a balcony.

After Commander Jones's death his widow built a tower at Shooter's Hill, by Woolwich Common, to perpetuate the memory of her husband who had rid the Indian Ocean of the tyrant Angria.

The following lines are from the pen of Robert Bloomfield, and allude to this monument :

> Yon far-famed monumental tower
> Records the achievements of the brave,
> And Angria's subjugated power,
> Who plunder'd on the Eastern Wave.

ANSTIS, Captain Thomas.

The first mention of the name of this notorious pirate occurs in the year 1718, when we hear of him shipping himself at Providence in a sloop called the *Buck* in company with five other rascals who were conspiring together to seize the vessel and with her go " a-pyrating."

Of these five, one was Howel Davis, who was afterwards killed in an affair at the Island of Princes; another, Denman Topping, who was killed in the taking of a rich Portuguese ship on the coast of Brazil; a third, Walter Kennedy, was eventually hanged at Execution Dock, while the two others, who escaped the usual end of pirates—that is, by hanging, shooting, or drowning in saltwater or rum—disappeared into respectable obscurity in employment of some sort in the City of London.

This party of six conspirators was the nucleus of a very powerful combination of pirates, which eventually came under the command of the famous Captain Roberts.

Anstis's pirate career began as did most others. They cruised about amongst the West India Islands, seizing and plundering all merchant ships they chanced upon, and, if we are to believe some of the stories that were circulated at the time of their treatment of their prisoners, they appear to have been an even rougher lot of scoundrels than was usual.

Before long they seized a very stout ship, the *Morning Star,* bound from Guinea to Carolina, and fitted her up with thirty-two cannons taken from

another prize; manned her with a crew of one hundred
men, and put Captain John Fenn in command.
Anstis, as the elder officer, could have had command
of this newer and larger ship, but he was so in love
with his own vessel, the *Good Fortune,* which was an
excellent sailer, that he preferred to remain in her.

The party now had two stout ships, but, as so often
happened, trouble began to ferment amongst the crew.
A large number of these had been more or less forced
to "go a-pyrating," and were anxious to avoid the
consequences, so they decided to send a round-
robin—that is, a petition—signed by all with their
names in a circle so that no rogue could be held to be
more prominent than any other, to ask for the King's
pardon.

This round-robin was addressed to "his most
sacred Majesty George, by the Grace of God, of Great
Britain, France, and Ireland, King, Defender of the
Faith," etc.

This petition was sent to England by a merchant
vessel then sailing from Jamaica, while the crews hid
their ships amongst the mangrove swamps of a small
uninhabited island off the coast of Cuba. Here they
waited for nine months for an answer to their petition
to the King, living on turtle, fish, rice, and, of course,
rum *ad lib.* as long as it lasted.

To pass the time various diversions were instigated,
particularly dancing—a pastime in great favour
amongst pirates. We have a most amusing account
left us of a mock court of justice held by them to try
one another of piracy, and he who was on one day
tried as the prisoner would next day take his turn at
being Judge.

This shows a grim sense of humour, as most of
those who took part in these mock trials were certain
to end their careers before a real trial unless they came
to a sudden and violent end beforehand.

Here is an account of one such mock-trial as given
to Captain Johnson, the historian of the pirates, by
an eyewitness :

"The Court and Criminals being both appointed,
as also Council to plead, the Judge got up in a Tree,
and had a dirty Taurpaulin hung over his shoulder ;
this was done by Way of Robe, with a Thrum Cap
on his Head, and a large Pair of Spectacles upon his
Nose. Thus equipp'd, he settled himself in his Place ;
and abundance of Officers attending him below, with
Crows, Handspikes, etc., instead of Wands, Tip-
staves, and such like. . . . The Criminals were brought
out, making a thousand sour Faces ; and one who
acted as Attorney-General opened the Charge against
them ; their Speeches were very laconick, and their
whole Proceedings concise. We shall give it by Way
of Dialogue.

"Attor. Gen. : 'An't please your Lordship, and
you Gentlemen of the Jury, here is a Fellow before you
that is a sad Dog, a sad sad Dog ; and I humbly hope
your Lordship will order him to be hang'd out of the
Way immediately. . . . He has committed Pyracy
upon the High Seas, and we shall prove, an't please
your Lordship, that this Fellow, this sad Dog before
you, has escaped a thousand Storms, nay, has got
safe ashore when the Ship has been cast away, which
was a certain Sign he was not born to be drown'd ;
yet not having the Fear of hanging before his Eyes,
he went on robbing and ravishing Man, Woman and
Child, plundering Ships Cargoes fore and aft, burning and sinking Ship, Bark and Boat, as if the Devil
had been in him. But this is not all, my Lord, he has
committed worse Villanies than all these, for we shall
prove, that he has been guilty of drinking Small-Beer ;
and your Lordship knows, there never was a
sober Fellow but what was a Rogue. My Lord, I
should have spoke much finer than I do now, but that

as your Lordship knows our Rum is all out, and how should a Man speak good Law that has not drank a Dram. . . . However, I hope, your Lordship will order the Fellow to be hang'd.'

" Judge : '. . . Hearkee me, Sirrah . . . you lousy, pittiful, ill-look'd Dog ; what have you to say why you should not be tuck'd up immediately, and set a Sun-drying like a Scare-crow ? . . . Are you guilty, or not guilty ?'

" Pris. : ' Not guilty, an't please your Worship.'

" Judge : 'Not guilty ! say so again, Sirrah, and I'll have you hang'd without any Tryal.'

" Pris. : ' An't please your Worship's Honour, my Lord, I am as honest a poor Fellow as ever went between Stem and Stern of a Ship, and can hand, reef, steer, and clap two Ends of a Rope together, as well as e'er a He that ever cross'd salt Water ; but I was taken by one George Bradley ' (the Name of him that sat as Judge,) ' a notorious Pyrate, a sad Rogue as ever was unhang'd, and he forc'd me, an't please your Honour.'

" Judge : ' Answer me, Sirrah. . . . How will you be try'd ?'

" Pris. : ' By G—— and my Country.'

" Judge : ' The Devil you will. . . . Why then, Gentlemen of the Jury, I think we have nothing to do but to proceed to Judgement.'

" Attor. Gen. : ' Right, my Lord ; for if the Fellow should be suffered to speak, he may clear himself, and that's an Affront to the Court.'

" Pris. : ' Pray, my Lord, I hope your Lordship will consider . . .'

" Judge : ' Consider ! . . . How dare you talk of considering ? . . . Sirrah, Sirrah, I never consider'd in all my Life. . . . I'll make it Treason to consider.'

" Pris. : ' But, I hope, your Lordship will hear some reason.'

"Judge : ' D'ye hear how the Scoundrel prates?
. . . What have we to do with the Reason? . . .
I'd have you to know, Raskal, we don't sit here to
hear Reason . . . we go according to Law. . . . Is
our Dinner ready ?'

" Attor. Gen. : ' Yes, my Lord.'

" Judge : ' Then heark'ee you Raskal at the Bar;
hear me, Sirrah, hear me . . . You must suffer, for
three reasons; first, because it is not fit I should
sit here as Judge, and no Body be hanged. . . .
Secondly, you must be hanged, because you have a
damn'd hanging Look. . . . And thirdly, you must
be hanged, because I am hungry; for, know, Sirrah,
that 'tis a Custom, that whenever the Judge's Dinner
is ready before the Tryal is over, the Prisoner is to be
hanged of Course. . . . There's Law for you, ye
Dog. . . . So take him away Gaoler.' "

In August, 1722, the pirates sailed out from their
hiding-place and waylaid the ship which was returning to Jamaica with the answer to the petition, but to
their disappointment heard that no notice had been
taken of their round-robin by the Government at
home.

No time was lost in returning to their old ways, for
the very next day both pirate ships left their hiding-
place and sailed out on the " grand account."

But now their luck deserted them, for the *Morning
Star* was run aground on a reef by gross neglect on
the part of the officers and wrecked. Most of the crew
escaped on to an island, where Captain Anstis found
them next day, and no sooner had he taken aboard
Captain Fenn, Phillips, the carpenter, and a few
others, than all of a sudden down upon them came two
men-of-war, the *Hector* and the *Adventure,* so that
Anstis had barely time to cut his cables and get away
to sea, hotly pursued by the *Adventure.* The latter,
in a stiff breeze, was slowly gaining on the brigantine

when all of a sudden the wind dropped, the pirates got
out the sweeps, and thus managed, for the time being,
to escape. In the meantime the *Hector* took prisoner
the forty pirates remaining on the island.

Anstis soon got to work again, and captured several
prizes. He then sailed to the Island of Tobago to
clean and refit his ship. Just when all the guns and
stores had been landed and the ship heeled, as ill-luck
would have it, the *Winchester*, man-of-war, put into
the bay; and the pirates had barely time to set their
ship on fire and to escape into the woods. Anstis had
by now lost all authority over his discontented crew,
and one night was shot while asleep in his hammock.

ANTONIO.

Captain of the Darien Indians and friend to the
English buccaneers.

ARCHER, John Rose.

He learnt his art as a pirate in the excellent school
of the notorious Blackbeard.

In 1723 he was, for the time being, in honest employment in a Newfoundland fishing-boat, which was
captured by Phillips and his crew. As Phillips was
only a beginner at piracy, he was very glad to get the
aid of such an old hand at the game as John Archer,
whom he promptly appointed to the office of quartermaster in the pirate ship. This quick promotion
caused some murmuring amongst Phillips's original
crew, the carpenter, Fern, being particularly out-
spoken against it.

Archer ended his days on the gallows at Boston on
June 2nd, 1724, and we read that he "dy'd very
penitent, with the assistance of two grave Divines to
attend him."

ARGALL.

Licensed and titled buccaneer.

Believed to have buried a rich treasure in the Isles of Shoals, off Portsmouth, New Hampshire, in the seventeenth century.

ARMSTRONG.

Born in London. A deserter from the Royal Navy. One of Captain Roberts's crew taken by H.M.S. *Swallow,* from which ship he had previously deserted.

In an account of his execution on board H.M.S. *Weymouth* we read : " Being on board a Man of War there was no Body to press him to an Acknowledgement of the Crime he died for, nor of sorrowing in particular for it, which would have been exemplary, and made suitable Impressions on seamen ; so that his last Hour was spent in lamenting and bewailing his Sins in general, exhorting the Spectators to an honest and good life, in which alone they could find Satisfaction."

This painful scene ended by the condemned singing with the spectators a few verses of the 140th Psalm : at the conclusion of which, at the firing of a gun, " he was tric'd up at the Fore Yard."

Died at the age of 34.

ARNOLD, Sion.

A Madagascar pirate, who was brought to New England by Captain Shelley in 1699.

ASHPLANT, Valentine.

Born in the Minories, London. He served with Captain Howell Davis, and later with Bartholomew Roberts. He was one of the leading lights of Roberts's crew, a member of the " House of Lords."

He took part in the capture and plundering of the

King Solomon at Cape Apollonia, North-West Coast of Africa, in January, 1719, when the pirates, in an open boat, attacked the ship while at anchor. Ashplant was taken prisoner two years later by H.M.S. *Swallow*. Tried for piracy at Cape Coast Castle and found guilty in March, 1722, and hanged in chains there at the age of 32.

ATWELL.

A hand aboard the brig *Vineyard* in 1830, he took part with Charles Gibbs and others in a mutiny in which both the captain and mate was murdered.

AUGUR, CAPTAIN JOHN.

A pirate of New Providence, Bahama Islands. He accepted the royal pardon in 1718, and impressed the Governor, Woodes Rogers, so favourably that he was placed in command of a sloop to go and trade amongst the islands. A few days out Augur met with two sloops, "the sight of which dispelled all memory of their late good intention," and turning pirates once more, they seized the two sloops and took out of them money and goods to the value of £500.

The pirates now sailed for Hispaniola, but with bad luck, or owing to retribution, a sudden hurricane arose which drove them back to the one spot in the West Indies they must have been most anxious to avoid—that is, the Bahama Islands. Here the sloop became a total wreck, but the crew got ashore and for a while lay hidden in a wood. Rogers, hearing where they were, sent an armed sloop to the island, and the captain by fair promises induced the eleven marooned pirates to come aboard. Taking these back to Providence, Rogers had them all tried before a court of lately converted pirates, and they were condemned to

be hanged. While standing on the gallows platform
the wretched culprits reproached the crowd of
spectators, so lately their fellow-brethren in piracy,
for allowing their old comrades to be hanged, and
urging them to come to the rescue. But virtue was
still strong in these recent converts, and all the comfort the criminals got was to be told " it was their
Business to turn their Minds to another World, and
sincerely to repent of what Wickedness they had done
in this." " Yes," answered the now irritated and in
no-wise abashed Augur, " I *do* heartily repent : I
repent I have not done more Mischief, and that we
did not cut the Throats of them that took us, and I
am extremely sorry that you an't all hang'd as well as
we."

AUSTIN, James.

Captured with the rest of Captain John Quelch's
crew in the brigantine *Charles*. Escaped for a time,
but was caught and secured in the gaol at Piscataqua,
and later on tried for piracy at the Star Tavern at
Boston in June, 1704.

AVERY, Captain John, *alias* Henry Every, *alias*
    Captain Bridgeman. Nicknamed "Long Ben,"
    or the " Arch-Pirate."

In the year 1695, when at the height of his career,
Avery caught the public's fancy as no other pirate
ever did, with the possible exception of Captain Kidd.
So much so that his achievements, or supposed
achievements, formed the plot of several popular
novels and plays.

Charles Johnson wrote a play called " The Successful Pyrate," which work ran into several editions, and
was acted at the Theatre Royal in Drury Lane.

The scene in this play was laid in the Island of

Madagascar, and the hero was modelled on Captain Avery.

This pirate was a Devonshire man, being born near Plymouth about the year 1665, and was bred to the sea. He sailed on several voyages as mate aboard a merchantman. He was later appointed first officer in an armed privateer *The Duke,* Commander Captain Gibson, which sailed from Bristol for Spain, being hired by the Spaniards for service in the West Indies against the French pirates.

Avery soon plotted a mutiny, which was carried out while *The Duke* lay at anchor in Cadiz Harbour; the ship was seized, and the captain put ashore. Avery was elected captain, and he renamed the ship the *Charles the Second.* For more than a year Avery sailed in this vessel, preying without distinction upon persons of all nations and religions.

After leaving Spain he first sailed to the Isle of May, holding the Portuguese governor for ransom till provisions were sent on board. He took near here three English ships, then sailed to the coast of Guinea to procure slaves. To catch these Avery would anchor off a village and hoist English colours. The trusting negroes would then paddle off to the ship in canoes, bringing gold to traffic with. At a given signal these natives would be seized, clapped in irons, and thrown into the hold.

Avery next sailed to the Island of Princes, where he attacked two Danish ships, and took them both. The next place the pirates touched at was Madagascar, from there they sailed to the Red Sea to await the fleet expected from Mocha. To pass the time and to earn an honest penny the pirates called in at a town called Meat, there to sell to the natives some of their stolen merchandise. But the cautious inhabitants refused to do any business with these suspicious looking merchants, so in order to punish them the pirates burnt down their town. They next visited Aden, where they met two other English pirate ships, and were soon joined by three others from America, all on the same enterprise.

Expecting the Mocha fleet to come along, they waited here, but the fleet slipped past the pirates in the night. Avery was after them the next morning, and catching them up, singled out the largest ship, fought her for two hours, and took her. She proved to be the *Gunsway*, belonging to the Great Mogul himself, and a very valuable prize, as out of her they took 100,000 pieces of eight and a like number of chequins, as well as several of the highest persons of the court who were passengers on a pilgrimage to Mecca. It was rumoured that a daughter of the Great Mogul was also on board. Accounts of this exploit eventually reached England, and created great excitement, so that it soon became the talk of the town that Captain Avery had taken the beautiful young princess to Madagascar, where he had married her and was living in royal state, the proud father of several small princes and princesses.

The Mogul was naturally infuriated at this outrage on his ship, and threatened in retaliation to lay waste all the East India Company's settlements.

Having got a vast booty, Avery and his friends sailed towards Madagascar, and on the way there Avery, as admiral of the little fleet, signalled to the captain of the other sloops to come aboard his vessel. When they arrived Avery put before them the following ingenious scheme. He proposed that the treasures in the two sloops should, for safety, be put into his keeping till they all three arrived in Madagascar. This, being agreed to, was done, but during the night, after Avery had explained matters to his own men, he altered his course and left the sloops, and never saw them again. He now sailed away with all the

plunder to the West Indies, arriving safely at New
Providence Island in the Bahamas, where he offered
the Governor a bribe of twenty pieces of eight and
two pieces of gold to get him a pardon.   Avery
arrived in 1696 at Boston, where he appears to have
successfully bribed the Quaker Governor to let him
and some of his crew land with their spoils unmolested.
But the pirate did not feel quite safe, and also thought
it would be wellnigh impossible to sell his diamonds
in the colony without being closely questioned as to
how he came by them.   So, leaving America, he
sailed to the North of Ireland, where he sold the sloop.
Here the crew finally dispersed, and Avery stopped
some time in Dublin, but was still unable to dispose of
his stolen diamonds.   Thinking England would be a
better place for this transaction, he went there, and
settled at Bideford in Devon.   Here he lived very
quietly under a false name, and through a friend com-
municated with certain merchants in Bristol.   These
came to see him, accepted his diamonds and some gold
cups, giving him a few pounds for his immediate
wants, and took the valuables to Bristol to sell,
promising to send him the money procured for them.
Time dragged on, but nothing came from the Bristol
merchants, and at last it began to dawn on Avery that
there were pirates on land as well as at sea.   His
frequent letters to the merchants brought at the most
but a few occasional shillings, which were immediately swallowed up by the payment of his debts
for the bare necessities of life at Bideford.   At length,
when matters were becoming desperate, Avery was
taken ill and died " not being worth as much as would
buy him a coffin."   Thus ended Avery, " the Grand
Pirate," whose name was known all over Europe, and
who was supposed to be reigning as a king in Madagascar when all the while he was hiding and starving
in a cottage at Bideford.

AYLETT, CAPTAIN.

This buccaneer was killed by an explosion of gunpowder on board the *Oxford* during a banquet of Morgan's captains off Hispaniola in 1669.

BAILY, JOB, or BAYLEY.
Of London.

One of Major Stede Bonnet's crew. Hanged at Charleston in 1718.

BAKER, CAPTAIN.

One of Gasparilla's gang up to 1822, when they were broken up by the United States Navy. His favourite hunting-ground was the Gulf of Mexico.

BALL, ROGER.

One of Captain Bartholomew's crew in the *Royal Fortune*. Captured by H.M.S. *Swallow* off the West Coast of Africa. He had been terribly burnt by an explosion of a barrel of gunpowder, and while seated "in a private corner, with a look as sullen as winter," a surgeon of the king's ship came up and asked him how he came to be blown up in that frightful manner. "Why," says he, "John Morris fired a pistol into the powder, and if he had not done it, I would." The surgeon, with great kindness, offered to dress the prisoner's wounds, but Ball, although in terrible pain, refused to allow them to be touched. He died the same night.

BALLET, JOHN. Buccaneer.

Third mate on board Woodes Rogers's ship, the *Duke*, but was by profession a surgeon, in which latter capacity he had sailed on a previous voyage with Dampier.

BALTIZAR, CAPTAIN.

A terror to all shipping in the Gulf of Mexico in the early part of the nineteenth century. Brought to Boston as a prisoner in 1823, taken thence to Kingston, Jamaica, and there hanged. For some extraordinary reason the American juries seldom would condemn a pirate to death, so that whenever possible the pirate prisoners were handed over to the English, who made short shift with them.

BANNISTER, CAPTAIN.

Ran away from Port Royal, Jamaica, in June, 1684, on a " privateering " venture in a ship of thirty guns. Caught and brought back by the frigate *Ruby*, and put on trial by the Lieutenant-Governor Molesworth, who was at that time very active in his efforts to stamp out piracy in the West Indies.

Bannister entirely escaped punishment, capital or otherwise, as he was released by the grand jury on a technical point, surely most rare good fortune for the captain in days when the law was elastic enough to fit most crimes, and was far from lenient on piracy. Six months later the indefatigable captain again eluded the forts, and for two years succeeded in dodging the frigates sent out by Governor Molesworth to capture him. Finally, in January, 1687, Captain Spragge sailed victoriously into Port Royal with Bannister and three other buccaneers hanging at the yard-arm, " a spectacle of great satisfaction to all good people, and of terror to the favourers of pirates."

BARBAROSSA, or " REDBEARD " (his real name was URUJ). Barbary Corsair.

Son of a Turkish renegade and a Christian mother. Born in the Island of Lesbon in the Ægean Sea, a stronghold of the Mediterranean pirates.

In 1504 Barbarossa made his headquarters at Tunis,

in return for which he paid the Sultan one-fifth of all the booty he took. One of his first and boldest exploits was the capture of two richly laden galleys belonging to Pope Julius II., on their way from Genoa to Civita Vecchia. Next year he captured a Spanish ship with 500 soldiers on board. In 1512 he was invited by the Moors to assist them in an attempt to retake the town and port of Bujeya from the Spaniards. After eight days of fighting, Barbarossa lost an arm, and the siege was given up, but he took away with him a large Genoese ship. In 1516 Barbarossa changed his headquarters to Jijil, and took command of an army of 6,000 men and sixteen galliots, with which he attacked and captured the Spanish fortress of Algiers, of which he became Sultan. Barbarossa was by now vastly rich and powerful, his fleets bringing in prizes from Genoa, Naples, Venice, and Spain.

Eventually Charles V. of Spain sent an army of 10,000 troops to North Africa, defeated the corsairs, and Barbarossa was slain in battle.

BARBE, CAPTAIN NICHOLAS.

Master of a Breton ship, the *Mychell,* of St. Malo, owned by Hayman Gillard. Captured by an English ship in 1532. Her crew was made up of nine Bretons and five Scots.

BARNARD, CAPTAIN. Buccaneer.

In June, 1663, this buccaneer sailed from Port Royal to the Orinoco. He took and plundered the town of Santo Tomas, and returned the following March.

BARNES, CAPTAIN.

In 1677 several English privateers surprised and sacked the town of Santa Marta in the Spanish Main.

To save the town from being burnt, the Governor and Bishop became hostages until a ransom had been paid. These the pirates, under the command of Captains Barnes and Coxon, carried back to Jamaica and delivered up to Lord Vaughan, the Governor of the island. Vaughan treated the Bishop well, and hired a vessel specially to send him back to Castagona, for which kindness "the good old man was exceedingly pleased."

BARNES, HENRY.
   Of Barbadoes.

   Tried for piracy at Newport in 1723, but found to be not guilty.

BARROW, JAMES.

   Taken by Captain Roberts out of the *Martha* snow (Captain Lady). Turned pirate and served in the *Ranger* in 1721.

BELLAMY, CAPTAIN CHARLES.   Pirate, Socialist, and orator.   A famous West Indian filibuster.

   He began life as a wrecker in the West Indies, but this business being uncertain in its profits, and Bellamy being an ambitious young man, he decided with his partner, Paul Williams, to aim at higher things, and to enter the profession of piracy. Bellamy had now chosen a calling that lent itself to his undoubted talents, and his future career, while it lasted, was a brilliant one.

   Procuring a ship, he sailed up and down the coast of Carolina and New England, taking and plundering numerous vessels; and when this neighbourhood became too hot for him he would cruise for a while in the cooler climate of Newfoundland.

   Bellamy had considerable gifts for public speaking, and seldom missed an opportunity of addressing the

assembled officers and crews of the ships he took,
before liberating or otherwise disposing of them.

His views were distinctly Socialistic. On one occasion, in an address to a Captain Beer, who had
pleaded to have his sloop returned to him, Captain
Bellamy, after clearing his throat, began as follows :
"I am sorry," he said, "that you can't have your
sloop again, for I scorn to do anyone any mischief—
when it is not to my advantage—though you are a
sneaking puppy, and so are all those who will submit
to be governed by laws which rich men have made for
their own security, for the cowardly whelps have not
the courage otherwise to defend what they get by their
knavery. But damn ye altogether for a pack of crafty
rascals, and you, who serve them, for a parcel of hen-
hearted numbskulls ! They vilify us, the scoundrels
do, when there is the only difference that they rob
the poor under cover of the law, forsooth, and we
plunder the rich under the protection of our own
courage. Had you not better make one of us than
sneak after these villains for employment ?"

Bellamy's fall came at last at the hands of a whaler
captain. At the time he was in command of the
Whidaw and a small fleet of other pirate craft, which
was lying at anchor in the Bay of Placentia in Newfoundland. Sailing from Placentia for Nantucket
Shoals, he seized a whaling vessel, the *Mary Anne*.
As the skipper of the whaler knew the coast well,
Bellamy made him pilot of his small fleet. The
cunning skipper one night ran his ship on to a sand-
bank near Eastman, Massachusetts, and the rest of
the fleet followed his stern light on to the rocks.
Almost all the crews perished, only seven of the
pirates being saved. These were seized and brought
to trial, condemned, and hanged at Boston in 1726.
The days spent between the sentence and the hanging
were not wasted, for we read in a contemporary

account that " by the indefatigable pains of a pious and learned divine, who constantly attended them, they were at length, by the special grace of God, made sensible of and truly penitent for the enormous crimes they had been guilty of."

BELVIN, JAMES.

Bo'son to Captain Gow, the pirate. He had the reputation of being a good sailor but a bloodthirsty fellow. Was hanged at Wapping in June, 1725.

BEME, FRANCIS.

In 1539 this Baltic pirate was cruising off Antwerp, waiting to waylay English merchant vessels.

BENDALL, GEORGE, or BENDEALL.

A flourishing pirate, whose headquarters, in the early eighteenth century, were in New Providence Island.

In the year 1717, King George offered a free pardon to all freebooters who would come in and give themselves up. But the call of the brotherhood was too strong for a few of the " old hands," and Bendall, amongst others, was off once again to carry on piracy around the Bahama and Virgin Islands. Within a few years these last " die-hards " were all killed, drowned, caught, or hanged.

BENNETT, WILLIAM.

An English soldier, who deserted from Fort Loyal, Falmouth, Marne, in 1689, and joined the pirate Pounds. Was sent to prison at Boston, where he died.

BILL, PHILIP.

Belonged to the Island of St. Thomas.

One of Captain Roberts's crew. Hanged at the age of 27.

BISHOP.

An Irishman. Chief mate to the pirate Captain Cobham.

BISHOP, Captain.

In 1613, Bishop and a few other English seamen set up as pirates at Marmora on the Barbary Coast.

BISHOP, William.

One of Avery's crew. Hanged at Execution Dock in 1691.

BLADS, William.
Born in Rhode Island.

One of Captain Charles Harris's crew. Hanged at Newport on July 19th, 1723. Age 28.

BLAKE, Benjamin.

A Boston boy, taken prisoner with Captain Pounds's crew at Tarpaulin Cove.

BLAKE, James.

One of Captain Teach's crew. Hanged in 1718 at Virginia.

BLEWFIELD, Captain, or Blauvelt.

In 1649 this Dutch pirate brought a prize into Newport, Rhode Island. In 1663 was known to be living among the friendly Indians at Cape Gratia de Dios on the Spanish Main. He commanded a barque carrying three guns and a crew of fifty men. He was very active in the logwood cutting in Honduras. Whether the town and river of Bluefield take their name from this pirate is uncertain, but the captain must many a time have gone up the river into the forests of Nicaragua on his logwood cutting raids.

BLOT, Captain. French filibuster.

In 1684 was in command of *La Quagone*, ninety men, eight guns.

BOLIVAR, Lieutenant.

This Portuguese pirate was first officer to Captain Jonnia. He was a stout, well-built man of swarthy complexion and keen, ferocious eyes, huge black whiskers and beard, and a tremendously loud voice. He took the Boston schooner *Exertion* at Twelve League Key on December 17th, 1821.

BOND, Captain.
Of Bristol.

In 1682 arrived at the Cape Verde Islands. Having procured leave to land on Mayo Island, on the pretence of being an honest merchant in need of provisions, particularly of beef and goats, Bond and his crew seized and carried away some of the principal inhabitants. A year later John Cooke and Cowley arrived at Mayo in the *Revenge,* but were prevented by the inhabitants from landing owing to their recent treatment at the hands of Bond.

BONNET, Major Stede, *alias* Captain Thomas, *alias* Edwards.

The history of this pirate is both interesting and unique. He was not brought up to the seafaring life; in fact, before he took to piracy, he had already retired from the Army, with the rank of Major. He owned substantial landed property in Barbadoes, lived in a fine house, was married, and much respected by the quality and gentry of that island. His turning pirate naturally greatly scandalized his neighbours, and they found it difficult at first to imagine whatever had caused this sudden and extraordinary resolution, particularly in a man of his position in Society. But when the cause at last came to be known, he was more pitied than blamed, for it was understood that the Major's mind had become unbalanced owing to the unbridled nagging of Mrs. Bonnet. Referring to this, the historian Captain Johnson writes as follows: "He was afterwards rather pitty'd than condemned, by those that were acquainted with him, believing that this Humour of going a-pyrating proceeded from a Disorder in his Mind, which had been but too visible in him, some Time before this wicked Undertaking; and which is said to have been occasioned by some Discomforts he found in a married State; be that as it will, the Major was but ill qualified for the Business, as not understanding maritime Affairs." Whatever the cause of the Major's "disorder of mind," the fact remains that at his own expense he fitted out a sloop armed with ten guns and a crew of seventy men. The fact that he honestly paid in cash for this ship is highly suspicious of a deranged mind, since no other pirate, to the writer's knowledge, ever showed such a nicety of feeling, but always stole the ship in which to embark "on the account." The Major, to satisfy the curious, gave out that he intended to trade between the islands, but one night, without a word of farewell to Mrs. Bonnet, he sailed out of harbour in the *Revenge*, as he called his ship, and began to cruise off the coast of Virginia. For a rank amateur, Bonnet met with wonderful success, as is shown by a list of the prizes he took and plundered in this first period of his piracy:

The *Anne*, of Glasgow (Captain Montgomery).

The *Turbet*, of Barbadoes, which, after plundering, he burnt, as he did all prizes from Barbadoes.

The *Endeavour* (Captain Scott).

The *Young*, of Leith.

The plunder out of these ships he sold at Gardiner Island, near New York.

Cruising next off the coast of Carolina, Bonnet took a brace of prizes, but began to have trouble with his unruly crew, who, seeing that their captain knew nothing whatever of sea affairs, took advantage of the fact and commenced to get out of hand. Unluckily for Bonnet, he at this time met with the famous Captain Teach, or Blackbeard, and the latter, quickly appreciating how matters stood, ordered the Major to come aboard his own ship, while he put his lieutenant, Richards, to command Bonnet's vessel. The poor Major was most depressed by this undignified change in his affairs, until Blackbeard lost his ship in Topsail Inlet, and finding himself at a disadvantage, promptly surrendered to the King's proclamation and allowed Bonnet to reassume command of his own sloop. But Major Bonnet had been suffering from qualms of conscience latterly, so he sailed to Bath Town in North Carolina, where he, too, surrendered to the Governor and received his certificate of pardon. Almost at once news came of war being declared between England and France with Spain, so Bonnet hurried back to Topsail, and was granted permission to take back his sloop and sail her to St. Thomas's Island, to receive a commission as a privateer from the French Governor of that island. But in the meanwhile Teach had robbed everything of any value out of Bonnet's ship, and had marooned seventeen of the crew on a sandy island, but these were rescued by the Major before they died of starvation. Just as the ship was ready to sail, a bumboat came alongside to sell apples and cider to the sloop's crew, and from these they got an interesting piece of news. They learnt that Teach, with a crew of eighteen men, was at that moment lying at anchor in Ocricock Inlet. The Major, longing to revenge the insult he had

suffered from Blackbeard, and his crew remembering
how he had left them to die on a desert island, went
off in search of Teach, but failed to find him. Stede
Bonnet having received his pardon in his own name,
now called himself Captain Thomas and again took
to piracy, and evidently had benefited by his apprenticeship with Blackbeard, for he was now most successful, taking many prizes off the coast of Virginia,
and later in Delaware Bay.

Bonnet now sailed in a larger ship, the *Royal
James,* so named from feelings of loyalty to the
Crown. But she proved to be very leaky, and the
pirates had to take her to the mouth of Cape Fear
River for repairs. News of this being carried to the
Council of South Carolina, arrangements were made
to attempt to capture the pirate, and a Colonel
William Rhet, at his own expense, fitted out two
armed sloops, the *Henry* (eight guns and seventy
men) and the *Sea Nymph* (eight guns and sixty men),
both sailing under the direct command of the gallant
Colonel. On September 25th, 1718, the sloops arrived
at Cape Fear River, and there sure enough was the
Royal James, with three sloops lying at anchor behind
the bar. The pirate tried to escape by sailing out, but
was followed by the Colonel's two vessels until all
three ran aground within gunshot of each other. A
brisk fight took place for five hours, when the Major
struck his colours and surrendered. There was great
public rejoicing in Charleston when, on October 3rd,
Colonel Rhet sailed victoriously into the harbour with
his prisoners. But next day Bonnet managed to
escape out of prison and sailed to Swillivant's Island.
The indefatigable Colonel Rhet again set out after
the Major, and again caught him and brought him
back to Charleston.

The trial of Stede Bonnet and his crew began on
October 28th, 1718, at Charleston, and continued till

November 12th, the Judge being Nicholas Trot. Bonnet was found guilty and condemned to be hanged. Judge Trot made a speech of overwhelming length to the condemned, full of Biblical quotations, to each of which the learned magistrate gave chapter and verse. In November, 1718, the gallant, if unfortunate, Major was hanged at White Point, Charleston.

Apart from the unusual cause for his turning pirate, Bonnet is interesting as being almost the only case known, otherwise than in books of romance, of a pirate making his prisoners walk the plank.

BONNY, ANNE. Female pirate.

Anne was born in County Cork, and her father was an Attorney-at-Law, who practised his profession in that city, her mother being lady's maid to the attorney's lawful wife.

The story of the events which led to the existence of Anne may be read in Johnson's "History of the Pyrates," where it is recounted in a style quite suggestive of Fielding. In spite of its sad deficiency in moral tone, the narrative is highly diverting. But as this work is strictly confined to the history of the pirates and not to the amorous intrigues of their forbears, we will skip these pre-natal episodes and come to the time when the attorney, having lost a once flourishing legal practice, sailed from Ireland to Carolina to seek a fortune there, taking his little daughter Anne with him. In new surroundings fortune favoured the attorney, and he soon owned a rich plantation, and his daughter kept house for him.

Anne was now grown up and a fine young woman, but had a "fierce and courageous temper," which more than once led her into scrapes, as, on one occasion, when in a sad fit of temper, she slew her English servant-maid with a case-knife. But except for these occasional outbursts of passion she was a good and dutiful girl. Her father now began to think of finding a suitable young man to be a husband for Anne, which would not be hard to do, since Anne, besides her good looks, was his heir and would be well provided for by him. But Anne fell in love with a good-looking young sailor who arrived one day at Charleston, and, knowing her father would never consent to such a match, the lovers were secretly married, in the expectation that, the deed being done, the father would soon become reconciled to it. But on the contrary, the attorney, on being told the news, turned his daughter out of doors and would have nothing more to do with either of them. The bridegroom, finding his heiress worth not a groat, did what other sailors have done before and since, and slipped away to sea without so much as saying good-bye to his bride. But a more gallant lover soon hove in sight, the handsome, rich, dare-devil pirate, Captain John Rackam, known up and down the coast as " Calico Jack." Jack's methods of courting and taking a ship were similar—no time wasted, straight up alongside, every gun brought to play, and the prize seized. Anne was soon swept off her feet by her picturesque and impetuous lover, and consented to go to sea with him in his ship, but disguised herself in sailor's clothes before going on board. The lovers sailed together on a piratical honeymoon until certain news being conveyed to Captain Rackam by his bride, he sailed to Cuba and put Anne ashore at a small cove, where he had a house and also friends, who he knew would take good care of her. But before long Anne was back in the pirate ship, as active as any of her male shipmates with cutlass and marlinspike, always one of the leaders in boarding a prize.

However, the day of retribution was at hand. While cruising near Jamaica in October, 1720, the pirates were surprised by the sudden arrival of an armed sloop, which had been sent out by the Governor of that island for the express purpose of capturing Rackam and his crew. A fight followed, in which the pirates behaved in a most cowardly way, and were soon driven below decks, all but Anne Bonny and another woman pirate, Mary Read, who fought gallantly till taken prisoners, all the while flaunting their male companions on their cowardly conduct. The prisoners were carried to Jamaica and tried for piracy at St. Jago de la Vega, and convicted on November 28th, 1720. Anne pleaded to have her execution postponed for reasons of her condition of health, and this was allowed, and she never appears to have been hanged, though what her ultimate fate was is unknown. On the day that her lover Rackam was hanged he obtained, by special favour, permission to see Anne, but must have derived little comfort from the farewell interview, for all he got in the way of sympathy from his lady love were these words—that " she was sorry to see him there, but if he had fought like a Man, he need not have been hang'd like a Dog."

BOON, John.

Member of the Council of Carolina under Governor Colleton, and expelled from it " for holding correspondence with pirates," 1687.

BOOTH, Samuel.
Of Charleston, Carolina.

One of Major Bonnet's crew. Hanged at Charleston, South Carolina, in 1718.

BOURNANO, Captain, or de Bernanos.

In 1679 this famous French filibuster commanded a ship of ninety tons, armed with six guns, and manned

by a crew of eighty-six French sailors. Joined
Captain Bartholomew Sharp when he was preparing
his expedition to assault the town of Santa Maria.
Bournano was a useful ally, as he was much liked by
the Darien Indians, but his crew quarrelled with the
English buccaneers, and they left Sharp's company.
In the year 1684, Bournano, known by then as Le
Sieur de Bernanos, commanded a ship, *La Schite*,
carrying a crew of sixty men and armed with eight
guns.

LA BOUSE, CAPTAIN OLIVER, or DE LA BOUCHE.
     French pirate.

When Captain Howel Davis had taken and sacked
the fort at Gambia and with his crew was spending
a day in revelry, a ship was reported, bearing down
on them in full sail. The pirates prepared to fight
her, when she ran up the Black Flag and proved to
be a French pirate ship of fourteen guns and sixty-
four hands, half French and half negroes, commanded by Captain La Bouse. A great many
civilities passed between the two captains, and they
agreed to sail down the coast together. Arriving at
Sierra Leone, they found a tall ship lying at anchor.
This ship they attacked, firing a broadside, when she
also ran up the Black Flag, being the vessel of the
notorious Captain Cocklyn. For the next two days
the three captains and their crews " spent improving
their acquaintance and friendship," which was the
pirate expression for getting gloriously drunk. On
the third day they attacked and took the African
Company's Fort. Shortly afterwards the three captains quarrelled, and each went his own way. In
1718 La Bouse was at New Providence Island. In
1720 this pirate commanded the *Indian Queen,*
250 tons, armed with twenty-eight guns, and a crew
of ninety men. Sailing from the Guinea Coast to the

East Indies, de la Bouche lost his ship on the Island of Mayotta, near Madagascar.

The captain and forty men set about building a new vessel, while the remainder went off in canoes to join Captain England's pirates at Johanna.

BOWEN.

A Bristol man. In 1537, when the Breton pirates were becoming very daring along the south coast of England and Wales, Bowen contrived to capture fourteen of these robbers, who had landed near Tenby, and had them put in prison.

BOWEN, CAPTAIN JOHN.

The practice of this South Sea pirate extended from Madagascar to Bengal. He commanded a good ship, the *Speaker*, a French vessel, owned by an English company interested in the slave trade, which Bowen had captured by a cunning ruse. He afterwards lost his ship off Mauritius, but was well treated by the Dutch Governor, who supplied doctors, medicine, and food to the shipwrecked pirates. After three months' hospitality on the island, Bowen procured a sloop, and in March, 1701, sailed for Madagascar. As a parting friendly gift to the Governor, he gave him 2,500 pieces of eight and the wreck of the *Speaker*, with all the guns and stores. On arriving at Madagascar, Bowen erected a fort and built a town. Shortly after this a ship, the *Speedy Return,* and a brigantine were so very thoughtless as to put into the port, and paid for this thoughtlessness by being promptly seized by Bowen. With these two vessels Bowen and his merry men went " a-pyrating " again, and with great success, for in a short time they had gathered together over a million dollars in coin, as well as vast quantities of valuable merchandise. The pirates then, most wisely, considering that they had

succeeded well enough, settled down amongst their
Dutch friends in the Island of Mauritius to a quiet
and comfortable life on shore.

BOWMAN, WILLIAM.

A seaman; one of the party which crossed the
Isthmus of Darien on foot with Dampier in 1681.
Wafer records that Bowman, "a weakly Man, a
Taylor by trade," slipped while crossing a swollen
river, and was carried off by the swift current, and
nearly drowned by the weight of a satchel he carried
containing 400 pieces of eight.

BOYD, ROBERT.
Of Bath Town, North Carolina.

Sailed with Major Stede Bonnet in the *Royal
James*.   Hanged on November 8th, 1718, at
Charleston.

BOYZA.
A Columbian.

One of Captain Gilbert's crew in the *Panda*.
Hanged at Boston in June, 1835.

BRADISH, CAPTAIN JOSEPH.

A notorious pirate. Born at Cambridge, Massachusetts, on November 28th, 1672. In March, 1689,
was in London out of a berth, and shipped as mate
in the hake-boat *Adventure*, bound for Borneo on an
interloping trade.

In September, 1698, when most of the officers and
passengers were ashore at the Island of Polonais,
Bradish and the crew cut the cable and ran away
with the ship. The crew shared the money which
was found in the bread-room, and which filled nine
chests, amounting to about 3,700 Spanish dollars.

Bradish sailed the *Adventure* to Long Island, arriv-

ing there on March 19th, 1699. After leaving their
money and jewels on Nassau Island, they sank their
ship. Most of the crew bought horses at the neighbouring farmhouses and disappeared. Bradish and
a few others were rash enough to go to Massachusetts,
where they were promptly arrested and placed in the
Boston Gaol. But the gaolkeeper, one Caleb Ray,
was a relation of Bradish, and allowed him to escape.
An offer of a reward of £200 brought the escaped
prisoner back, and he sailed in irons on H.M.S.
Advice, with Kidd and other pirates, to England,
and was hanged in chains in London at Hope Dock
in 1700.

BRADLEY, GEORGE.

Master of Captain Fenn's ship, the *Morning Star*,
wrecked on the Grand Caymans in August, 1722.
The crew got ashore on an island and hid in the
woods. Bradley and the other pirates afterwards
surrendered themselves to an English sloop, and
were carried to Bermuda. Bradley escaped to
England, and was last heard of at Bristol.

BREAKES, CAPTAIN HIRAM.

This Dutch pirate was the second son of a well-to-
do councillor of the Island of Saba in the West Indies.
Hiram was appointed in the year 1764 to a ship which
traded between that island and Amsterdam. In the
latter port, Hiram, who was now 19 years of age and
a handsome fellow standing over six feet in height,
fell in love with a certain Mrs. Snyde.

Getting command of a small ship that traded
between Schiedam, in Holland, and Lisbon, Breakes
for some time sailed between these ports. Returning
to Amsterdam, he and Mrs. Snyde murdered that
lady's husband, but at the trial managed to get
acquitted.

Breakes's next exploit was to steal his employer's ship and cargo and go out as a pirate, naming his vessel the *Adventure*. His first exploit was a daring one. Sailing into Vigo Harbour in full view of the forts, he seized a vessel, the *Acapulco,* lately come from Valparaiso, and took her off. On plundering her they found 200,000 small bars of gold, each about the size of a man's finger. The captain and crew of this Chilian vessel were all murdered. Breakes preferred the *Acapulco* to his own ship, so he fitted her up and sailed in her to the Mediterranean.

Breakes was one of the religious variety of pirate, for after six days of robbing and throat-slitting he would order his crew to clean themselves on the Sabbath and gather on the quarter-deck, where he would read prayers to them and would often preach a sermon " after the Lutheran style," thus fortifying the brave fellows for another week of toil and bloodshed.

Gifted with unlimited boldness, Breakes called in at Gibraltar and requested the Governor to grant him a British privateer's commission, which the Governor did " for a consideration." Sailing in the neighbourhood of the Balearic Islands, he took a few ships, when one day, spying a nunnery by the sea-shore in Minorca, he proposed to his crew that they should fit themselves out with a wife apiece.

This generous offer was eagerly accepted, and the crew, headed by Captain Breakes, marched up to the nunnery unopposed, and were welcomed at the door by the lady abbess. Having entered the peaceful cloister, each pirate chose a nun and marched back to the ship with their spoils. Soon after this Breakes decided to retire from piracy, and returned to Amsterdam to claim Mrs. Snyde. But he found that she had but lately been hanged for poisoning her little son, of which the pirate was father. This tragedy so preyed upon the mind of Captain Breakes that he turned "melancholy mad" and drowned himself in one of the many dykes with which that city abounds.

BRECK, JOHN.

One of the crew of the brigantine *Charles* (Captain John Quelch). Tried for piracy at Boston in 1704.

BREHA, CAPTAIN, *alias* LANDRESSON.

BRENNINGHAM, CAPTAIN.
Of Jamaica and Tortuga.

In 1663 commanded a frigate of six guns and seventy men.

BRIERLY, JOHN, *alias* TIMBERHEAD.
Of Bath Town in North Carolina.

One of the crew of the *Royal James*. Hanged at Charleston in November, 1718.

BRIGHT, JOHN.
Of St. Margaret's, Westminster.

One of the crew of Captain Charles Harris. Hanged at Newport, Rhode Island, in July, 1723, at the age of 25.

BRINKLEY, JAMES.
Of Suffolk, England.

One of Captain Charles Harris's crew. Hanged for piracy at Newport, Rhode Island, on July 19th, 1723. Age 28.

BRODLEY, CAPTAIN JOSEPH, or BRADLEY, sometimes called "Lieutenant-Colonel." "An ancient and expert pirate."

Appointed Vice-Admiral by Morgan in his expedition up the Chagre River. He was a tough old pirate, and had proved himself a terror to the Spaniards, particularly when Mansvelt took the Isle of St. Catharine. In 1676 Brodley was sent by Morgan to capture the Castle of Chagre, a very strongly garrisoned fort. All day the pirates kept up a furious attack, but were driven back. At last, when it seemed impossible for the pirates ever to succeed in entering the castle, a remarkable accident happened which altered the whole issue. One of the pirates was wounded by an arrow in his back, which pierced his body and came out the opposite side. This he instantly pulled out at the side of his breast; then, taking a little cotton, he wound it about the arrow, and, putting it into his musket, he shot it back into the castle. The cotton, kindled by the powder, set fire to several houses within the castle, which, being thatched with palm-leaves, took fire very easily. This fire at last reached the powder magazine, and a great explosion occurred. Owing to this accident of the arrow the pirates were eventually able to take the Castle of Chagre. This was one of the finest and bravest defences ever made by the Spaniards. Out of 314 Spanish soldiers in the castle, only thirty survived, all the rest, including the Governor, being killed. Brodley was himself severely wounded in this action and died as a consequence ten days later.

BROOKS, JOSEPH (senior).

One of Blackbeard's crew in the *Queen Ann's Revenge*. Killed on November 22nd, 1718, at North Carolina.

BROOKS, JOSEPH (junior).

One of Blackbeard's crew in the *Queen Ann's Revenge*. Taken prisoner by Lieutenant Maynard on November 22nd, 1718. Carried to Virginia, where he was tried and hanged.

BROWN, Captain.

A notorious latter-day pirate, who "worked" the east coast of Central America in the early part of the nineteenth century.

BROWN, Captain.

On July 24th, 1702, sailed from Jamaica in command of the *Blessing*—ten guns and crew of seventy-nine men, with the famous Edward Davis on board—to attack the town of Tolu on the Spanish Main. The town was taken and plundered, but Brown was killed, being shot through the head.

BROWN, Captain Nicholas.

Surrendered to the King's pardon for pirates at New Providence, Bahamas, in 1718. Soon afterwards he surrendered to the Spanish Governor of Cuba, embraced the Catholic faith, and turned pirate once more; and was very active in attacking English ships off the Island of Jamaica.

BROWN, John.
Of Durham, England.

One of Captain Charles Harris's crew. Hanged at the age of 29 years at Newport, Rhode Island, in 1723.

BROWN, John.
Of Liverpool.

One of Captain Harris's crew. Found guilty of piracy at Newport, Rhode Island, in 1723, but recommended to the King's favour, perhaps in view of his age, being but 17 years old.

BROWNE, Captain James.
A Scotchman.

In 1677, when in command of a mixed crew of English, Dutch, and French pirates, he took a Dutch ship trading in negroes off the coast of Cartagena. The Dutch captain and several of his crew were killed, while the cargo of 150 negroes was landed in a remote bay on the coast of Jamaica.

Lord Vaughan sent a frigate, which captured about a hundred of the negro slaves and also Browne and eight of his pirate crew. The captain and crew were tried for piracy and condemned. The crew were pardoned, but Browne was ordered to be executed. The captain appealed to the Assembly to have the benefit of the Act of Privateers, and the House of Assembly twice sent a committee to the Governor to beg a reprieve. Lord Vaughan refused this and ordered the immediate execution of Browne. Half an hour after the hanging the provost-marshal appeared with an order, signed by the Speaker, to stop the execution.

BROWNE, EDWARD.

Of York River, Virginia.

One of Captain Pounds's crew. Wounded at Tarpaulin Cove in 1689.

BROWNE, JOHN, *alias* MAMME.

An English sailor who joined the Barbary pirates at Algiers and turned Mohammedan. Taken in the *Exchange* in 1622 and carried a prisoner to Plymouth.

BROWNE, RICHARD. Surgeon.

Surgeon-General in Morgan's fleet which carried the buccaneers to the Spanish Main. He wrote an account of the disastrous explosion on board the *Oxford* during a banquet given to Morgan and the buccaneer commanders on January 2nd, 1669, off Cow Island to the south of Hispaniola, at which the details were being discussed for an attack on Cartagena.

Browne writes : " I was eating my dinner with the rest when the mainmasts blew out and fell upon Captains Aylett and Bigford and others and knocked them on the head. I saved myself by getting astride the mizzenmast." Only Morgan and those who sat on his side of the dinner-table were saved.

Browne, who certainly was not biased towards Morgan in his accounts of his exploits, is one of the few narrators who gives the buccaneer Admiral credit for moderation towards his prisoners, particularly women.

BUCK, ELEAZER.

One of Captain Pounds's crew. Tried at Boston in 1689 for piracy and found guilty, but pardoned on payment of a fine of twenty marks.

BUCKENHAM, CAPTAIN.

In 1679 sailed from England to the West Indies. He was taken by the Spaniards off Campeachy and carried to Mexico. A seaman, Russel, also a prisoner there, and who escaped afterwards, reported to Lionel Wafer that he last saw Captain Buckenham with a log chained to his leg and a basket on his back, crying bread about the streets of the city of Mexico for his master, a baker.

BULL, CAPTAIN DIXEY.

Born in London of a respectable family, and in 1631 went to Boston, where he received a grant of land at York on the coast of Maine. Became a " trader for bever " in New England. In June, 1632, while in Penobscot Bay, a French pinnace arrived and seized his shallop and stock of " coats, ruggs, blanketts, bisketts, etc." Annoyed by this high-handed behaviour, Bull collected together a small crew and turned pirate, thus being the very first pirate on the New England coast. Bull took several small vessels, and was not caught by the authorities, who sent out small armed sloops to search for him, and nothing more was heard of this pioneer pirate after 1633, although rumour said that he had reached England in safety.

BULL, Mr.

A member of the crew of Coxon's canoe, he was killed in the famous attack by the buccaneers on the Spanish Fleet off Panama in 1680.

BULLOCK. Surgeon.

One of the crew at the second disastrous attack by Captain Sharp on the town of Arica, when the buccaneers were driven out of the town. All escaped who could, except the surgeons, who, in a most unprofessional way, had been indulging somewhat freely in the wines of the country during the battle, and consequently were in no condition to take their places with the retreating force. The surgeons, after being taken prisoner, were persuaded to disclose to the Spaniards the prearranged signals by smoke from two fires, which was to be given in case of a successful taking of the town, to bring up the boats that were hiding on the shore, ready to take the buccaneers back to their ships. Fortunately the buccaneers on the shore arrived just as the canoes were getting under way, otherwise the whole remnant of them would have perished. The only one of these disreputable surgeons whose name we know is Dr. Bullock. Some months afterwards it was ascertained, through a prisoner, that the Spaniards " civilly entertained these surgeons, more especially the women." Surgeons, even such surgeons as these, were considered to be valuable in those days in the out-of-the-way Spanish colonies.

BUNCE, CHARLES.
Born at Exeter; died at the age of 26.

Taken by Captain Roberts out of a Dutch galley in 1721, he joined the pirates, to be eventually hanged in 1722. He made a moving speech from the gallows, "disclaiming against the guilded Bates of Power, Liberty, and Wealth that had ensnared him amongst the pirates," earnestly exhorting the spectators to remember his youth, and ending by declaring that "he stood there as a beacon upon a Rock" (the gallows standing on one) "to warn erring Marriners of Danger."

BURDER, WILLIAM.
Mayor of Dover.

It may seem strange to accuse the mayor of so important a seaport as Dover of being a pirate, but it is difficult to see how William Burder is to escape the accusation when we learn that in the year 1563 he captured 600 French vessels and a large number of neutral craft, which he plundered, and also no fewer than sixty-one Spanish ships, to the very natural annoyance of the King of Spain, whose country was at this time at peace with England.

BURGESS, CAPTAIN SAMUEL SOUTH.

Born and bred in New York, he was a man of good education, and began his career on a privateer in the West Indies. Later on he was sent by a Mr. Philips, owner and shipbuilder, to trade with the pirates in Madagascar. This business Burgess augmented with a little piracy on his own account, and after taking several prizes he returned to the West Indies, where he disposed of his loot. He then proceeded to New York, and, purposely wrecking his vessel at Sandy Hook, landed in the guise of an honest shipwrecked mariner.

Burgess settled down for a time to a well-earned rest, and married a relative of his employer, Mr. Philips.

Philips sent him on two further voyages, both of which were run on perfectly honest lines, and were most successful both to owner and captain. But a later voyage had an unhappy ending. After successfully trading with the pirates in Madagascar, Burgess was returning home, carrying several pirates as passengers, who were returning to settle in America, having made their fortunes. The ship was captured off the Cape of Good Hope by an East Indiaman, and taken to Madras. Here the captain and passengers were put in irons and sent to England to be tried. The case against Burgess fell through, and he was liberated. Instead of at once getting away, he loitered about London until one unlucky day he ran across an old pirate associate called Culliford, on whose evidence Burgess was again arrested, tried, and condemned to death, but pardoned at the last moment by the Queen, through the intercession of the Bishop of London. After a while he procured the post of mate in the *Neptune*, a Scotch vessel, which was to go to Madagascar to trade liquors with the pirates who had their headquarters in that delectable island. On arrival at Madagascar a sudden hurricane swept down, dismasted the *Neptune,* and sank two pirate ships. The chief pirate, Halsey, as usual, proved himself a man of resource. Seeing that without a ship his activities were severely restricted, he promptly, with the help of his faithful and willing crew, seized the *Neptune,* this satisfactory state of affairs being largely facilitated by the knowledge that the mate, Burgess, was all ripe to go on the main chance once more. The first venture of this newly formed crew was most successful, as they seized a ship, the *Greyhound,* which lay in the bay, the owners of which had but the previous day bought—and paid for—a valuable loading of merchandise from the pirates. This was now taken back by the pirates, who, having refitted the *Neptune,* set forth seeking fresh adventures and prizes. The further history of Burgess is one of constant change and disappointment.

While serving under a Captain North, he was accused of betraying some of his associates, and was robbed of all his hard-earned savings. For several years after this he lived ashore at a place in Madagascar called Methalage, until captured by some Dutch rovers, who soon after were themselves taken by French pirates. Burgess, with his former Dutch captain, was put ashore at Johanna, where, under the former's expert knowledge, a ship was built and sailed successfully to Youngoul, where Burgess got a post as third mate on a ship bound to the West Indies. Before sailing, Burgess was sent, on account of his knowledge of the language, as ambassador to the local King. Burgess, unfortunately for himself, had in the past said some rather unkind things about this particular ruler, and the offended monarch, in revenge, gave Burgess some poisoned liquor to drink, which quickly brought to an end an active if chequered career.

BURGESS, Captain Thomas.

One of the pirates of the Bahama Islands who surrendered to King George in 1718 and received the royal pardon. He was afterwards drowned at sea.

BURK, Captain.

An Irishman, who committed many piracies on the coast of Newfoundland. Drowned in the Atlantic during a hurricane in 1699.

CACHEMARÉE, Captain. French filibuster.

Commanded the *St. Joseph*, of six guns and a crew of seventy men. In 1684 had his headquarters at San Domingo.

CÆSAR.

A negro. One of Teach's crew hanged at Virginia in 1718. Cæsar, who was much liked and trusted by Blackbeard, had orders from him to blow up the *Queen Ann's Revenge* by dropping a lighted match into the powder magazine in case the ship was taken by Lieutenant Maynard. Cæsar attempted to carry out his instructions, but was prevented from doing so by two of the surrendered pirates.

CÆSAR, Captain.

One of Gasparilla's gang of pirates who hunted in the Gulf of Mexico. His headquarters were on Sanibel Island.

CALLES, Captain John, or Callis.

A notorious Elizabethan pirate, whose activities were concentrated on the coast of Wales.

We quote Captain John Smith, the founder of Virginia, who writes: "This Ancient pirate Callis, who most refreshed himselfe upon the Coast of Wales, who grew famous, till Queene Elizabeth of Blessed Memory, hanged him at Wapping."

Calles did not die on the gallows without an attempt at getting let off. He wrote a long and ingenious letter to Lord Walsyngham, bewailing his former wicked life and promising, if spared, to assist in ridding the coast of pirates by giving particulars of "their roads, haunts, creeks, and maintainers." One of the chief of these "maintainers," or receivers of stolen property, was Lord O'Sullivan, or the Sulivan

Bere of Berehaven. In spite of a long and very plausible plea for pity, this "ancient and wicked pyrate" met his fate on the gibbet at Wapping.

CAMMOCK, William.

A seaman under Captain Bartholomew Sharp. He died at sea on December 14th, 1679, off the coast of Chile. "His disease was occasioned by a sunfit, gained by too much drinking on shore at La Serena; which produced in him a *celenture,* or malignant fever and a hiccough." He was buried at sea with the usual honours of "three French vollies."

CANDOR, Ralph.

Tried for piracy with the rest of Captain Lowther's crew at St. Kitts in March, 1723, and acquitted.

CANNIS, *alias* Cannis Marcy.

A Dutch pirate who acted as interpreter to Captain Bartholomew Sharp's South Sea Expedition. Captain Cox and Basil Ringmore took him with them after the sacking of Hilo in 1679, to come to terms with the Spanish cavalry over the ransoming of a sugar mill. On Friday, May 27th, 1680, while ashore with a watering party in the Gulf of Nicoya, the interpreter, having had, no doubt, his fill of buccaneering, ran away.

CARACCIOLI, Signor, *alias* D'Aubigny.

An Italian renegade priest, who became an atheist, Socialist, and revolutionist, and was living at Naples when Captain Fourbin arrived there in the French man-of-war *Victoire.*

Caraccioli met and made great friends with a young French apprentice in the ship, called Misson, and a place was found for him on board. The ex-priest proved himself to be a brave man in several engagements with the Moors and with an English warship, and was quickly promoted to be a petty officer.

Caraccioli, by his eloquence, soon converted most of the crew to believe in his theories, and when Captain Fourbin was killed in an action off Martinique with an English ship, Misson took command and appointed the Italian to be his Lieutenant, and continued to fight the English ship to a finish. The victorious crew then elected Misson to be their captain, and decided to " bid defiance to all nations " and to settle on some out-of-the-way island. Capturing another English ship off the Cape of Good Hope, Caraccioli was put in command of her, and the whole of the English crew voluntarily joined the pirates, and sailed to Madagascar. Here they settled, and the Italian married the daughter of a black Island King; an ideal republic was formed, and our hero was appointed Secretary of State.

Eventually Caraccioli died fighting during a sudden attack made on the settlement by a neighbouring tribe.

CARMAN, Thomas.
Of Maidstone in Kent.
Hanged at Charleston in 1718 with the rest of Major Bonnet's crew.

CARNES, John.
One of Blackbeard's crew. Hanged at Virginia in 1718.

CARR, John.
A Massachusetts pirate, one of Hore's crew, who was hiding in Rhode Island in 1699.

CARTER, DENNIS.

Tried for piracy in June, 1704, at the Star Tavern in Boston. One of John Quelch's crew.

CARTER, JOHN.

Captured by Major Sewall in the *Larimore* galley, and brought into Salem. One of Captain Quelch's crew. Tried at Boston in 1704.

CASTILLO.

A Columbian sailor in the schooner *Panda*. Hanged for piracy at Boston on June 11th, 1835.

LA CATA.

A most blood-thirsty pirate and one of the last of the West Indian gangs.

In 1824, when La Cata was cruising off the Isle of Pines, his ship was attacked by an English cutter only half his size. After a furious fight the cutter was victorious, and returned in triumph to Jamaica with the three survivors of the pirates as prisoners. One of these was found out at the trial to be La Cata himself. Hanged at Kingston, Jamaica.

CHANDLER, HENRY, *alias* RAMMETHAM RISE.

Born in Devonshire, his father kept a chandler's shop in Southwark. An English *renegado* at Algiers, who had turned Mohammedan and had become an overseer in the pirates' shipyards. He was a man of some authority amongst the Moors, and in 1621 he appointed a slave called Goodale to become master of one of the pirate ships, the *Exchange*, in which one Rawlins also sailed. Owing to the courage and ingenuity of the latter, the European slaves afterwards seized the ship and brought her into Plymouth; Chandler being thrown into gaol and afterwards hanged.

CHEESMAN, EDWARD.

Taken prisoner out of the *Dolphin*, on the Banks of Newfoundland, by the Pirate Phillips in 1724. With the help of a fisherman called Fillmore, he killed Phillips and ten other pirates and brought the ship into Boston Harbour.

CHEVALLE, DANIEL.

One of Captain John Quelch's crew. Tried for piracy at Boston in 1704.

CHILD, THOMAS.

In the year 1723, at the age of 15, he was tried for piracy at Newport, Rhode Island. This child must have seen scores of cold-blooded murders committed while he sailed with Low and Harris. Found to be not guilty.

CHRISTIAN, CAPTAIN.

In 1702 the town of Tolu was sacked by Captain Brown of the *Blessing*. Brown was killed, and Christian was elected to be captain in his stead. Davis tells us that " Christian was an old experienced soldier and privateer, very brave and just in all his actions." He had lived for a long while amongst the Darien Indians, with whom he was on very friendly terms.

CHULY, DANIEL.

Tried for piracy at Boston, Massachusetts, in 1706.

CHURCH, CHARLES.
Of St. Margaret's, Westminster.

One of Captain Charles Harris's crew. Hanged on July 19th, 1723, at Newport, Rhode Island. Age

CHURCH, EDWARD.

In 1830 he served in the brig *Vineyard,* from New Orleans to Philadelphia. Took part in the mutiny which was planned by the notorious pirate Charles Gibbs.

CHURCH, WILLIAM.
Of the *Gertrwycht* of Holland.

At the trial at West Africa in 1722 of the crew of Bartholomew Roberts's, four of the prisoners—W. Church, Phil. Haak, James White, and Nicholas Brattle—were proved to have " served as Musick on board the *Royal Fortune,* being taken out of several merchant ships, having had an uneasy life of it, having sometimes their Fiddles, and often their Heads broke, only for excusing themselves, as saying they were tired, when any Fellow took it in his Head to demand a Tune." Acquitted.

CHURCHILL, JOHN.

One of Captain George Lowther's crew. Captured by the *Eagle* sloop at the Island of Blanco, not far from Tortuga.

Hanged on March 11th, 1722, at St. Kitts.

CLARKE, JONATHAN.
Of Charleston, South Carolina.

One of Major Stede Bonnet's crew. Tried for piracy at Charleston in 1718, and found to be not guilty.

CLARKE, RICHARD, *alias* JAFAR.

A renegade English sailor, who turned " Turk "— that is, became a Mohammedan—and was appointed chief gunner on one of the Barbary pirate ships.

Captured in the *Exchange*, and brought into Plymouth in 1622. He was hanged.

CLARKE, ROBERT.

Governor of New Providence, Bahama Islands. Instead of trying to stamp out the pirates, he did all he could to encourage them, by granting letters of marque to such men as Coxon, to go privateering, these letters being quite illegal. The proprietors of the Bahama Islands turned Clarke out and appointed in his place Robert Lilburne in 1682.

CLIFFORD, JOHN.

One of Captain John Quelch's crew; tried at the Star Tavern at Boston in 1704 for piracy. All the accused pleaded "Not guilty" except Clifford and two others who turned Queen's evidence.

CLINTON, CAPTAIN.

One of the notorious sixteenth century pirates " who grew famous until Queene Elizabeth of blessed memory, hanged them at Wapping."

COBHAM, CAPTAIN.
Of Poole in Dorsetshire.

At the age of 18 he took to smuggling. His biographer tells us that even at this comparatively early age Cobham " was cautious and prudent, and though he intrigued with the ladies, he managed to keep it secret." Cobham was very successful as a smuggler, on one occasion landing a cargo of ten thousand gallons of brandy at Poole. But a little later on his vessel was captured by a King's cutter. This annoyed the young captain, and he bought a cutter

at Bridport, mounted fourteen guns in her, and turned
pirate. Out of his very first prize, an Indiaman,
which he boarded off the Mersey, he took a sum of
£40,000, and then scuttled the ship and drowned the
crew.

Cobham, calling in at Plymouth, met a damsel
called Maria, whom he took on board with him,
which at first caused some murmuring amongst his
crew, who were jealous because they themselves were
not able to take lady companions with them on their
voyages, for, as the same biographer sagely remarks,
"where a man is married the case is altered, no man
envies him his happiness; but where he only keeps a
girl, every man says, ' I have as much right to one as
he has.' " Nevertheless, Maria proved herself a great
success, for when any member of the crew was to be
punished Maria would use her influence with the captain to get him excused or his punishment lessened,
thus winning the affection of all on board. The English Channel becoming too dangerous for Cobham,
he sailed across the Atlantic and lay in wait for vessels
between Cape Breton and Prince Edward Isle, and
took several prizes. In one of these he placed all the
crew in sacks and threw them into the sea. Maria,
too, took her part in these affairs, and once stabbed
to the heart, with her own little dirk, the captain of
a Liverpool brig, the *Lion,* and on another occasion,
to indulge her whim, a captain and his two mates
were tied up to the windlass while Maria shot them
with her pistol. Maria always wore naval uniform,
both at sea and when in port; in fact, she entered
thoroughly into the spirit of the enterprise.

Cobham now wished to retire from the sea, but
Maria urged him to further efforts, as she had set her
heart on his buying her a beautiful place in England
called Mapleton Hall, near Poole.

Maria's last act at sea was to poison the whole crew

of an Indiaman, who were prisoners in irons aboard the pirate ship.

Cobham having made a vast fortune, at last decided to settle down, and he bought a large estate near Havre from the Duc de Chartres. It was on the coast, and had a snug little harbour of its own, where the retired pirate kept a small pleasure yacht in which he and Maria used to go for fishing expeditions. One day, when they were out on one of these picnics, a West India brig lay becalmed near by, and Cobham and his crew went on board to visit the captain of the merchant ship. But the temptation proved too strong, and Cobham suddenly shooting the captain, Maria and the yacht's crew quickly despatched the rest. Carrying the prize to Bordeaux, he sold her for a good price. This was Cobham's last act of piracy, and soon afterwards he was made a magistrate, and presided at the county courts. Maria, it was thought, possibly owing to remorse, poisoned herself with laudanum and died. Cobham lived to a good old age, and eventually passed away, leaving many descendants, who, a hundred years ago, "were moving in the first grade at Havre."

COBHAM, Mrs. Maria.

A bloodthirsty and ambitious woman pirate, the wife of Captain Cobham, late of Poole in Dorset.

COCKLYN, Captain Thomas.

In 1717 was in the Bahama Islands when Woodes Rogers arrived at New Providence Island with King George's offer of pardon to those pirates who came in and surrendered themselves. Cocklyn, like many others, after surrendering, fell again into their wicked ways, and ended by being hanged. Only a year after receiving the royal pardon we hear of him being in

company with Davis and La Bouse and several other
notorious pirates at Sierra Leone, when he was in
command of a tall ship of twenty-four guns.

Cocklyn ended his life on the gallows.

COFRECINA, Captain.

A notorious Spanish-American pirate who was very
troublesome in the South Atlantic in the early part of
the last century. Eventually captured by Midshipman
Hull Foot of the U.S. Navy in March, 1825, at St.
Thomas Isle. Executed in Porto Rico by the
terrible Spanish method of the garotte.

COLE, Captain John.

Commander of the *Eagle, alias* the *New York
Revenge's Revenge.* Tried, condemned, and hanged
in 1718 at Charleston. His was a brilliant career
while it lasted, but was cut short after a brief and
meteoric spell.

COLE, Samuel.

One of Captain Fly's crew. Tried and condemned
for piracy at Boston in 1726. On the way to the
gallows the culprits were taken to church, where they
had to listen to a long sermon from Dr. Colman,
bringing home to the wretched creatures their dread-
ful sins and their awful future.

COLLIER, Captain Edward.

Commanded the *Oxford,* a King's ship, which was
sent from England to Jamaica at the earnest request
of Governor Modyford, for a " nimble frigate," to
help keep control over the increasingly turbulent
buccaneers. Collier's first act was to seize a French
man-of-war, a privateer called the *Cour Volent,* of La
Rochelle, commanded by M. la Vivon, his excuse

being that the Frenchmen had robbed an English vessel of provisions. Collier was appointed to be Morgan's Vice-Admiral, and a few days later the *Oxford* was blown up accidentally while a conference of buccaneer captains was taking place.

In 1670, with six ships and 400 men, the buccaneers sailed for the Spanish Main and sacked the city of Rio de la Hacha. Collier led the left wing in the famous and successful attack on Panama City with the rank of colonel.

Richard Brown reports that Collier could on occasions be very cruel, and that he even executed a Spanish friar on the battlefield after quarter had been given to the vanquished. On their return to the coast after the sacking of Panama, Collier was accused, with Morgan and the other commanders, of having cheated the seamen of their fair share of the plunder, and of deserting them, and then sailing off in the ships with the supplies of food as well as the plunder.

COLLINS, Thomas.

This Madagascar pirate was a carpenter by trade, who had by 1716 retired from the sea and lived in splendour in that island. Collins was made Governor of the pirate colony, and built a small fort for its defence, which the pirates armed with the guns taken out of their ship, which had by long use grown old and crazy, and was of no further use to them.

COMRY, Adam.

Surgeon to the ship *Elizabeth*, taken by Captain Bartholomew Roberts's squadron. Gave evidence at the trial of George Wilson and another sea-surgeon, Scudamore, that the former had borrowed from Comry a "clean shirt and drawers, for his better appearance and reception." When visiting Captain

Bartholomew Roberts's ship, Comry was forced to
serve as surgeon on board one of Roberts's vessels.

CONDENT, CAPTAIN, *also* CONGDON or CONDEN.
  Born at Plymouth in Devonshire.

  Condent was quartermaster in a New York sloop,
at the Island of New Providence, when Governor
Woodes Rogers arrived there in 1718. The captain
of the sloop seems to have thought best to leave rather
than wait to welcome the new Governor. When only
a few days out, one of the crew, an Indian, who had
been cruelly treated, attempted, in revenge, to blow
up the ship. This was prevented by Condent, who
with great courage leapt into the hold and shot the
Indian, but not before the latter had fired at him and
broken his arm. The crew, to show the relief they
felt at being saved from a sudden death, hacked to
pieces the body of the Indian, while the gunner,
ripping open the dead man's belly, tore out his heart,
which he boiled and ate.

  Turning their attention from cannibalism to piracy,
the pirates took a prize, the *Duke of York,* but disputes arising, the captain and part of the crew sailed
in the prize, while Condent was elected captain of the
sloop, and headed across the Atlantic for the Cape
Verde Islands, where he found the salt fleet, of twenty
small vessels, lying at anchor off the Island of Mayo,
all of which he took. Sailing next to the Island of
St. Jago, he took a Dutch ship. This proving a better
ship than the sloop, Condent transferred himself and
crew into her, and named her the *Flying Dragon,*
presenting the sloop to the mate of an English prize,
who he had forced to go with him. From thence
Condent sailed away for the coast of Brazil, taking
several Portuguese ships which, after plundering, he
let go. After cleaning the *Flying Dragon* on Ferdinando Island, the pirates took several more prizes,

and then one day met with a Portuguese man-of-war
of seventy guns.   Coming up with her, the Portuguese hailed the pirates, and they answered " from
London bound for Buenos Ayres."   The man-of-war,
to pay a compliment to the ship of her English ally,
manned the shrouds and cheered him, and while this
amicable demonstration of marine brotherly feeling
was taking place, Captain Condent came up alongside
and suddenly fired a broadside and a volley of small
arms into the man-of-war, and a smart engagement
followed, in which the pirates were worsted, and were
lucky to escape.

Sailing away round the Cape of Good Hope, Con-
dent arrived at the pirate stronghold at the Island of
Johanna, where he took on board some of Captain
Halsey's crew, and, reinforced by these skilled
masters in the craft of piracy, took several rich East
Indiamen off the Malabar coast.

Calling in at the Isle of St. Mary, one of the
Mascerenas group, he met with another Portuguese
ship of seventy guns, which he was fortunate enough
to make a prize of.   In this ship they found amongst
the passengers the Viceroy of Goa.   Carrying this
rich prize to Zanzibar, they plundered her of a large
amount of money.

Having now gathered a vast fortune, they thought
it time to give up piracy, so they returned to the
Island of St. Mary, where they made a share of their
plunder, and the company broke up, many of them
settling down amongst the natives.   Captain Condent
and some others sent from here a petition to the
Governor of Mauritius asking for a pardon, and received answer that he would take them into his protection if they would destroy their ships.   Having
done this, they sailed to Mauritius, where they settled
down, and Captain Condent married the Governor's
sister-in-law.

A few years later the captain and his wife left the island and sailed to France, settling at St. Malo, where Condent drove a considerable trade as a merchant.

COOK, Captain Edward, or Edmund.

Was on the Pacific coast with Captains Sharp and Sawkins, 1680. Being unable to keep order amongst his unruly crew, he resigned his ship and command to Captain John Cox, a New Englander. He commanded a barque in the successful sacking of Porto Bello in the same year in company with Sharp, Coxon, and others.

On land engagements his flag was a red one striped with yellow, on which was a device of a hand and sword.

COOK, George, alias Ramedam.

An English renegade amongst the Barbary pirates of Algiers. Was gunner's mate when captured in the *Exchange* in 1622. Brought to Plymouth and hanged.

COOK, William.

Servant to Captain Edmund Cook, and was found, on being searched, to have on him a paper with the names of all his fellow pirates written on it, and was suspected of having prepared it to give to some of the Spanish prisoners. For this, Captain Walters put him in irons on January 7th, 1681.

He died on board ship on Monday, February 14th, 1681, off the coast of Chile.

COOKE, Captain John.

This buccaneer was born in the Island of St. Christopher. "A brisk, bold man," he was promoted to the rank of quartermaster by Captain Yankey. On taking a Spanish ship, Cooke claimed the command of her, which he was entitled to, and would have gone in her with an English crew had not the French members of the crew, through jealousy, sacked the ship and marooned the Englishmen on the Island of Avache. Cooke and his men were rescued by another French buccaneer, Captain Tristram, and taken to the Island of Dominica. Here the English managed to get away with the ship, leaving Tristram and his Frenchmen behind on land. Cooke, now with a ship of his own, took two French ships loaded with wine. With this valuable cargo he steered northward, and reached Virginia in April, 1683. He had no difficulty in selling his wine for a good price to the New Englanders, and with the profits prepared for a long voyage in his ship, the *Revenge*. He took on board with him several famous buccaneers, including Dampier and Cowley, the latter as sailing master. They first sailed to Sierra Leone, then round the Horn to the Island of Juan Fernandez. Here Cooke was taken ill. His next stop was at the Galapagos Islands. Eventually Cooke died a mile or two off the coast of Cape Blanco in Mexico. His body was rowed ashore to be buried, accompanied by an armed guard of twelve seamen. While his grave was being dug three Spanish Indians came up, and asked so many questions as to rouse the suspicions of the pirates, who seized them as spies, but one escaping, he raised the whole countryside.

COOPER, Captain.

Commanded a pirate sloop, the *Night Rambler*. On November 14th, 1725, he took the *Perry* galley (Captain King, commander), three days out from Barbadoes, and the following day a French sloop, and carried both prizes to a small island called Aruba, near Curaçao, where they plundered them and divided the spoil amongst the crew. The crews of the two prizes were kept on the island by Cooper for seventeen days, and would have starved if the pirate's doctor had not taken compassion on them and procured them food.

Upton, boatswain in the *Perry*, joined the pirates, and was afterwards tried and hanged in England.

COOPER, Captain.

On October 19th, 1663, he brought into Port Royal, Jamaica, two Spanish prizes, one the *Maria of Seville*, a royal azogue carrying 1,000 quintals of quicksilver for the King of Spain's mines in Mexico, besides oil, wine, and olives. Also a number of prisoners were taken, including several friars on their way to Campeachy and Vera Cruz. The buccaneers always rejoiced at capturing a priest or a friar, and these holy men generally experienced very rough treatment at the hands of the pirates.

Cooper's ship was a frigate of ten guns, and a crew of eighty men.

CORBET, Captain.

Sailed with Captain Heidon from Bantry Bay in the *John of Sandwich* in 1564 to search for a good prize in which he might go a-pirating on his own account. The ship was wrecked on the Island of Alderney, and all the crew arrested. Corbett and several others escaped in a small boat.

CORNELIUS, Captain.

A contemporary of Howard Burgess North and other Madagascar pirates.

DE COSSEY, Stephen James.

With three other pirates was tried and convicted in June, 1717, before the Vice-Admiralty Court at

Charleston. The President of the Court was Judge Trot, a terror to all pirates, as he never failed to hang a guilty one. De Cossey and the other prisoners were found guilty of piratically taking the vessels *Turtle Dove, Penelope,* and the *Virgin Queen.*

COWARD, WILLIAM.

In November, 1689, with three men and a boy he rowed out to the ketch *Elinor* (William Shortrigs, master), lying at anchor in Boston Harbour, and seized the vessel and took her to Cape Cod. The crew of the ketch could make no resistance as they were all down with the smallpox. The pirates were caught and locked up in the new stone gaol in Boston. Hanged on January 27th, 1690.

COWLEY, CAPTAIN C.
M.A. Cantab.

A man of high intelligence and an able navigator. In the year 1683 he sailed from Achamach or Cape Charles in Virginia for Dominica as sailing master of a privateer, the *Revenge* (eight guns and fifty-two men), in company with Dampier and Captain John Cooke. As soon as they were away from the land, they turned buccaneers or pirates, and sailed to Sierra Leone in West Africa. Thence to the coast of Brazil, round the Horn, where Cowley mentions that owing to the intense cold weather the crew were able, each man, to drink three quarts of burnt brandy a day without becoming drunk.

On February 14th the buccaneers were abreast of Cape Horn, and in his diary Cowley writes : " We were choosing valentines and discoursing on the Intrigues of Woman, when there arose a prodigious storm," which lasted till the end of the month, driving them farther south than any ship had ever been before ;

"so that we concluded the discoursing of Women at sea was very unlucky and occasioned the storm." Cowley, who was addicted to giving new names to islands, not only named one Pepys Island, but when he arrived at the Galapagos Islands, he rechristened them most thoroughly, naming one King Charles Island, while others he named after the Dukes of York, Norfolk, and Albemarle, and Sir John Narborough. Feeling, no doubt, that he had done enough to honour the great, and perhaps to have insured himself against any future trouble with the authorities when he returned home, he named one small island "Cowley's Enchanted Isle."

The Earl of Alington, Lord Culpepper, Lord Wenman, all had islands in this group christened with their names and titles.

In September, 1684, Cowley, now in the *Nicholas*, separated from Davis, and sailed from Ampalla for San Francisco, and then started west to cross the Pacific Ocean. On March 14th, 1685, at seven o'clock in the morning, after a voyage of 7,646 miles, land was at last seen, which proved to be the Island of Guan.

The Spanish Governor was most friendly to the visitors, and when complaint was made to him that the buccaneers had killed some of his Indian subjects he "gave us a Toleration to kill them all if we would." Presents were exchanged, Cowley giving the Governor a valuable diamond ring, one, no doubt, taken off the hand of some other loyal subject of the King of Spain. Here the pirates committed several atrocious cruelties on the Indians, who wished to be friends with the foreigners.

In April they arrived at Canton to refit, and while there, thirteen Tartar ships arrived laden with Chinese merchandise, chiefly valuable silks. Cowley wanted to attack and plunder them, but his crew refused to do so, saying "they came for gold and silver, and not to be made pedlars, to carry packs on their backs," to Cowley's disgust, for he complains, " had Reason but ruled them, we might all have made our Fortunes and have done no Christian Prince nor their subjects any harm at all." Thence they sailed to Borneo, the animals and birds of which island Cowley describes. Sailing next to Timor, the crew mutinied, and Cowley and eighteen others bought a boat and sailed in her to Java, some 300 leagues. Here they heard of the death of King Charles II., which caused Cowley to get out his map of the Galapagos Islands, and to change the name of Duke of York Island to King James Island. At Batavia Cowley procured a passage in a Dutch ship to Cape Town. In June, 1686, he sailed for Holland after much health drinking and salutes of 300 guns, arriving in that country in September, and reaching London, "through the infinite Mercy of God," on October 12th, 1686.

COX, CAPTAIN JOHN. Buccaneer.

Born in New England, and considered by some of his fellow buccaneers "to have forced kindred upon Captain Sharp "—the leader of the fleet—" out of old acquaintance, only to advance himself." Thus he was made Vice-Admiral to Captain Sharp, in place of Captain Cook, whose crew had mutinied and refused to sail any longer under his command. Cox began his captaincy by getting lost, but after a fortnight rejoined the fleet off the Island of Plate, on the coast of Peru, "to the great joy of us all." This island received its name from the fact that Sir Francis Drake had here made a division of his spoils, distributing to each man of his company sixteen bowlfuls of doubloons and pieces of eight. The buccaneers rechristened it Drake's Island.

Cox took part in the attack on the town of Hilo

in October, 1679, sacked the town and burnt down
the large sugar factory outside. He led a mutiny
against his relative and benefactor, Captain Sharp, on
New Year's Day, 1681, being the "main promoter of
their design" to turn him out. Sharp afterwards
described his old friend as a "true-hearted dis-
sembling New-England Man," who he had promoted
captain "merely for old acquaintance-sake."

COXON, Captain John. Buccaneer.
   One of the most famous of the "Brethren of the
   Coast."

   In the spring of 1677, in company of other English
buccaneers, he surprised and plundered the town of
Santa Marta on the Spanish Main, carrying away the
Governor and the Bishop to Jamaica.
   In 1679 Coxon, with Sharp and others, was fitting
out an expedition in Jamaica to make a raid in the
Gulf of Honduras, which proved very successful, as
they brought back 500 chests of indigo, besides cocoa,
cochineal, tortoiseshell, money, and plate.
   Coxon was soon out again upon a much bolder
design, for in December, 1679, he met Sharp, Essex,
Allinson, Row, and other buccaneer chiefs at Point
Morant, and in January set sail for Porto Bello. Landing some twenty leagues from the town, they marched
for four days, arriving in sight of the town on February 17th, "many of them being weak, being three days
without any food, and their feet cut with the rocks for
want of shoes." They quickly took and plundered the
town, hurrying off with their spoils before the arrival
of strong Spanish reinforcements. The share of each
man in this enterprise came to one hundred pieces of
eight. A warrant was issued by Lord Carlisle, the
Governor of Jamaica, for the apprehension of Coxon
for plundering Porto Bello, and another was issued
soon after by Morgan, when acting as Governor, but

nothing seems to have resulted from these. Sailing
north to Boca del Toro, they careened their ships, and
were joined by Sawkins and Harris. From this place
the buccaneers began, in April, 1680, to land and
cross the Isthmus of Darien, taking the town of Santa
Maria on the way. Quarrels took place between
Coxon, who was, no doubt, a hot-tempered man, and
Harris, which led to blows. Coxon was also jealous
of the popular young Captain Sawkins, and refused
to go further unless he was allowed to lead one of the
companies. After sacking the town of Santa Maria,
the adventurers proceeded in canoes down the river to
the Pacific. Seizing two small vessels they found
there, and accompanied by a flotilla of canoes, they
steered for Panama, and, with the utmost daring,
attacked, and eventually took, the Spanish fleet of
men-of-war—one of the most remarkable achievements
in the history of the buccaneers.

Coxon now quarrelled again with his brother
leaders, and began a march back across the isthmus;
his party of seventy malcontents including Dampier
and Wafer, who each published accounts of their
journey. By 1682 Coxon seems to have so ingratiated
himself with the Jamaican authorities as to be sent in
quest of a troublesome French pirate, Jean Hamlin,
who was playing havoc with the English shipping in
his vessel, *La Trompeuse*.

Later in the same year Coxon procured letters of
marque from Robert Clarke, the Governor of New
Providence Island, himself nothing better than a
pirate, to go cruising as a " privateer." Coxon was
continually being arrested and tried for piracy, but
each time he managed to escape the gallows. We do
not know the name of the ship Coxon commanded
at this date, but it was a vessel of eighty tons, armed
with eight guns, and carrying a crew of ninety-seven
men.

COYLE, CAPTAIN RICHARD.
Born at Exeter in Devonshire.

An honest seafaring man until, when sailing as
mate with Captain Benjamin Hartley, they arrived at
Ancona with a cargo of pilchards. Here the captain
took on board a new carpenter, called Richardson,
who soon became a close friend of the mate's. These
two brought about a mutiny, attacked the captain, and
threw him, still alive, over the side to drown. Coyle
was elected captain, and they sailed as pirates, in
which capacity they were a disgrace to an ancient
calling. After a visit to Minorca, which ended with
ignominy, they sailed to Tunis, where Coyle told such
a plausible yarn as to deceive the Governor into believing that he had been the master of a vessel lost in
a storm off the coast of Sardinia. The pirates were
supplied with money by the British Consul in Tunis;
but Coyle, while in his cups, talked too freely, so that
the true story of his doings got to the Consul's ears,
who had him arrested and sent to London to be lodged
in the Marshalsea Prison. Tried at the Old Bailey,
he was sentenced to death, and was hanged at Execution Dock on January 25th, 1738.

CRACKERS, CAPTAIN.

A retired pirate who settled at Sierra Leone, and
was living there in 1721. He had been famous in his
day, having robbed and plundered many a ship. He
owned the best house in the settlement, and was distinguished by having three cannons placed before his
door, which he was accustomed to fire salutes from
whenever a pirate ship arrived or left the port. He
was the soul of hospitality and good fellowship, and
kept open-house for all pirates, buccaneers, and
privateersmen.

CRISS, Captain John, *alias* " Jack the Bachelor."
A native of Lorne in the North of Ireland.

His father was a fisherman, and little Jack used to go out with him, and then help him sell his fish at Londonderry. The lad grew up into a bold and handsome young fellow, " and many a girl cocked cap at him and he had great success amongst the ladies, and intrigued with every woman that gave him any encouragement."

Tiring of the monotony and low profits of a fisherman's calling, Jack turned smuggler, carrying cargoes of contraband goods from Guernsey to Ireland. Making a tidy sum at this, he bought himself a French galliot, and sailing from Cork, he began to take vessels off the coast of France, selling them at Cherbourg. The young pirate took no risks of information leaking out, for he drowned all his prisoners. Cruising in the Mediterranean, Criss met with his usual success, and, not content with taking ships, he plundered the seaport of Amalfi on the coast of Calabria. Calling at Naples, Criss put up at the Ferdinand Hotel, where one morning he was found dead in his bed. It was discovered afterwards that, in spite of his nickname, he was married to three wives.

CULLEN, Andrew.
Of Cork in Ireland.

Brother of Pierce Cullen. One of the crew of Captain Roche's ship. After the crew had mutinied and turned pirate he posed as the supercargo.

CULLEN, Pierce.
Of Cork in Ireland.

One of Captain Philip Roche's gang.

CULLIFORD, CAPTAIN, of the *Mocha*.

A Madagascar pirate.

Little is known of him except that one day in the streets of London he recognized and denounced another pirate called Burgess.

CUMBERLAND, GEORGE, THIRD EARL OF, 1558-1605.

M.A., Trinity College, Cambridge.

After taking his degree at Cambridge he migrated to Oxford for the purpose of studying geography.

So many books have been written about this picturesque and daring adventurer that it is not necessary to do more than mention his name here, as being perhaps the finest example of a buccaneer that ever sacked a Spanish town.

He led twelve voyages to the Spanish Main, fitting them out at his own expense, and encountering the same dangers and hardships as his meanest seaman.

He married in 1577 at the age of nineteen, and sailed on his first voyage in 1586. Cumberland was greatly esteemed by Queen Elizabeth, and always wore in his hat a glove which she had given him.

There is sufficient evidence to show that the Earl was not prompted to spend his life and fortune on buccaneering voyages merely by greed of plunder, but was chiefly inspired by intense love of his country, loyalty to his Queen, and bitter hatred of the Spaniards.

CUNNINGHAM, CAPTAIN WILLIAM.

Had his headquarters at New Providence Island, in the Bahamas. Refused the royal offer of pardon to the pirates in 1717, and was later caught and hanged.

CUNNINGHAM, PATRICK.

Found guilty at Newport in 1723, but reprieved.

CURTICE, Joseph.

One of Captain Teach's crew in the *Queen Ann's Revenge*. Killed on November 22nd, 1718, off the coast of North Carolina.

DAMPIER, Captain William. Buccaneer, explorer, and naturalist.
Born at East Coker in the year 1652.

Brought up at first to be a shopkeeper, a life he detested, he was in 1669 apprenticed to a ship belonging to Weymouth, and his first voyage was to France. In the same year he sailed to Newfoundland, but finding the bitter cold unbearable, he returned to England. His next voyage, which he called " a warm one," was to the East Indies, in the *John and Martha,* and suited him better.

Many books have been written recounting the voyages of Dampier, but none of these are better reading than his own narrative, published by James and John Knapton in London. This popular book ran into many editions, the best being the fourth, published in 1729, in four volumes. These volumes are profusely illustrated by maps and rough charts, and also with crude cuts, which are intended to portray the more interesting and strange animals, birds, fishes, and insects met with in his voyages round the globe.

In 1673 Dampier enlisted as a seaman in the *Royal Prince,* commanded by the famous Sir Edward Spragge, and fought in the Dutch war.

A year later he sailed to Jamaica in the *Content,* to take up a post as manager of a plantation belonging to a Colonel Hellier. His restless spirit soon revolted against this humdrum life on a plantation, and Dampier again went to sea, sailing in a small trading vessel amongst the islands,

Dampier's first step towards buccaneering was taken when he shipped himself on a small ketch which was sailing from Port Royal to load logwood at the Bay of Campeachy. This was an illegal business, as the Spanish Government claimed the ownership of all that coast, and did their best to prevent the trade. Dampier found some 250 Englishmen engaged in cutting the wood, which they exchanged for rum. Most of these men were buccaneers or privateers, who made a living in this way when out of a job afloat. When a ship came into the coast, these men would think nothing of coming aboard and spending thirty and forty pounds on rum and punch at a single drinking bout.

Dampier returned afterwards to take up logwood cutting himself, but met with little success, and went off to Beef Island. He had by this time begun to take down notes of all that appeared to him of interest, particularly objects of natural history. For example, he described, in his own quaint style, an animal he found in this island.

"The Squash is a four-footed Beast, bigger than a Cat. Its Head is much like a Foxes, with short Ears and a long Nose. It has pretty short Legs and sharp Claws, by which it will run up trees like a Cat. The flesh is good, sweet, wholesome Meat. We commonly skin and roast it; and then we call it pig; and I think it eats as well. It feeds on nothing but good Fruit; therefore we find them most among the Sapadillo-Trees. This Creature never rambles very far, and being taken young, will become as tame as a Dog, and be as roguish as a Monkey."

Dampier's first act of actual piracy was when he joined in an attack on the Spanish fort of Alvarado, but although the fort was taken, the townspeople had time to escape with all their valuables before the pirates could reach them. Returning to England in

1678, he did not remain long at home, for in the beginning of 1679 he sailed for Jamaica in a vessel named the *Loyal Merchant*. Shortly after reaching the West Indies, he chanced to meet with several well-known buccaneers, including Captains Coxon, Sawkins, and Sharp. Joining with these, he sailed on March 25th, 1679, for the Province of Darien, "to pillage and plunder these parts." Dampier says strangely little about his adventures for the next two years, but a full description of them is given by Ringrose in his "Dangerous Voyage and Bold Adventures of Captain Sharp and Others in the South Sea," published as an addition to the "History of the Buccaneers of America" in 1684.

This narrative tells how the buccaneers crossed the isthmus and attacked and defeated the Spanish Fleet off Panama City. After the death of their leader, Sawkins, the party split up, and Dampier followed Captain Sharp on his "dangerous and bold voyage" in May, 1680.

In April, 1681, after various adventures up and down the coast of Peru and Chile, further quarrels arose amongst the buccaneers, and a party of malcontents, of which number Dampier was one, went off on their own account in a launch and two canoes from the Island of Plate, made famous by Drake, and landed on the mainland near Cape San Lorenzo. The march across the Isthmus of Darien has been amusingly recounted by the surgeon of the party, Lionel Wafer, in his book entitled "A New Voyage and Description of the Isthmus of America," published in London in 1699.

On reaching the Atlantic, Dampier found some buccaneer ships and joined them, arriving at Virginia in July, 1682. In this country he resided for a year, but tells little about it beyond hinting that great troubles befell him. In April, 1683, he joined a

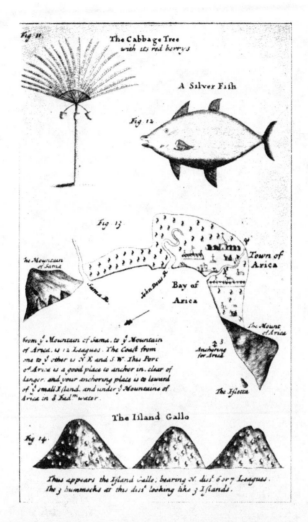

A PAGE FROM THE LOG-BOOK OF CAPTAIN DAMPIER.

To face p. 98.

privateer vessel, the *Revenge*, but directly she was out of sight of land the crew turned pirates, which had been their intention all along. Two good narratives have been written of this voyage, one by Dampier, and the other by Cowley, the sailing-master. This venture ended in the famous circumnavigation of the world, and Dampier described every object of interest he met with, including the country and natives of the north coast of Australia, which had never been visited before by Europeans. Dampier must have found it very difficult to keep his journal so carefully and regularly, particularly in his early voyages, when he was merely a seaman before the mast or a petty officer. He tells us that he carried about with him a long piece of hollow bamboo, in which he placed his manuscript for safe keeping, waxing the ends to keep out the sea water.

After almost endless adventures and hardships, he arrived back in England in September, 1691, after a voyage of eight years, and an absence from England of twelve, without a penny piece in his pocket, nor any other property except his unfortunate friend Prince Jeoly, whom he sold on his arrival in the Thames, to supply his own immediate wants. Dampier's next voyage was in the year 1699, when he was appointed to command H.M.S. *Roebuck*, of twelve guns and a crew of fifty men and boys, and victualled for twenty months' cruise. The object of this voyage was to explore and map the new continent to the south of the East Indies which Dampier had discovered on his previous voyage. Had he in this next voyage taken the westward course, as he originally intended, and sailed to Australia round the Horn, it is possible that Dampier would have made many of the discoveries for which James Cook afterwards became so famous, and by striking the east coast of Australia would very likely have antedated the civilisation of that continent by fifty years. But he was persuaded, partly by his timid crew, and perhaps in some measure by his own dislike of cold temperatures, to sail by the eastward route and to double the Cape of Good Hope. The story of this voyage is given by Dampier in his book, published in 1709, " A Voyage to New Holland, etc., in the Year 1699."

After spending some unprofitable weeks on the north coast of Australia, failing to find water or to make friends with the aboriginals, scurvy broke out amongst his somewhat mutinous crew, and he sailed to New Guinea, the coast of which he saw on New Year's Day, 1700.

By this time the *Roebuck* was falling to pieces, her wood rotten, her hull covered with barnacles. Eventually, using the pumps day and night, they arrived, on February 21st, 1701, at Ascension Island, where the old ship sank at her anchors. Getting ashore with their belongings, they waited on this desolate island until April 3rd, when four ships arrived, three of them English men-of-war.

I was told, only the other day, by a friend who lives in the Island of St. Helena, and whose duties take him at least once each year to Ascension Island, that a story still survives amongst the inhabitants of these islands that there is hidden somewhere in the sandhills a treasure, which Dampier is believed to have put there for safe keeping, but for some reason never removed. But poor Dampier never came by a treasure in this or any other of his voyages, and though the legend is a pleasant one, it is a legend and nothing more. Dampier went on board one of the men-of-war, the *Anglesea*, with thirty-five of his crew. Taken to Barbadoes, he there procured a berth in another vessel, the *Canterbury*, in which he sailed to England.

Dampier had now made so great a name for himself

by his two voyages round the globe that he was
granted a commission by Prince George of Denmark
to sail as a privateer in the *St. George,* to prey on
French and Spanish ships, the terms being : " No
purchase, no pay." Sailing as his consort was the
Cinque Ports, whose master was Alexander Selkirk,
the original of Robinson Crusoe. This voyage, fully
recounted in Dampier's book, is a long tale of adventure, hardship, and disaster, and the explorer eventually returned to England a beggar. However, his
travels made a great stir, and he was allowed to kiss
the Queen's hand and to have the honour of relating
his adventures to her.

Dampier's last voyage was in the capacity of pilot
or navigating officer to Captain Woodes Rogers in
the *Duke,* which sailed with another Bristol privateer,
the *Duchess,* in 1708. The interesting narrative of
this successful voyage is told by Rogers in his book,
" A Cruising Voyage Round the World," etc., published in 1712. Another account was written by the
captain of the *Duchess,* Edward Cooke, and published
in the same year. This last voyage round the world
ended at Erith on October 14th, 1711, and was the
only one in which Dampier returned with any profit
other than to his reputation as an explorer and navigator.

Dampier was now fifty-nine years of age, and
apparently never went to sea again. In fact, he
henceforth disappears from the stage altogether, and
is supposed to have died in Colman Street in London,
in the year 1715. Of Dampier's early life in England
little is known, except that he owned, at one time, a
small estate in Somersetshire, and that in 1678 he
married "a young woman out of the family of the
Duchess of Grafton." There is an interesting picture
of Dampier in the National Portrait Gallery, painted
by T. Murray, and I take this opportunity to thank

the directors for their kind permission to reproduce this portrait.

One other book Dampier wrote, called a "Discourse of Winds," an interesting work, and one which added to the author's reputation as a hydrographer. There is little doubt that Defoe was inspired by the experiences and writings of Dampier, not only in his greatest work, "Robinson Crusoe," but also in "Captain Singleton," "Colonel Jack," "A New Voyage Round the World," and many of the maritime incidents in "Roxana" and "Moll Flanders."

DAN, JOSEPH.

One of Avery's crew. Turned King's witness at his trial in 1696, and was not hanged.

DANIEL, CAPTAIN. A French filibuster.

The name of this bloodthirsty pirate will go down to fame as well as notoriety by his habit of combining piracy with strict Church discipline. Harling recounts an example of this as follows, the original account of the affair being written by a priest, M. Labat, who seems to have had rather a weak spot in his heart for the buccaneer fraternity :

"Captain Daniel, in need of provisions, anchored one night off one of the 'Saintes,' small islands near Dominica, and landing without opposition, took possession of the house of the curé and of some other inhabitants of the neighbourhood. He carried the curé and his people on board his ship without offering them the least violence, and told them that he merely wished to buy some wine, brandy and fowls. While these were being gathered, Daniel requested the curé to celebrate Mass, which the poor priest dared not refuse. So the necessary sacred vessels were sent for and an altar improvised on the deck for the service, which they chanted to the best of their ability. As at

Martinique, the Mass was begun by a discharge of artillery, and after the Exaudiat and prayer for the King, was closed by a loud ' Vive la Roi !' from the throats of the buccaneers. A single incident, however, somewhat disturbed the devotions. One of the buccaneers, remaining in an indecent attitude during the Elevation, was rebuked by the captain, and instead of heeding the correction, replied with an impertinence and a fearful oath. Quick as a flash Daniel whipped out his pistol and shot the buccaneer through the head, adjuring God that he would do as much to the first who failed in his respect to the Holy Sacrifice. The shot was fired close by the priest, who, as we can readily imagine, was considerably agitated. ' Do not be troubled, my father,' said Daniel; ' he is a rascal lacking in his duty and I have punished him to teach him better.' " A very efficacious means, remarks Labat, of preventing his falling into another like mistake. After the Mass the body of the dead man was thrown into the sea, and the curé was recompensed for his pains by some goods out of their stock and the present of a negro slave.

DANIEL, Stephen.

One of Captain Teach's crew. Hanged for piracy in Virginia in 1718.

DANSKER, Captain.

A Dutch pirate who cruised in the Mediterranean in the sixteenth century, using the North African coast as his base. He joined the Moors and turned Mohammedan. In 1671 Admiral Sir Edward Spragge was with a fleet at Bougie Bay, near Algiers, where, after a sharp fight, he burnt and destroyed a big fleet of the Moorish pirates, amongst those killed being the renegade Dansker.

DARBY, JOHN.

A Marblehead fisherman, one of the crew of the ketch *Mary*, of Salem, captured by Captain Pound. He joined the pirates, and was killed at Tarpaulin Cove.

DAVIS, CAPTAIN EDWARD. Buccaneer and pirate. Flourished from 1683-1702. According to Esquemiling, who knew Davis personally, his name was John, but some authorities call him Edward, the name he is given in the " Dictionary of National Biography."

In 1683 Davis was quartermaster to Captain Cook when he took the ship of Captain Tristian, a French buccaneer, of Petit Guave in the West Indies. Sailed north to cruise off the coast of Virginia. From there he sailed across the Atlantic to West Africa, and at Sierra Leone came upon a Danish ship of thirty-six guns, which he attacked and took. The pirates shifted their crew into this ship, christening her the *Bachelor's Delight*, and sailed for Juan Fernandez in the South Pacific, arriving there in March, 1684. Here they met with Captain Brown, in the *Nicholas,* and together sailed to the Galapagos Islands. About this time Captain Cook died, and Davis was elected captain in his place. Cruising along the coasts of Chile and Peru, they sacked towns and captured Spanish ships. On November 3rd Davis landed, and burnt the town of Paita. Their principal plan was to waylay the Spanish Fleet on its voyage to Panama. This fleet arrived off the Bay of Panama on May 28th, 1685, but the buccaneers were beaten and were lucky to escape with their lives. At the Gulf of Ampalla, Davis had to put his sick on shore, as spotted fever raged amongst the crew. Davis then cruised for a while with the buccaneer Knight, sacking several towns.

Deciding to return to the West Indies with their plunder, several of the crew, who had lost all their share by gambling, were left, at their own request, on the Island of Juan Fernandez. Davis then sailed round the Horn, arriving safely at Jamaica with a booty of more than 50,000 pieces of eight, besides quantities of plate and jewels.

At Port Royal, after he had accepted the offer of pardon of King James II., Davis sailed to Virginia and settled down at Point Comfort. We hear no more of him for the next fourteen years, until July 24th, 1702, when he sailed from Jamaica in the *Blessing* (Captain Brown ; twenty guns, seventy-nine men), to attack the town of Tolu on the Spanish Main, which was plundered and burnt. Davis next sailed to the Samballoes, and, guided by the Indians, who were friendly to the buccaneers, but hated the Spaniards, they attacked the gold-mines, where, in spite of most cruel tortures, they got but little gold. The crew next attacked Porto Bello, but found little worth stealing in that much harassed town.

Davis is chiefly remarkable for having commanded his gang of ruffians in the Pacific for nearly four years. To do this he must have been a man of extraordinary personality and bravery, for no other buccaneer or pirate captain ever remained in uninterrupted power for so long a while, with the exception of Captain Bartholomew Roberts.

DAVIS, Captain Howel.

This Welsh pirate was born at Milford in Monmouthshire. He went to sea as a boy, and eventually sailed as chief mate in the *Cadogan* snow, of Bristol, to the Guinea Coast. His ship was taken off Sierra Leone by the pirate England, and the cáptain murdered. Davis turned pirate, and was given command of this old vessel, the *Cadogan,* in which to go " on the account." But the crew refused to turn pirate, and sailed the ship to Barbadoes, and there handed Davis over to the Governor, who imprisoned him for three months and then liberated him. As no one on the island would offer him employment, Davis went to New Providence Island, the stronghold of the West India pirates.

Arrived there, he found that Captain Woodes Rogers had only lately come from England with an offer of a royal pardon, which most of the pirates had availed themselves of. Davis got employment under the Governor, on board the sloop, the *Buck,* to trade goods with the French and Spanish settlements. The crew was composed of the very recently reformed pirates, and no sooner was the sloop out of sight of land than they mutinied and seized the vessel, Davis being voted captain, on which occasion, over a bowl of punch in the great cabin, the new captain made an eloquent speech, finishing by declaring war against the whole world. Davis proved himself an enterprising and successful pirate chief, but preferred, whenever possible, to use strategy and cunning rather than force to gain his ends. His first prize was a big French ship, which, although Davis had only a small sloop and a crew of but thirty-five men, he managed to take by a bold and clever trick. After taking a few more ships in the West Indies, Davies sailed across the Atlantic to the Island of St. Nicholas in the Cape Verde Islands. Here he and his crew were a great social success, spending weeks on shore as the guests of the Governor and chief inhabitants. When Davis reluctantly left this delightful spot, five of his crew were missing, "being so charmed with the Luxuries of the Place, and the Conversation of some Women, that they stayed behind."

Davis now went cruising and took a number of vessels, and arrived eventually at St. Jago. The

Portuguese Governor of this island did not take at
all kindly to his bold visitor, and was blunt enough
to say he suspected Davis of being a pirate. This
suspicion his crew took exception to, and they decided
they could not let such an insult pass, so that very
night they made a sudden attack on the fort, taking
and plundering it.

Davis sailed away next morning to the coast and
anchored off the Castle of Gambia, which was
strongly held for the African Company by the
Governor and a garrison of English soldiers. Davis,
nothing daunted, proposed to his merry men a bold
and ingenious stratagem by which they could take
the castle, and, the crew agreeing, it was carried out
with so much success that they soon had the castle,
Governor, and soldiers in their possession, as well as
a rich spoil of bars of gold; and all these without a
solitary casualty on either side. After this brilliant
coup, many of the soldiers joined the pirates. The
pirates were attacked shortly afterwards by a French
ship commanded by Captain La Bouse, but on both
ships hoisting their colours, the Jolly Roger, they
understood each other and fraternized, and then sailed
together to Sierra Leone, where they attacked a tall
ship they found lying there at anchor. This ship also
proved to be a pirate, commanded by one Captain
Cocklyn, so the three joined forces and assaulted the
fort, which, after a sharp bombardment, surrendered.
Davis was then elected commander of the pirate fleet,
but one night, when entertaining the other captains
in his cabin, all having drunk freely of punch, they
started to quarrel, and blows were threatened, when
Davis, with true Celtic eloquence, hiccupped out the
following speech :

" Hearke ye, you Cocklyn and La Bouse. I find
by strengthening you I have put a rod into your
Hands to whip myself, but I'm still able to deal with

you both; but since we met in Love, let us part in
Love, for I find that three of a Trade can never
agree." Alone once more, Davis had prodigious
success, taking prize after prize, amongst others the
Princess, the second mate in which was one Roberts,
soon to become a most famous pirate. Off Anamaboe
he took a very rich prize, a Hollander ship, on board
of which was the Governor of Accra and his retinue,
as well as £15,000 sterling and rich merchandise.
Arriving next at the Portuguese Island of Princes,
Davis posed as an English man-of-war in search of
pirates, and was most warmly welcomed by the
Governor, who received him in person with a guard
of honour and entertained him most hospitably.
Davis heard that the Governor and the chief persons
of the island had sent their wives to a village a few
miles away, so the pirate and a few chosen spirits
decided to pay a surprise visit on these ladies. However, the ladies, on perceiving their gallant callers,
shrieked and ran into the woods and, in fact, made
such a hullabaloo that the English Don Juans were
glad to slink away, and " the Thing made some noise,
but not being known was passed over."

Davis, ever a cunning rogue, now formed a pretty
scheme to take the Governor and chief inhabitants
prisoners and to hold them for a big ransom. This
plan was spoilt by a Portuguese slave swimming
to shore and telling the Governor all about it, and
worse, telling him about the little affair of Davis and
his visit to the ladies in the wood. The Governor
now laid his plans, and with such success that Davis
walked unsuspecting into the trap, and was " shot in
the bowels," but it is some consolation to know that
he " dyed like a game Cock," as he shot two of the
Portuguese with his pistols as he fell.

Thus died a man noted during his lifetime by his
contemporaries for his " affability and good nature,"

which only goes to show how one's point of view is apt to be influenced by circumstances.

DAVIS, GABRIEL.

Tried for piracy at the Star Tavern in Boston, Massachusetts, in 1704.

DAVIS, WILLIAM.
A Welshman.

Arrived at Sierra Leone in honest employ in the *Ann* galley. Quarrelling with the mate, whom he beat, he deserted his ship and went to live ashore with the negroes, one of whom he married, with whom he settled down. One evening, the weather being hot, and Davis being very thirsty, he sold his bride for some punch. His wife's relations, being indignant, seized Davis, who told them, being, perhaps, still a little under the influence of the punch, that he did not care if they took his head off. But his "in-laws" knew a more profitable way of being revenged than that, and sold him to Seignior Joffee, a Christian black. Soon afterwards Captain Roberts, in the *Royal Fortune*, arrived in the bay, and Davis ran away and joined the pirates.

Hanged at the age of 23.

DAWES. Corsair.
An English renegade.

When Roberts was cast away on June 12th, 1692, in Nio, a small island in the Grecian Archipelago, in His Majesty's hired ship the *Arcana* galley, most of the crew escaped in a French prize they had taken. Roberts remained behind, hoping to save some of his valuables, which were in the *Arcana*. But on June 15th a crusal, or corsair, appeared in the harbour, which Roberts's five companions went on board of.

Various designs were made by the corsair captain to induce Roberts to come aboard. Eventually an Englishman named Dawes (a native of Saltash in Cornwall) was sent ashore. He had served for eight years in the corsair until taken out of her a short time previously by the *Arcana*. Roberts writes, in his frank style: " But Dawes, like a Dog returning to his Vomit, went on Board again." Eventually a party of the corsair's landed under the leadership of Dawes, and captured Roberts and carried him on board the pirate craft, where for many years he worked as a slave.

DAWES, ROBERT.

One of the mutineers on the brig *Vineyard* in 1830. It was the full confession of Dawes that brought about the conviction and execution of the ringleader, Charles Gibbs.

DAWSON, JOSEPH.

One of Captain Avery's crew of the *Charles the Second*. Tried at the Old Bailey in 1696 for piracy, and convicted. He pleaded to be spared and to be sent to servitude in India, but was hanged at Execution Dock.

DEAL, CAPTAIN ROBERT.

Mate to Captain Vane in 1718. He was very active off the coast of Carolina and New England, taking many prizes. In November, 1718, when cruising between Cape Meise and Cape Nicholas, on the look-out for ships, he met with and fired on a vessel that appeared to be a merchantman, at the same time running up the Jolly Roger. The apparently peaceful merchantman replied with a broadside, and proved to be a French man-of-war. A quarrel took place amongst the pirates, Vane and some of the crew,

including Deal, being for running away for safety,
while the rest, headed by Rackam, were in favour
of fighting it out. Vane insisted on their escaping,
which they did, but next day he, Deal, and some
others were turned out of the ship and sent away on
their own in a small sloop. Deal was put in command
of this sloop, but was soon afterwards captured by an
English man-of-war and brought to Jamaica, where
he was tried, convicted, and hanged.

DEANE, CAPTAIN JOHN. Buccaneer.

Commanded the *St. David*. He was accused by
the Governor of Jamaica in 1676 of having held up a
ship called the *John Adventure* and of taking out of
her several pipes of wine and a cable worth £100, and
of forcibly carrying the vessel to Jamaica. Deane was
also reported for wearing Dutch, French, and Spanish
colours without commission, and was tried and condemned to suffer death as a pirate. Owing to various
legal, or illegal, quibbles, Deane was reprieved.

DEDRAN, LE CAPITAINE. A French filibuster of
    French Domingo.

Commanded, in 1684, the *Chasseur* (120 men,
20 guns).

DEIGLE, RICHARD.

An Elizabethan pirate. Wrecked in the *John of
Sandwich* at Alderney in 1564, when he was arrested,
but escaped in a small boat.

DELANDER, CAPTAIN. Buccaneer.

Commanded a *chatas*, or small coasting craft. He
was sent by Morgan ahead of the main body when,
in January, 1671, he marched from San Lorenzo on
his great assault on Panama.

DELIZUFF. Barbary corsair.

In 1553, while Barbarossa was sailing from Algiers to Constantinople, he was joined by Delizuff with a fleet of eighteen pirate vessels.

Delizuff was killed in an affair at the Island of Biba, and, the crews of the two corsairs quarrelling, the ships of Delizuff stole away one dark night.

DELVE, JONATHAN.

One of Captain Lowther's crew in the *Happy Delivery*. Was hanged at St. Kitts in 1722.

DEMPSTER, CAPTAIN. Buccaneer.

In 1668 he was in command of several vessels and 300 men, blockading Havana.

DENNIS, HENRY.
Of Bideford in Devonshire.

At first a pirate with Captain Davis, he afterwards joined Captain Roberts's crew. Was tried for piracy at Cape Coast Castle in 1722, and found guilty, but for some reason was reprieved and sold for seven years to serve the Royal African Company on their plantations.

DERDRAKE, CAPTAIN JOHN, *alias* JACK OF THE
    BALTIC. A Danish pirate, of Copenhagen.

When a carpenter in the King's Dockyard at Copenhagen he was dismissed for drunkenness. After making a few voyages to London as a ship's carpenter, his parents died and left their son a fortune of 10,000 rix-dollars. With this money Derdrake built himself a fast sailing brig sheathed with copper, and for a while traded in wood between Norway and London. Becoming impatient of the smallness of the profits in this trade, he offered his services and ship to Peter the Great. This monarch, as was his custom, examined the ship in person, and, approving of her, bought her, and at the same time appointed Derdrake to be a master shipwright in the royal dockyards on the Neva. The carpenter, always a man of violent temper, one day quarrelled with one of his superiors, seized an axe, and slew him. His ship then happening to be in the roads, Derdrake hurried on board her and made sail, and went off with the cargo, which he sold in London. Arming his vessel with twelve guns, he sailed for Norway, but on the way he was attacked by a big Russian man-of-war. The Russian was defeated and surrendered, and Derdrake went into her in place of his own smaller ship, giving his new craft the ominous name of the *Sudden Death*. With a fine, well-armed ship and a crew of seventy desperadoes, one-half English, and the rest Norwegian and Danish, he now definitely turned pirate. Lying in wait for English and Russian ships carrying goods to Peter the Great, the pirates took many valuable prizes, with cargoes consisting of fittings for ships, arms, and warm woollen clothing. For these he found a ready market in Sweden, where no questions were asked and "cash on delivery" was the rule.

Derdrake drowned all his prisoners, and was one of the very few pirates, other than those found in works of fiction, who forced his victims to "walk the plank." Not long afterwards the pirates met with and fought an armed Swedish vessel, which was defeated, but the captain and crew escaped in the long-boat, and, getting to shore, spread the tidings of the pirates' doings. On hearing the news, the Governor of St. Petersburg, General Shevelling, sent out two ships to search for and take the pirates, offering a reward of 4,000 rix-dollars for Derdrake's head. The pirates had just heard of this when they happened to take a Russian vessel bound for Cronstadt, on board of which was a passenger, a sister of

the very General Shevelling. This poor lady, after
being reproached by the pirates for her brother's
doings, was stabbed to death in the back by Derdrake.
At this time there was aboard the *Sudden Death* a
Danish sailor, who, having been severely flogged for
being drunk at sea, shammed sickness and pretended
to have lost the use of his limbs. The captain was
deceived, and sent the sailor, well supplied with
money, to a country house at Drontheim in Sweden,
to recover. No sooner had Jack of the Baltic left
than the Danish sailor set off post-haste for St. Petersburg, where he saw the Governor and told him of
his sister's murder, and also that the pirates were to
be found at Strothing in Sweden. Two well-armed
vessels were immediately despatched, which, finding
the *Sudden Death* at anchor, fought and sunk her,
though unfortunately Derdrake was on shore and so
escaped; but the whole crew were hung up alive by
hooks fixed in their ribs and sent to drift down the
Volga. Derdrake, who had a large sum of money
with him, bought an estate near Stralsund, and lived
there in luxury for fourteen years, until one day, a
servant having robbed him of a sum of money, Derdrake followed him to Stockholm, where he was recognized by the captain of the Swedish ship who had
first given information against him, and the pirate
was at once arrested, tried, and hanged.

DEW, Captain George.
    Of Bermuda.

He commanded a Bermuda ship and sailed in
company with Captain Tew, when they were caught
in a storm off that island, and Captain Dew, having
sprung his mast, was compelled to put back to the
island for repairs. Captain Tew continued his
journey to Africa, but what became of Captain Dew
is not known.

DIABOLITO.

A Central American pirate who became very famous in the early part of the last century. Commanded the *Catalina* in 1823 off the coast of Cuba.

DIEGO, or DIEGO GRILLO.
   A mulatto of Havana.

After the general amnesty to pirates, given in 1670, Diego, Thurston, and others continued to attack Spanish ships and to carry their prizes to their lair at Tortuga Island. Diego commanded a vessel carrying fifteen guns. He succeeded in defeating three armed ships in the Bahama Channel, which had been sent to take him, and he massacred all the Spaniards of European birth that he found among the crews. He was caught in 1673 and hanged.

DIPPER, HENRY.

One of the English soldiers who deserted from the Fort Loyal, Falmouth, Maine, and joined Captain Pound, the pirate. Killed in the fight at Tarpaulin Cove in 1689.

DOLE, FRANCIS.

Was one of Hore's crew. Lived with his wife, when not " on the account," at his house at Charleston, near Boston. The pirate Gillam was found hiding there by the Governor's search-party on the night of November 11th, 1699. Dole was committed to gaol at Boston.

DOROTHY, JOHN.

One of Captain John Quelch's crew. Tried for piracy at Boston in June, 1704.

DOVER, DOCTOR THOMAS.
  Born 1660; died 1742.

  This many-sided character was educated at Caius
College, Cambridge, where he took the degree of
Bachelor of Medicine. Many years afterwards, in
1721, the Royal College of Physicians made him a
licentiate. For many years Dover practised as a
physician at Bristol, until the year 1708, when he
sailed from Bristol as " second captain " to Captain
Woodes Rogers, with the *Duke* and the *Duchess,*
two privateer ships fitted out for a South Sea cruise
by some Bristol merchants. Dover had no knowledge whatever of navigation, but, having a considerable share in the adventure, he insisted on being given
a command. Sailing round the Horn, the two ships
arrived, on the night of February 1st, 1709, off the
Island of Juan Fernandez, where they observed a
light. Next morning Dover went ashore in a boat,
to find and rescue the solitary inhabitant of the island,
Alexander Selkirk, the original of Robinson Crusoe.
Sailing north, a Spanish ship was taken and rechristened the *Bachelor,* and Dover was put in command of her. He sacked Guayaquil in April, 1709,
many of the crew contracting plague from sleeping in
a church where some bodies had recently been buried.
Dover undertook to treat the sick with most heroic
measures, bleeding each sick man and drawing off
100 ounces of blood.

  He also took the famous *Acapulco* ship, with a
booty worth more than a million pounds sterling.
Dover returned to Bristol in October, 1711, with a
prize of great value, after sailing round the world.

  Giving up piracy, he settled in practice in London,
seeing his patients daily at the Jerusalem Coffee-
house in Cecil Street, Strand. He wrote a book
called " The Ancient Physician's Legacy to His
Country," which ran into seven or eight editions,

in which he strongly recommended the administration of large doses of quicksilver for almost every malady that man is subject to. This book won him the nickname of the "Quicksilver Doctor." He invented a diaphoretic powder containing ipecacuanha and opium, which is used to this day, and is still known as Dover's powder.

Dover died at the age of 82, in the year 1742, and should always be remembered for having invented Dover's powders, commanded a company of Marines, rescued Alexander Selkirk, written a most extraordinary medical book, and for having been a successful pirate captain.

DOWLING, CAPTAIN WILLIAM.
   Of New Providence, Bahamas.

Hanged for piracy in the early part of the eighteenth century.

DRAGUT. Barbary corsair.

Started life as a pirate, and was eventually put in command of twelve large galleys by Kheyr-ed-din. Pillaged and burnt many towns on the Italian coast, and destroyed ships without number. Was taken prisoner by the younger Doria, and condemned to row in the galleys for four years until ransomed for 3,000 ducats by Kheyr-ed-din. Appointed Admiral of the Ottoman Fleet. Ended a bloodthirsty but very successful career in 1565 by being killed at the Siege of Malta.

DRAKE, SIR FRANCIS.
   Born about 1540.

The life of the famous Admiral is too well known to require more than a bare notice in these pages. Although the Spaniards called him "the Pirate," he was more strictly a buccaneer in his early voyages, when he sailed with the sole object of spoiling the Spaniards. His first command was the *Judith,* in John Hawkins's unfortunate expedition in 1567. Drake made several voyages from Plymouth to the West Indies and the Spanish Main.

In 1572 he burnt Porto Bello, and a year later sacked Vera Cruz. He served with the English Army in Ireland under Lord Essex in 1574 and 1575. In 1578 he sailed through the Straits of Magellan, plundered Valparaiso, and also captured a great treasure ship from Acapulco. Sailing from America, he crossed the Pacific Ocean, passed through the Indian Archipelago, rounded the Cape of Good Hope, and arrived at Deptford in England in 1581. At the conclusion of this voyage he was knighted by Queen Elizabeth, being the first Englishman to sail round the world. Drake's voyages after this were sailed under commission and letters of marque, and so lose any stigma of being buccaneering adventures.

Drake died at Porto Bello in the year 1596.

DROMYOWE, PETER. A Breton pirate.

One of the crew of Captain du Laerquerac, who in 1537 took several English ships in the Bristol Channel.

DRUMMOND, *alias* TEACH, THATCH, or BLACK-
BEARD.

DUNBAR, NICHOLAS. Pirate.

One of the crew of the brigantine *Charles* (Captain Quelch). Tried for piracy at Boston in 1704.

DUNKIN, GEORGE.
Of Glasgow.

One of Major Stede Bonnet's crew. Hanged at Charleston, South Carolina, in November, 1718. Buried in the marsh below low-water mark.

DUNN, WILLIAM.
One of Captain Pound's crew.

DUNTON, CAPTAIN.

A citizen of London, taken prisoner by the Sallee pirates in 1636. Being a good navigator and seaman, and the Moorish pirates being as yet inexperienced in the management of sailing ships, Dunton was put into a Sallee ship as pilot and master, with a crew of twenty-one Moors and five Flemish renegadoes. He was ordered to go to the English coast to capture Christian prisoners. When off Hurst Castle, near the Needles in the Isle of Wight, his ship was seized and the crew carried to Winchester to stand their trial for piracy. Dunton was acquitted, but he never saw his little son of 10 years old, as he was still a slave in Algiers.

EASTON, CAPTAIN.

Joined the Barbary pirates in the sixteenth century, succeeding so well as to become, according to John Smith, the Virginian, a " Marquesse in Savoy," whatever that may have been.

EASTON, CAPTAIN PETER.

One of the most notorious of the English pirates during the reign of James I.
In the year 1611 he had forty vessels under his command. The next year he was on the Newfoundland coast, where he plundered the shipping and fishing settlements, stealing provisions and munitions, as well as inducing one hundred men to join his fleet.
A year later, in 1613, he appears to have joined the English pirates who had established themselves at Mamora on the Barbary coast.

EATON, EDWARD.
Of Wrexham in Wales.

One of Captain Harris's crew. Hanged at Newport, Rhode Island, on July 19th, 1723. Age 38.

ECHLIN.

An English pirate, of the *Two Brothers,* a Rhode Island built vessel, commanded in 1730 by a one-armed English pirate called Captain Johnson.

EDDY, WILLIAM.
Of Aberdeen.

One of Major Stede Bonnet's crew. Hanged at White Point, Charleston, South Carolina, on November 8th, 1718, and buried in the marsh below low-water mark.

ENGLAND, CAPTAIN.

Sailing in 1718 as mate in a sloop from Jamaica, he was taken prisoner by the pirate Captain Winter. England joined the pirates, and was given the command of a vessel. In this ship he sailed to the coast of West Africa, and the first prize he took was the *Cadogan* snow (Captain Skinner), at Sierra Leone. Some of England's crew knew Skinner, having served in his ship, and, owing to some quarrel, had been handed over to a man-of-war, and deprived of the wages due to them. These men afterwards deserted the man-of-war and joined the pirates. On Captain Skinner coming aboard England's ship, these men took him and bound him to the windlass, and then pelted him with glass bottles, after which they whipped him up and down the deck, eventually one of them shooting him through the head. This brutal treatment was none of England's doing, who was generally kind to his prisoners.

England's next prize was the *Pearl*, which he exchanged for his own sloop; fitted her up for the "pyratical Account," and christened her the *Royal James*. Captain England was most successful, taking a number of prizes, which he plundered. One ship he captured so took the eye of England that he fitted her up and changed into her, naming her the *Victory*. This he did in the harbour at Whydah, where he met with another pirate, called la Bouche. The two pirates and their crews spent a holiday at this place where, according to the well-informed Captain Johnson, "they liv'd very wantonly for several Weeks, making free with the Negroe Women and committing such outrageous Acts, that they came to an open Rupture with the Natives, several of whom they kill'd and one of their Towns they set on Fire." Leaving here, no doubt to the great relief of the negroes, it was put to the vote of the crew to decide where they should go, and the majority were for visiting the East Indies. Rounding the Cape of Good Hope, they arrived at Madagascar early in 1720, where they only stopped for water and provisions, and then sailed to the coast of Malabar in India. Here they took several country ships, and one Dutch one, but soon returned to Madagascar, where they went on shore, living in tents, and hunting hogs and deer. While on this island they looked for Captain Avery's crew, but failed to discover them. While the pirates were here they managed to take a ship commanded by a Captain Mackra, but not without a desperate fight. The pirates were for killing Mackra, but, owing to the efforts of Captain England, he managed to escape.

The pirates had several times complained of the weakness, or humanity, of their commander towards his prisoners, and they now turned him out and elected a new captain, and marooned England and

three others on the Island of Mauritius. The captain
and his companions set about building a small boat
of some old staves and pieces of deal they found
washed up on the beach. When finished they sailed
to Madagascar, where, when last heard of, they were
living on the charity of some other pirates.

ERNADOS, EMANUEL.

A Carolina pirate who was hanged at Charleston in
1717.

ESMIT, ADOLF.

A Danish buccaneer, who afterwards became
Governor of the Danish island of St. Thomas, one
of the Virgin Islands. The population of this island
consisted of some 350 persons, most of whom were
English. Esmit did all he could to assist the pirates,
paid to fit out their ships for them, gave sanctuary to
runaway servants, seamen, and debtors, and refused
to restore captured vessels. Adolf had taken advantage of his popularity with the inhabitants to turn out
his brother, who was the rightful Governor appointed
by the Danish Government.

ESSEX, CAPTAIN CORNELIUS. Buccaneer.

In December, 1679, he met with several other well-
known buccaneers in four barques and two sloops at
Point Morant, and on January 7th set sail for Porto
Bello. The fleet was scattered by a terrible storm,
but eventually they all arrived at the rendezvous.
Some 300 men went in canoes and landed about
twenty leagues from the town of Porto Bello, and
marched for four days along the sea-coast.

The buccaneers, "many of them were weak, being
three days without any food, and their feet cut with
the rocks for want of shoes," entered the town on

February 17th, 1680. The buccaneers, with prisoners and spoil, left the town just in time, for a party of 700 Spanish soldiers was near at hand coming to the rescue. The share to each man came to one hundred pieces of eight. In 1679 Essex was brought a prisoner by a frigate, the *Hunter,* to Port Royal, and tried with some twenty of his crew for plundering on the Jamaican coast. Essex was acquitted, but two of his crew were hanged.

EUCALLA, Domingo.

A negro. Hanged at Kingston, Jamaica, on February 7th, 1823. Made a moving harangue to the spectators from the gallows, ending with a prayer. Of the ten pirates executed this day, Eucalla showed the greatest courage.

EVANS, Captain John. Welsh pirate.

Was master of a sloop belonging to the Island of Nevis. Afterwards being in Jamaica and out of employment, and berths being scarce, he decided to go "on the account," and in September, 1722, rowed out of Port Royal in a canoe with a few chosen companions. They began piracy in a small way, by paddling along the coast and landing at night to break into a house or two and robbing these of anything they could carry away.

At last at Dun's Hole they found what they were looking for, a small Bermuda sloop lying at anchor. Evans stepped aboard and informed the crew of the sloop that he was captain of their vessel, "which was a piece of news they knew not before." Going on shore, Evans stood treat to his crew at the village inn, spending three pistols on liquid refreshment. He so took the fancy of the publican by his open-handed ways that he was invited to call again. This Evans and his companions did, in the middle of the same night, and rifled the house and took away all they could carry aboard their sloop.

Mounting four guns and christening their little vessel the *Scowerer,* they set sail for Hispaniola. Good luck immediately followed, as on the very next day they took their first prize, a Spanish sloop, an extraordinarily rich prize for her size, for the crew were able to share a sum of £150 a man. For a while all was *coleur de rose,* prize after prize simply falling into their hands. But an unhappy accident was soon to bring an end to Evans's career. The boatswain was a noisy, surly fellow, and on several occasions the captain had words with him about his disrespectful behaviour. The boatswain on one of these occasions so far forgot himself as not only to use ill language to his captain but to challenge him to a fight on the next shore they came to with pistol and sword. On reaching land the cowardly boatswain refused to go ashore or to fight, whereupon the captain took his cane and gave him a hearty drubbing, when the boatswain, all of a sudden drawing a pistol, shot Evans through the head, so that he fell down dead. Thus was brought to a tragic and sudden end a career that showed early signs of great promise. The boatswain jumped overboard and swam for the shore, but a boat put off and brought him back to the vessel. A trial was at once held, but the chief gunner, unable to bear with the slow legal procedure any further, stepped forward and shot the prisoner dead.

The crew of thirty men now shared their plunder of some £9,000 and broke up, each going his own way.

EVERSON, Captain Jacob, *alias* Jacobs.

In January, 1681, Sir Henry Morgan, then Lieutenant-Governor of Jamaica, received information that a famous Dutch buccaneer, Everson, was

anchored off the coast in an armed sloop, in company
with a brigantine which he had lately captured. This
was more than the ex-pirate Governor could tolerate,
so he at once set out in a small vessel with fifty picked
men. The sloop was boarded at midnight, but Everson and a few others escaped by leaping overboard
and swimming to the shore. Most of the prisoners
were Englishmen, and were convicted of piracy and
hanged.

EXQUEMELIN, ALEXANDER OLIVIER, or ESQUE-
    MELING in English, ŒXMELIN in French.
    Buccaneer.

A surgeon with the most famous buccaneers,
Exquemelin will always be known as the historian
who recorded the deeds of the buccaneers in his
classic book, "Bucaniers of America, or a true
account of the assaults committed upon the coasts of
the West Indies, etc.," published by W. Cooke,
London, 1684. This book was first published in
Dutch at Amsterdam in 1678, then in German in
1679, in Spanish in 1681. Since then almost in-
numerable editions and reprints have appeared.

The author was a Fleming, who arrived at Tortuga
Island in 1666 as an engagé of the French West India
Company. After serving for three years under an
inhuman master he became so ill that he was sold
cheaply to a surgeon. By the kind treatment of his
new master Exquemelin soon regained his health,
and at the same time picked up the rudiments of the
craft of barber surgeon. He was in all the great
exploits of the buccaneers, and writes a clear, entertaining, and apparently perfectly accurate first-hand
account of these adventures. He returned to
Europe in 1674, and shortly afterwards published
his book.

FALL, John.

This buccaneer was one of Captain Sharp's crew. On the death of John Hilliard, the ship's master, Fall was promoted to the larboard watch. Nothing further is known of this man.

FARRINGTON, Thomas.

One of John Quelch's crew on the brigantine *Charles*. Tried for piracy at Boston in June, 1704, at the Star Tavern.

FENN, Captain John.

In the year 1721 Captain Anstis took prize a stout ship, the *Morning Star*, bound from Guiney to Carolina. This ship the pirates armed with thirty-two pieces of cannon, manned her with a crew of one hundred men, and placed Fenn in command, who had until then been gunner in Anstis's ship, the *Good Fortune*. Fenn was a one-handed man. By carelessness, or perhaps because of Fenn only having one hand, the *Morning Star* was run on to a reef in the Grand Caymans and lost. Fenn and a few others had just been taken on board by his consort when two King's ships arrived, and the *Good Fortune* barely escaped capture.

Fenn was soon given another ship, one armed with twenty-four guns. In April, 1723, while cleaning their ship at the Island of Tobago, they were suddenly surprised by the arrival of a man-of-war, the *Winchelsea*. Setting fire to their ship, the crew ran to hide in the woods. Fenn was caught a few days later struggling through the jungle with his gunner.

FERDINANDO, Lewis.

In 1699 he captured a sloop belonging to **Samuel Salters**, of Bermuda.

FERN, THOMAS.

A Newfoundland fish-splitter.

In August, 1723, joined with John Phillips in stealing a small vessel, which they called the *Revenge,* and went "on the account." Fern was appointed carpenter. Fern gave trouble afterwards over the promotion of a prisoner, an old pirate called Rose Archer, to the rank of quartermaster.

Later on Fern headed a mutiny and attempted to sail off on his own in one of the prize vessels. He was caught, brought back, and forgiven, but on attempting to run away a second time, Captain Phillips killed him, "pursuant to the pirates articles."

FERNON, WILLIAM.

A Somersetshire man.

Taken from a Newfoundland ship, he became a seaman aboard Bartholomew Roberts's *Royal Fortune.* Died at the age of 22.

FIFE, CAPTAIN JAMES.

Surrendered to Governor Woodes Rogers at New Providence Island, Bahamas, in June, 1718, and received the royal pardon to pirates. Was afterwards killed by his own crew.

FILLMORE, JOHN.

A fisherman of Ipswich.

Taken out of the *Dolphin* when fishing for cod off the Banks of Newfoundland in 1724 by the pirate Captain Phillips, and forced to join the pirates. Having no other means of escape he, with two others, suddenly killed Phillips and two more pirates and brought the vessel into Boston Harbour. Millard Fillmore, thirteenth President of the United States, was the great grandson of John Fillmore.

FITZERRALD, John.
Of Limerick.

This Irish pirate was hanged at Newport, Rhode Island, in 1723, at the age of 21.

FLEMING, Captain. Pirate.

This notorious Elizabethan pirate did his country a great service by bringing to Plymouth the first tidings of the approach of the Spanish Armada in 1585.

To quote John Smith, the great Elizabethan traveller and the founder of the colony of Virginia, "Fleming was an expert and as much sought for as any pirate of the Queen's reign, yet such a friend to his Country, that discovering the Spanish Armada, he voluntarily came to Plymouth, yielded himself freely to my Lord Admirall, and gave him notice of the Spaniards coming : which good warning came so happily and unexpectedly, that he had his pardon, and a good reward."

FLETCHER, John.
Of Edinburgh.

Tried at Newport, Rhode Island, for piracy in 1723, found "not guilty." His age was only 17 years.

FLY, Captain William. Pirate and prizefighter.

He was boatswain in the *Elizabeth,* of Bristol, in 1726, bound for Guinea. Heading a mutiny on May 27th, he tossed the captain over the ship's side, and slaughtered all the officers except the ship's surgeon. Fly was unanimously elected captain by the crew. His first prize was the *John and Hannah* off the coast of North Carolina. The next the *John and Betty,* Captain Gale, from Bardadoes to Guinea. After taking several other vessels, he cruised off the coast of Newfoundland where he took a whaler. Fly was caught by a piece of strategy on the part of the whaler captain, who carried him and his crew in chains in their own ship to Great Brewster, Massachusetts, in June, 1726. On July 4th Fly and the other pirates were brought to trial at Boston, and on the 16th were executed. On the day of execution Fly refused to go to church before the hanging to listen to a sermon by Dr. Coleman. On the way to the gallows he bore himself with great bravado, jumping briskly into the cart with a nosegay in his hands bedecked with coloured ribbons like a prizefighter, smiling and bowing to the spectators. He was hanged in chains at Nix's Mate, a small island in Boston Harbour, and thus was brought to a close a brief though brilliant piratical career of just one month.

FORREST, WILLIAM.

One of the mutinous crew of the *Antonio* hanged at Boston in 1672.

FORSEITH, EDWARD.

One of Captain Avery's crew. Hanged at Execution Dock, 1696.

FOSTER. Buccaneer and poet.

Only two facts are known about this adventurer. One is that he was reproved on a certain occasion by Morgan (who thought nothing of torturing his captives) for " harshness " to his prisoners, and the other that he wrote sentimental verse, particularly one work entitled " Sonneyettes of Love."

FRANKLYN, CHARLES.

This Welsh pirate was a Monmouthshire man, and one of Captain Howel Davis's crew. While at the

Cape Verde Islands, Franklyn " was so charmed with the luxuries of the place and the free conversation of the Women," that he married and settled down there.

FREEBARN, MATTHEW.

One of Captain Lowther's crew. Hanged at St. Kitts on March 11th, 1722.

FROGGE, WILLIAM. Buccaneer.

Was with Morgan in his attacks on Porto Bello and Panama in 1670. He kept a diary of the chief events of these exploits, and distinctly states that the Spaniards, and not Morgan, set fire to the city. But he was greatly enraged against Morgan for cheating the buccaneers out of their plunder, and giving each man only about £10 as his share.

FULWORTH, MRS. ANNE.

This lady accompanied Anne Bonny to New Providence Island from Carolina in the guise of her mother. When Captain Rackam and Anne Bonny were intriguing to run away from the latter's husband, " a pardoned pirate, a likely young fellow and of a sober life," Mrs. Fulworth offered sympathy and advice to the lovers. The scandal being brought to the ears of Governor Woodes Rogers by a pirate called Richard Turnley, he sent for the two ladies, " and examining them both upon it, and finding they could not deny it, he threaten'd, if they proceeded further in it, to commit them both to Prison, and order them to be whipp'd, and that Rackam, himself, should be their Executioner."

GARCIA.

One of Gilbert's crew in the *Panda*. Hanged at Boston in June, 1835.

GARDINER.

Although at one time a pirate, by some means or other he became appointed to the office of Deputy Collector at Boston in 1699. Accepted a bribe of stolen gold from the pirate Gillam, which caused some gossip in the town.

GASPAR, Captain José, *alias* "Gasparilla" or "Richard Cœur de Lion."

Was an officer of high rank in the Spanish Navy till 1782, when, having been detected in stealing some jewels belonging to the Crown, he stole a ship and turned pirate. Settling at Charlotte Harbour, he built a fort, where he kept his female prisoners, all the male ones being killed. Here he lived in regal state as king of the pirates, on Gasparilla Island. In 1801 he took a big Spanish ship forty miles from Boca Grande, killed the crew, and took a quantity of gold and twelve young ladies. One of these was a Spanish princess, whom he kept for himself; the eleven Mexican girls he gave to his crew.

Gaspar was described as having polished manners and a great love of fashionable clothes, and being fearless in fight; but in spite of all these attractive qualities, the little Spanish princess would have none of him, and was murdered.

By the year 1821 the United States Government had made matters so hot for Gaspar that the pirate kingdom was broken up and their booty of 30,000,000 dollars divided.

As he was about to sail away, a big ship came into the bay, apparently an English merchantman. Gaspar at once prepared to attack her, when she ran up the Stars and Stripes, proving herself to be a heavily armed American man-of-war. The pirate ship was defeated, and Gaspar, winding a piece of anchor chain round his waist, jumped overboard and was drowned, his age being 65.

GATES, THOMAS.

Hanged in Virginia in 1718 with the rest of Captain Edward Teach's crew.

GAUTIER, FRANÇOIS, or GAUTIEZ, *alias* GEORGE SADWELL.
Native of Havre.

Cook on board the *Jane* schooner, commanded by Captain Thomas Johnson. While on a voyage from Gibraltar to Brazil with a valuable cargo, Gautier and the mate killed the captain and the helmsman and steered the vessel to Scotland, sinking her near Stornoway. Caught and tried at Edinburgh in November, 1821, found guilty, and hanged in January on the sands of Leith, his body being publicly dissected afterwards by the Professor of Anatomy to Edinburgh University. The age of this French pirate at his death was 23.

GAYNY, GEORGE, or GAINY.

One of Wafer's little party lost in the jungle of Darien in 1681. In attempting to swim across a swollen river with a line, he got into difficulties, became entangled in the line which was tied round his neck, and having also a bag containing 300 Spanish silver dollars on his back, he sank and was swept away. Some time afterwards Wafer found Gayny lying dead in a creek with the rope twisted about him and his money at his neck.

GENNINGS, CAPTAIN.

A renegade English pirate who joined the Barbary corsairs, turned Mohammedan, and commanded a

Moorish pirate vessel. Taken prisoner off the Irish coast, he was brought to London and hanged at Wapping.

GERRARD, Thomas.
Of the Island of Antigua.

One of Major Bonnet's crew of the *Royal James*. Tried for piracy at Charleston in 1718, but found "not guilty."

GIBBENS, Garrat.

Boatswain on board the *Queen Ann's Revenge*. Was killed at the same time as Captain Teach.

GIBBS, Charles.

Born at Rhode Island in 1794, he was brought up on a farm there. Ran away to sea in the United States sloop-of-war *Harriet*. Was in action off Pernambuco against H.M.S. *Peacock*, afterwards serving with credit on board the *Chesapeake* in her famous fight with the *Shannon;* but after his release from Dartmoor as a prisoner of war he opened a grocery shop in Ann Street, called the "Tin Pot," "a place full of abandoned women and dissolute fellows." Drinking up all the profits, he was compelled to go to sea again, and got a berth on a South American privateer. Gibbs led a mutiny, seized the ship and turned her into a pirate, and cruised about in the neighbourhood of Havana, plundering merchant vessels along the coast of Cuba. He slaughtered the crews of all the ships he took. In 1819 returned to private life in New York with 30,000 dollars in gold. Taking a pleasure trip to Liverpool, he was entrapped by a designing female and lost all his money.

In 1830 he took to piracy once more and shipped as a seaman in the brig *Vineyard* (Captain W. Thornby), New Orleans to Philadelphia, with a cargo of cotton, molasses, and 54,000 dollars in specie.

Gibbs again brought about a mutiny, murdering the captain and mate. After setting fire to and scuttling the ship, the crew took to their boats, landing at Barrow Island, where they buried their money in the sand.

He was hanged at New York as recently as 1831.

GIDDENS, PAUL.

One of Captain Quelch's crew. Tried at Boston in 1704.

GIDDINGS, JOHN.

Of York River, Virginia.

One of Captain Pound's crew. Wounded and taken prisoner at Tarpaulin Cove in 1689.

GILBERT, CAPTAIN.

Commanded the schooner *Panda.* On September 20th, 1832, he took and plundered a Salem brig, the *Mexican,* on her way from Salem to Rio de Janeiro. A few months later Gilbert and his crew were captured by Captain Trotter, of H.M. brig-of-war *Curlew,* and taken as prisoners to Salem and handed over to the United States authorities. Tried at Boston in December, 1834. Hanged at the same place on June 11th, 1835. This was the last act of piracy committed upon the Atlantic Ocean.

GILLAM, CAPTAIN JAMES, *alias* KELLY.

A notorious pirate. When serving on board the East Indiaman *Mocha,* he led a mutiny, and with his own hands murdered the commander, Captain Edge-comb, in his sleep. He came back to America with Captain Kidd, and was hiding, under the name of Kelly, when caught in 1699 at Charleston, opposite Boston, by the Governor of Massachusetts, who described him as "the most impudent, hardened villain I ever saw." It was said that Gillam had entered the service of the Mogul, turned Moham-medan, and been circumcised. To settle this last point, the prisoner was examined by a surgeon and a Jew, who both declared, on oath, that it was so.

GILLS, JOHN.

One of Captain Teach's crew. Hanged in Virginia in 1718.

GLASBY, HARRY.

Sailed as mate in the *Samuel,* of London (Captain Cary), which was taken in 1720 by Roberts, who made Glasby master on board the *Royal Fortune*.

Tried for piracy on the Guinea Coast in April and acquitted. Evidence was brought at his trial to show that Glasby was forced to serve with the pirates, for, being a "sea-artist" or sail-master, he was most use-ful to them. Twice he tried to escape in the West Indies, on one occasion being tried with two others by a drunken jury of pirates. The other deserters were shot, but Glasby was saved by one of his judges threatening to shoot anyone who made any attempt on him. Glasby befriended other prisoners and gave away his share of the plunder to them. When the *Royal Fortune* was taken by the *Swallow,* several of the most desperate pirates, particularly one James Philips, took lighted matches with which to ignite the powder magazine and blow up the ship. Glasby prevented this by placing trusted sentinels below.

GODEKINS, MASTER.

This notorious Hanseatic pirate, with another called Stertebeker, did fearful damage to English and other merchant shipping in the North Sea in the latter part of the fourteenth century.

On June 1st, 1395, he seized an English ship laden with salt fish off the coast of Denmark, her value being reckoned at £170. The master and crew of twenty-five men they slew, the only mariner saved being a boy, whom the pirates took with them to Wismar.

These same men took another English ship, the *Dogger* (Captain Gervase Cat). The *Dogger* was at anchor, and the crew fishing, when the pirates attacked them. The captain and crew were wounded, and damage was done to the tune of 200 nobles.

Another vessel taken was a Yarmouth barque, *Michael* (master, Robert Rigweys), while off Plymouth, the owner, Hugh ap Fen, losing 800 nobles. In 1394 these Hanseatic pirates, with a large fleet, attacked the town of Norbern in Norway, plundering the town and taking away all they could carry, as well as the merchants, who they held for ransom. The houses they burnt.

GOFFE, CHRISTOPHER.

Originally one of Captain Woollery's crew of Rhode Island pirates. In November, 1687, he surrendered himself at Boston, and was pardoned. In August, 1691, was commissioned by the Governor

to cruise with his ship, the *Swan*, between Cape Cod
and Cape Ann, to protect the coast from pirates.

GOLDSMITH, CAPTAIN THOMAS.
   Of Dartmouth in Devon.

During the reign of Queen Anne, Goldsmith commanded a privateer vessel, the *Snap Dragon*, of
Dartmouth.   He turned pirate and amassed great
riches.

This pirate would have been forgotten by now were
it not that he died in his bed at Dartmouth, and was
buried in the churchyard there.   The lines engraved
on his tombstone have been quoted in the Preface, but
may be repeated here :

> Men that are virtuous serve the Lord;
> And the Devil's by his friends ador'd;
> And as they merit get a place
> Amidst the bless'd or hellish race;
> Pray then, ye learned clergy show
> Where can this brute, Tom Goldsmith, go?
> Whose life was one continual evil,
> Striving to cheat God, Man, and Devil.

GOMEZ, JOHN, *alias* PANTHER KEY JOHN.
   Brother-in-law of the famous pirate Gasparilla.

Died, credited with the great age of 120 years, at
Panther Key in Florida in 1900.

GOODALE, JOHN.
   A Devonshire man.

Goodale, who was a renegade and had turned
Mohammedan, held a position of importance and
wealth amongst the Moors of Algiers.   In the year
1621 he bought from the Moors a British prize called
the *Exchange*, and also, for the sum of £7 10s., an
English slave, lately captain of an English merchant
ship, whom he got cheap owing to his having a
deformed hand.

GOODLY, Captain.

An English buccaneer of Jamaica, who in the year 1663 was in command of a "junk" armed with six guns and carrying a crew of sixty men.

GORDON, Captain Nathaniel.
Of Portland, Maine.

Commanded and owned the *Evie,* a small, full-rigged ship, which was fitted up as a "slaver." Made four voyages to West Africa for slaves. On his last voyage he was captured by the United States sloop *Mohican,* with 967 negroes on board. Tried in New York for piracy and found guilty and condemned to death. Great pressure was brought on President Lincoln to reprieve him, but without success, and Gordon was hanged at New York on February 22nd, 1862.

GOSS, Cuthbert.
Born at Topsham in Devon.

The compiler of these biographies regrets to have to record that this pirate was hanged, at the comparatively tender age of 21, outside the gates of Cape Coast Castle, within the flood-marks, in 1722. He was one of Captain Roberts's crew, having been taken prisoner by Roberts at Calabar in a prize called the *Mercy* galley, of Bristol, in 1721.

GOW, Captain John, *alias* Smith, *alias* Goffe.   A Scotch pirate, born at Thurso.

Although the short career of this pirate made a great noise at the time, he did little to merit the fame which he achieved. He had the honour of having an account of his piratical activities written by Defoe, and ninety years later was made the hero in a novel by Walter Scott, as Captain Cleveland.

Gow sailed from Amsterdam as a foremast hand in the *George* galley, commanded by Captain Ferneau, a Guernsey man. Being a brisk and intelligent man, he was soon promoted to be second mate. They called at Santa Cruz in Barbary to take in a cargo of beeswax to deliver at Genoa. Sailing from Santa Cruz on November 3rd, 1724, Gow and a few others conspired to mutiny and then to go "upon the account." The captain, as was his custom, had all hands, except the helmsman, into his cabin at eight o'clock each night for prayers. This particular night, after it was dark, the conspirators went below to the hammocks of the chief mate, the supercargo, and the surgeon and cut all their throats. They did the same to the captain, who was then thrown overboard though still alive.

Gow being now elected captain and one Williams, a thorough rogue, mate, they renamed the vessel the *Revenge,* armed her with eighteen guns, and cruised off the coast of Spain, taking an English sloop with a cargo of fish from Newfoundland, commanded by Captain Thomas Wise of Poole. Their second prize was a Glasgow ship loaded with herrings and salmon.

They next sailed to Madeira, where Gow presented the Governor with a box of Scotch herrings. About this time Williams, the first mate, insulted Gow by accusing him of cowardice because he had refused to attack a big French ship, and snapped his pistol at him. Two seamen standing near shot Williams, wounding him severely, and to get rid of him they put him aboard one of their prizes. Discussions now took place as to where to sail, and Gow, who was in love with a lass in the Orkney Islands, suggested sailing thither, as being a good place to traffic their stolen goods.

On arriving at Carristown they sold most of their cargo, and one of the crew, going on shore, bought a

horse for three pieces of eight and rode to Kirkwall
and surrendered himself. Next day ten more men
deserted, setting out in the long-boat for the mainland
of Scotland, but were taken prisoners in the *Forth*,
of Edinburgh. By now the whole countryside was
alarmed. Gow's next move was to land his men and
plunder the houses of the gentry. They visited a
Mrs. Honnyman and her daughter, but these ladies
managed to get their money and jewellery away in
safety. Gow's crew marched back to their ship with
a bagpiper playing at their head.

They now sailed to Calfsound, seized three girls
and took them aboard. Then to the Island of Eda
to plunder the house of Mr. Fea, an old schoolmate
of Gow's. Arriving there on February 13th, by bad
management they ran their vessel on the rocks. The
bo'son and five men went ashore and met Mr. Fea,
who entertained them at the local public-house. By
a simple stratagem, Mr. Fea seized first the bo'son
and afterwards the five men. Soon after this, Fea
trapped Gow and all the rest of his crew of twenty-
eight men. Help was sent for, and eventually the
Greyhound frigate arrived and took Gow and his crew
to London, arriving off Woolwich on March 26th,
1725. The prisoners were taken to the Marshalsea
Prison in Southwark, and there found their old companion, Lieutenant Williams. Four men turned
King's evidence—viz., George Dobson, Job Phinnies,
Tim Murphy, and William Booth.

The trial at Newgate began on May 8th, when Gow
was sullen and reserved and refused to plead. He
was ordered to be pressed to death, which was the
only form of torture still allowed by the law. At the
last moment Gow yielded, and pleaded " not guilty."
Gow was found guilty, and hanged on June 11th,
1725, but "as he was turned off, he fell down from
the Gibbit, the rope breaking by the weight of some

PRESSING A PIRATE TO PLEAD.

To face p. 140.

that pulled his leg. Although he had been hanging
for four minutes, he was able to climb up the ladder
a second time, which seemed to concern him very
little, and he was hanged again."

His body was then taken to Greenwich and there
hanged in chains, to be a warning to others.

GRAFF, LE CAPITAINE LAURENS DE. Filibuster.

Commanded *Le Neptune,* a ship armed with fifty-
four guns and a crew of 210 men, in the West Indies
in the seventeenth century.

GRAHAM, CAPTAIN.

Commanded a shallop, with a crew of fourteen
men, in 1685. Sailed in company with Captain Veale
up and down the coast of Virginia and New England.

GRAMBO.

Was "boss" of Barataria, the smugglers' stronghold off the Island of Grande Terre, near Louisiana,
until shot by Jean Lafitte in 1811.

GRAMMONT, SIEUR DE. French filibuster.

One of the great buccaneers. Born in Paris, he
entered the Royal Marines, in which he distinguished
himself in several naval engagements.

He commanded a frigate in the West Indies, and
captured near Martinique a Dutch ship with a cargo
worth £400,000, which he carried to Hispaniola, but
there lost all of it through gambling, and, not daring
to return to France, he joined the buccaneers.

He sailed to Curaçoa in 1678 with the Count
d'Estrees' fleet, which was wrecked on a coral reef
off the Isle d'Aves. De Grammont was left behind
to salve what he could from the wreck. After this,
with 700 men he sailed to Maracaibo, spending six

months on the lake, seizing the shipping and plundering all the settlements in the neighbourhood.

In June, 1680, de Grammont, with an obsolete commission and a small party of men, made a brilliant night assault on La Guayra, the seaport of Caracas. Only forty-seven men took part in the actual attack on the town, which was guarded by two forts and by cannon upon the walls. The pirates were attacked next day by 2,000 Spaniards from Caracas, but with the greatest skill and bravery de Grammont got almost all his party away, though wounded himself in the throat. He carried away with him amongst his prisoners the Governor of the town.

He retired to the Isle d'Aves to nurse his wound, and later went to Petit Goave.

In 1683 took part in the successful English and French attack on Vera Cruz, and afterwards, when Vanhorn died of gangrene, de Grammont, his lieutenant, carried his ship back to Petit Goave. In 1685 he received a fresh commission from de Cossey, the Governor of Dominica, and joined forces with the famous buccaneer Laurens de Graff at the Isle of Vache, and sailed with 11,000 men for Campeachy. Taking the town, he reduced it to ashes and blew up the fortress, returning with the plunder to Hispaniola. Before leaving, however, to celebrate the Festival of St. Louis, they burnt a huge bonfire, using 200,000 crowns worth of logwood.

Grammont at this time commanded a fine ship, *Le Hardy* (fifty guns and a crew of 300 men).

In 1686 de Grammont was granted a commission of "Lieutenant du Roi," in order to keep him from harassing the Spaniards, and yet not to lose his valuable services to his country.

In order to have one last fling at the old free buccaneering life before settling down to the more sedate and respectable calling of an officer in the French

King's navy, de Grammont sailed off with a party of
180 desperadoes, but was never heard of again.

GRAND, Pierre le.
A native of Dieppe in Normandy.

Le Grand was the man who, having made one
great and successful exploit, had the good sense to
retire. He was the first pirate to take up his quarters
at Tortuga Island, and was known amongst the English as " Peter the Great." His name will go down to
posterity for his " bold and insolent " action when in
a small open boat with a handful of men he seized a
great Spanish galleon.

Pierre had been out on the " grand account " for a
long while, meeting with no success. When almost
starving and in despair, a great Spanish fleet hove in
sight, and one ship, bigger than the rest, was observed
sailing at some little distance behind the other vessels.
The mad idea entered the head of the now desperate
pirate to take this ship. The pirates all took an oath
to their captain to fight without fear and never to
surrender. It was dusk, and in these tropical latitudes
night follows day very quickly. Before the attack,
orders were given to the surgeon to bore a hole in the
bottom of the boat so that it would quickly sink, thus
taking away any hope of escape should the enterprise
fail. This was done, and the boat was paddled quietly
alongside the great warship, when the crew, armed
only with a pistol and a sword a-piece, clambered up
the sides and jumped aboard. Quickly and silently
the sleeping helmsman was killed, while Pierre and a
party of his men ran down into the great cabin, where
they surprised the Spanish admiral playing cards with
his officers. The admiral, suddenly confronted by a
band of bearded desperadoes in his cabin with a pistol
aimed at his head, ejaculated " Jesus bless us ! are
these devils or what are they ?" While this was going

on others of the pirates had hurried to the gun-room, seized the arms, killing every Spaniard who withstood them. Pierre knew, as scarcely any other successful pirate or gambler ever did, the right moment to stop. He at once put ashore all the prisoners he did not want for working the ship, and sailed straight back to France; where he lived the rest of his life in comfortable obscurity, and never again returned to piracy.

The news of this exploit spread rapidly over the West Indies, and caused the greatest excitement amongst the pirate fraternity of Tortuga and Hispaniola.

Men left their work of killing and drying beef, while others deserted their plantations to go a-pirating on the Spaniards, in much the same way as men went to a gold rush years after. Those who had no boat would venture forth in canoes looking for rich Spanish treasure ships.

It was this wild deed of Pierre le Grand that was the beginning of piracy in the West Indies, towards the latter half of the seventeenth century.

GRANGE, ROGER.

One of Captain Lowther's crew of the *Happy Delivery*. Tried for piracy at St. Kitts in 1722, but acquitted.

DE GRAVES, CAPTAIN HERBERT.

This Dutch pirate sailed as captain of his own merchant vessel during the reign of King Charles II. He took to landing his crew on the south coast of England and raiding gentlemen's houses. The first he ever pillaged was that of a Mr. Sturt, in Sussex. In those days, when banks were almost unknown, the houses of the rich often contained great sums of money. De Graves was wont to sail along the Devonshire coast, sometimes landing and robbing a house, sometimes taking a ship, which he would carry to Rotterdam and sell. He made several daring raids into Cowes and Lowestoft, getting off with valuable plunder.

In the war between England and the Dutch, Graves was given command of a fire-ship. This vessel he handled very capably, and in the action off the Downs he ran her on board the *Sandwich*, setting her on fire. James, Duke of York, escaped from the *Sandwich* with great difficulty, while the Earl of Albemarle and most of the crew perished. At the conclusion of the war, De Graves returned to piracy, but his ship was wrecked in a storm close to Walmer Castle. The captain and a few of his crew were saved, and, being made prisoners, were hanged on a tree.

GREAVES, Captain, *alias* "Red Legs." West Indian pirate.

Born in Barbadoes of prisoners who had been sent there as slaves by Cromwell. Most of these slaves were natives of Scotland and Ireland, and, owing to their bare knees, generally went by the name of Red Legs. Young Greaves was left an orphan, but had a kind master and a good education. His master dying, the lad was sold to another and a cruel one. The boy ran away, swam across Carlisle Bay, but by mistake clambered on to the wrong ship, a pirate vessel, commanded by a notoriously cruel pirate called Captain Hawkins. Finding himself driven to the calling of piracy, Greaves became very efficient, and quickly rose to eminence. He was remarkable for his dislike of unnecessary bloodshed, torture of prisoners, and killing of non-combatants. These extraordinary views brought about a duel between himself and his captain, in which the former was victorious, and he was at once elected commander.

Greaves now entered a period of the highest

piratical success, but always preserved very strictly his reputation for humanity and morality. He never tortured his prisoners, nor ever robbed the poor, nor maltreated women.

His greatest success of all was his capture of the Island of Margarita, off the coast of Venezuela.

On this occasion, after capturing the Spanish Fleet, he turned the guns of their warships against the forts, which he then stormed, and was rewarded by a huge booty of pearls and gold.

Red Legs then retired to the respectable life of a planter in the Island of Nevis, but was one day denounced as a pirate by an old seaman. He was cast into a dungeon to await execution, when the great earthquake came which destroyed and submerged the town in 1680, and one of the few survivors was Greaves. He was picked up by a whaler, on board of which he served with success, and later on, for his assistance in capturing a gang of pirates, he received pardon for his earlier crimes.

He again retired to a plantation, and was noted for his many acts of piety and for his generous gifts to charities and public institutions, eventually dying universally respected and sorrowed.

GREENSAIL, RICHARD.

One of Blackbeard's crew in the *Queen Ann's Revenge*. Hanged in Virginia in 1718.

GREENVILLE, HENRY.

Hanged at Boston in 1726 with Captain Fly and Samuel Cole.

GRIFFIN, JACK.

Chief mate of a Bristol vessel. One of the chief mutineers on board the *Bird* galley in 1718, off Sierra Leone, when he befriended the captain of the *Bird*, with whom he had been at school. Took part in a feast to celebrate the success of the mutiny, the meal being cooked in a huge caldron in which the slaves' food was prepared. In this caldron were boiled, on this occasion, fowls, ducks, geese, and turkeys, which were unplucked; several Westphalian hams were added, and a "large sow with young embowled." The health of King James III., the Pretender, was drunk with full honours.

GRIFFIN, John.
Of Blackwall, Middlesex.

Taken out of the *Mercy* galley and appointed carpenter on board the *Royal Fortune* by Captain Roberts. Condemned to be hanged at Cape Coast Castle, but pardoned and sold to the Royal African Company as a slave for seven years.

GRIFFIN, Richard.
A gunsmith of Boston.

Sailed with Captain Pound. Wounded in a fight at Tarpaulin Cove, a bullet entering his ear and coming out through his eye.

GROGNIET, Captain.
A French buccaneer who in 1683 was in company with Captain L'Escayer, with a crew of some 200 French and 80 English freebooters. He joined Davis and Swan during the blockade of Panama in 1685, and was in the unsuccessful attempt in May, 1685, on the Spanish treasure fleet from Lima. In July of the same year Grogniet, with 340 French buccaneers, parted company from Davis at Quibo, plundered several towns, and then, foolishly, revisited Quibo, where they were discovered by a Spanish squadron in January, 1686, and their ship was burnt while the

crew was on shore. They were rescued by Townley, with whom they went north to Nicaragua, and sacked Granada. In May, 1686, Grogniet and half the Frenchmen crossed the isthmus. In the January following, Grogniet reappeared, and, joining with the English, again plundered Guayaquil, where he was severely wounded, and died soon afterwards.

GULLIMILLIT, Breti.

Taken with other South American pirates by H.M. sloop *Tyne,* and hanged at Kingston, Jamaica, in 1823.

GUTTEREZ, Juan.

Hanged at Kingston, Jamaica, on February 7th, 1823.

GUY, Captain.

Commanded the frigate *James* (fourteen guns, ninety men). Belonged to Tortuga Island and Jamaica in 1663.

HAINS, Richard.

One of Captain Low's crew. When Low took a Portuguese ship at St. Michael's in the Azores in 1723, he, with unusual kindness, simply burnt the ship and let the crew go to shore in a boat. While the prisoners were getting out the boat, Richard Hains happened to be drinking punch out of a silver tankard at one of the open ports, and took the opportunity to drop into the boat among the Portuguese and lie down in the bottom, so as to escape with them. Suddenly remembering his silver tankard, he climbed back, seized the tankard, and hid again in the boat, somehow, by great good fortune, being unobserved by those on the ship, and so escaped almost certain death both for himself and the Portuguese sailors.

HALSEY, CAPTAIN JOHN.

This famous South Sea pirate was born on March 1st, 1670, at Boston, and received a commission from the Governor of Massachusetts to cruise as a privateer on the Banks. No sooner was he out of sight of land than Halsey turned pirate. Taking a ship or two, he sailed to the Canary Islands, picking up a rich Spanish ship there. He next doubled the Cape of Good Hope, and paid a call on the "brethren" at Madagascar. He then sailed to the Red Sea, another happy hunting ground of the pirates, and met a big Dutch ship armed with sixty guns. Halsey astounded his men by announcing his sudden determination to attack only Moorish ships in the future. The indignant crew mutinied, threw Captain Halsey and his chief gunner in irons, and proceeded to attack the Dutchman. The mutinous pirates got the worst of the encounter, and released Halsey, who only just managed to get his ship away. Luck seems to have deserted Halsey for a while, for not a Moorish ship could he meet with, so much so that his scruples against taking Christian ships eased enough to permit him to bag a brace of English ships, the *Essex* and the *Rising Eagle*.

The captain of the former proved to be a very old and dear friend of Halsey's quartermaster, and to show a friendly feeling, Halsey allowed the captain to keep all his personal belongings. Nevertheless, they took a comfortable booty, comprising some fifty thousand pounds in English gold, out of the *Essex*, and another ten thousand out of the *Rising Eagle*.

The pirates, being strict business men, produced invoices and sold the two ships back to their legal owners for cash, and having settled this affair to everybody's satisfaction, Halsey and his consort returned to Madagascar. Here they were visited by the captain of a Scotch ship, the *Neptune*, which had come to trade liquor, probably rum, but possibly whisky, with the pirates. A sudden hurricane arose, destroying both the pirate ships and damaging the *Neptune*. Halsey, ever a man of resource, thereupon seized the Scotch ship, and, with even greater enterprise, at once attacked a ship, the *Greyhound*, which lay at anchor, which was loaded with stolen merchandise which the pirates had only just sold to the captain of the *Greyhound*, and for which they had been paid.

The end was now drawing near, for in 1716 Captain Halsey was taken ill of some tropical fever and died. He was a popular commander, respected, ever loved by his men, for he was a humane man, never killing his prisoners unless necessity compelled. A contemporary eyewitness of his funeral rites leaves the following account of his burial :

" With great solemnity, the prayers of the Church of England being read over him and his sword and pistols laid on his coffin, which was covered with a ship's Jack. As many minute guns were fired as he was old—viz., 46—and three English vollies and one French volley of small arms." The chronicler continues : " His grave was made in a garden of watermelons and fenced in to prevent his being rooted up by wild pigs."

This last a truly touching thought on the part of the bereaved.

HAMAN, CAPTAIN JOHN.

He lived all alone with his wife and family on a small and otherwise uninhabited island in the Bahamas.

About the year 1720, he sailed into New Providence Harbour in his 40-ton sloop, intending to settle there. Captain Rackam and Anne Bonny stole this vessel and eloped in her.

Writing of Captain Haman, Johnson tells us "his Livelihood and constant Employment was to plunder and pillage the Spaniards, whose Sloops and Launces he had often surprised about Cuba and Hispaniola, and sometimes brought off a considerable Booty, always escaping by a good Pair of Heels, insomuch that it became a Bye-Word to say, 'There goes John Haman, catch him if you can.' His Business to Providence now was to bring his Family there, in order to live and settle, being weary, perhaps, of living in that Solitude, or else apprehensive if any of the Spaniards should discover his Habitation, they might land, and be revenged of him for all his Pranks."

HAMLIN, CAPTAIN JEAN.
A famous French filibuster who turned pirate.

Set out in 1682 from Jamaica in a sloop with 120 other desperadoes in pursuit of a French ship that was "wanted" by the Jamaican Governor. Having overtaken the ship, *La Trompeuse,* he seized her, fitted her up as a man-of-war, and then started out on a wild piratical cruise, taking eighteen Jamaican vessels, barbarously ill-treating the crews, and completely demoralizing the trade of the island. Two other ships were now sent to find and destroy the new *La Trompeuse,* but Hamlin escaped and sailed to the Virgin Islands, and was most hospitably received by the Governor of the Danish Island of St. Thomas, one Adolf Esmit, who was himself a retired pirate. Using this island as his headquarters Hamlin cruised about and took several English ships.

In May, 1683, he appeared on the West Coast of Africa disguised as an English man-of-war. Off the coast of Sierra Leone, he took seventeen Dutch and English ships, returning to Dominica in July, 1683, finally reaching the friendly St. Thomas Island, being warmly welcomed back by the pirate Governor. Three days afterwards, H.M.S. *Francis* arrived on the look-out for pirates, and attacked and burnt Hamlin's ship. Hamlin, with the help of the Governor, managed to escape with his life.

HANDS, ISRAEL, also known as BASILICA HANDS.

Sailing-master with the famous Teach or Black-beard. One day when Teach was entertaining a pilot and Hands in his cabin, after they had been drinking and chatting awhile seated round the cabin table, on which stood a lighted candle, Blackbeard suddenly drew his pistols, blew out the candle, and crossing his arms, fired both his pistols under the table. Hands was shot in the knee, and crippled for life. Teach's explanation to the angry demands of his guests as to the reason for this extraordinary conduct produced the reply that ' if he did not shoot one or two of them now and then, they'd forget who he was." Hands after this deserted, but was captured at Bath in Caro-lina by Brand. Hands, probably in revenge for being wantonly shot by Teach, turned King's evidence at the inquiry held at Charleston, and brought very serious accusations against one of the most prominent men in the colony, Knight, who was secretary to the Chief Justice, and a deputy collector of Customs.

Hands was tried for piracy in Virginia in December, 1718, but pardoned. When last heard of was seen begging his bread in London.

HANSEL, CAPTAIN.

He behaved himself so courageously at the taking of Porto Bello in 1669, that a party of some 400 men, in four ships, chose Hansel to be their admiral in an attempt on the town of Comana, near Caracas. This attack was a most complete failure, the pirates being driven off "with great loss and in great confusion." When Hansel's party arrived back at Jamaica, they found the rest of Morgan's men had returned before them, who "ceased not to mock and jeer at them for their ill success at Comana, after telling them, 'Let us see what money you brought from Comana, and if it be as good silver as that which we bring from Maracaibo.'"

HARDING, Captain Thomas.

In 1653 he captured a rich prize, a Barbadoes vessel. For this he was tried for piracy at Boston.

HARDY, Richard.

One of Captain Bartholomew Roberts's crew. Hanged at Cape Coast Castle, West Coast of Africa, on April 6th, 1722, at the age of 25 years.

It is recorded that, owing to the lack of expert knowledge in the niceties of carrying out executions, Hardy was led to the scaffold with his hands tied behind him. This annoyed Hardy very much, and it is mentioned in the official account of his execution that the prisoner indignantly declared "that he had seen many a Man hang'd, but this Way of the Hands being ty'd behind them, he was a Stranger to, and never saw before in his Life."

HARPER, Abraham.

Born at Bristol.

He was cooper on board Captain Roberts's *Royal Fortune*. When the pirates took a prize, it was Harper's duty to see that all the casks and coopers' tools were removed from the prize to the pirate craft.

Hanged at the age of 23, with the rest of the crew, in 1722.

HARRIS, Captain.

Joined the Barbary corsairs during the reign of Queen Elizabeth, turned Mohammedan, and rose to command a Moorish pirate vessel. Cruised off the coast of Ireland, was taken prisoner by an English ship, and hanged at Wapping.

HARRIS, Hugh.
Of Corfe Castle, Dorsetshire.

One of Roberts's crew; tried and condemned to be hanged in 1722, but reprieved and sold to the Royal African Company to serve for seven years in their plantations.

HARRIS, James.
One of Roberts's crew.

HARRIS, Peter.
Born in Kent.

This buccaneer was known amongst the brethren of the coast as "a brave and Stout Soldier."

In 1680 he took a leading part in the march of the buccaneers across the Isthmus of Darien, but during the attack on the Spanish Fleet off Panama he was shot in both legs, and died of his wounds.

HARRIS, Richard.
A Cornishman.

One of Captain Roberts's crew and the oldest, being 45 years of age when he was hanged, an unusually advanced age to reach in this most "unhealthy" profession.

HARRISON, Captain.

Sailed in October, 1670, in company with Captains Prince and Ludbury, into Port Royal, after a successful expedition with 170 men up the San Juan River in Nicaragua, when they plundered the unfortunate city of Granada. This city had suffered so much from previous attacks from the buccaneers that the plunder came to only some £20 per man on this occasion.

Modyford, the Governor of Jamaica, " reproved the captains for acting without commissions, but did not deem it prudent to press the matter too far "; in fact, instead of arresting Harrison and his crew, he sent them to join Morgan the Buccaneer, who was then gathering together a great fleet of buccaneers at the Isle of Vache.

HARVEY, CAPTAIN.

Arrived at New London in 1685 in company with another pirate, Captain Veale; posed as an honest merchant, but, being recognized, left in great haste.

HARVEY, WILLIAM.

Tried for piracy with the rest of Gow's crew at Newgate in 1725, and acquitted.

HARWOOD, JOHN.

Tried for piracy at Boston in 1704. One of the crew of the brigantine *Charles* (Captain John Quelch, Commander).

HATTSELL, CAPTAIN.

This buccaneer served as an officer with Mansfield in his successful and daring night attack on the Island of Providence, when, with only 200 men, the fort was captured and the Spanish Governor taken prisoner. Captain Hattsell was left behind with thirty-five men to hold the island, while Mansfield sailed to the mainland with his prisoners, who had surrendered on condition that they should be safely conducted there.

HAWKINS, Captain.

A seventeenth-century Barbadoes pirate. Notorious for his cruelty, which led to his fighting a duel with one of his crew, Greaves, *alias* Red Legs, by whom he was defeated, his victor being elected captain in his place.

HAWKINS, Sir John.
Born in 1532.

This famous Elizabethan seaman sailed in 1561 to the Canary Islands, and traded in negro slaves between Africa and Hispaniola. Afterwards became an officer in the Royal Navy. Died at sea off Porto Bello, in 1595, when serving with Drake in the West Indies.

HAWKINS, Captain Thomas.

In the year 1689 cruised off the coast of New England, burning and plundering the shipping. The Bay colony sent out an armed sloop, the *Mary* (Samuel Pease, commander), in October of that year, to attempt to capture Hawkins. Pease found the pirate in Buzzard's Bay. Hawkins ran up a red flag and a furious engagement began. The crew of the *Mary* at last boarded the pirates, and the captain, Pease, was so severely wounded that he died.

HAWKINS, Thomas.
Born at Boston.

Turned pirate and cruised with Captain Pound. Tried for piracy at Boston in 1690, but reprieved. Sent to England, but on the voyage was killed in a fight with a French privateer.

HAYES, Captain, nicknamed "Bully Hayes." A South Sea pirate.

In 1870 was arrested by the English Consul at Samoa for piracy. There being no prison in this delightful island, the Consul ran Hayes's ship on shore, and waited for a man-of-war to call and take his prisoner away. Hayes spent his time, while under open arrest, attending native picnic parties, at which he was the life and soul, being, when off duty, a man of great charm of manner and a favourite with the ladies. Presently another pirate arrived, one Captain Pease, in an armed ship with a Malay crew. Hayes and Pease quarrelled violently, and the Consul had great trouble to keep the two pirates from coming to blows. This animosity was all a sham to throw dust in the Consul's eyes, for one night Pease sailed away with Hayes, whom he had smuggled on board his ship.

HAZEL, THOMAS.
Of Westminster.

Hanged in Rhode Island in 1723 at the advanced age, for a pirate, of 50. This is one of the longest lived pirates we have been able to hear of.

HEAMAN, PETER, *alias* ROGERS.
A French pirate, born in 1787.

Sailed from Gibraltar in May, 1821, as mate on board the schooner *Jane* (Captain Thomas Johnson), bound for Bahia, Brazil, with a very rich cargo of beeswax, silk, olives, and other goods, as well as eight barrels of Spanish dollars.

When about seventeen days out, in the middle of the night, Heaman attacked one of the crew, James Paterson, and beat him to death. On the captain coming up on deck to find out what all the noise was about, Heaman beat him to death with a musket, being assisted by the cook, Francis Gautier, also a Frenchman. The two conspirators then proceeded to imprison the rest of the crew in the forecastle, and threw the dead bodies of the captain and the sailor overboard. For two days the murderers tried to suffo-

cate the crew by burning pitch and blowing the smoke
into the forecastle. Failing to accomplish this they
let the crew out after each had sworn on the Bible not
to inform on them. The course was now altered, and
they sailed towards Scotland. The barrels of dollars
were broken open and the coins placed in bags. In
June they reached the Island of Barra, where Gautier
went ashore, wearing the late captain's green coat,
and bought a large boat. Next, they sailed to Stornoway, where they arrived in July, and here they sank
their schooner. The crew rowed ashore in the long-
boat, sharing out the dollars as they went, using an
old tin as a measure, each man getting 6,300 dollars
as his share. Their boat was smashed on the rocks
when landing, but they got their plunder safely ashore
and hid it amongst the stones on the beach. Early
next morning the mutineers were visited by the
Customs officer. After he had left, the cabin boy, a
Maltese, ran after him and told him the true story of
the murders and robbery. A party of islanders was
got together, the mutineers arrested and taken to
Edinburgh, where Heaman and Gautier were tried for
piracy and murder, and on November 27th found guilty
and condemned to death. They were both hanged on
January 9th, 1822, on the sands of Leith, within the
flood mark, and afterwards their bodies were delivered
to Dr. Alexander Munro, Professor of Anatomy in the
University of Edinburgh, to be publicly dissected by
him.

HEATH, Peleg.

One of William Coward's crew. Condemned to be
hanged at Boston in 1690, but afterwards reprieved.

HEIDON, Captain.

Arrested for piracy in 1564 for having captured a
Flemish ship. This vessel he manned with thirteen

Scotchmen in addition to his own crew, and sailed off the coast of Spain. Here he took a prize containing a cargo of wine, which he carried to the Island of Bere in Bantry Bay. The wine was sold to Lord O'Sullivan. Heidon now fitted up another ship, the *John of Sandwich*. Was wrecked in her on the Island of Alderney and Heidon was arrested, but managed to escape in a small boat with some others of the pirates.

HENLEY, Captain.

In 1683 sailed from Boston " bound for the Rack," afterwards going to the Red Sea, where he plundered Arab and Malabar ships.

HERDUE, Captain. Buccaneer.

Commanded a frigate of four guns, crew of forty men, at Tortuga Island, in 1663.

HERNANDEZ, Augustus.

Hanged at Kingston, Jamaica, in 1823.

HERNANDEZ, Juan.

Captured with nine other pirates by H.M. sloop-of-war *Tyne* and taken to Jamaica. Hanged on February 7th, 1823, at Kingston.

HERRIOTT, David.

Master of the *Adventure,* from Jamaica, taken by Teach in 1718. He joined the pirates, and later, when Major Stede Bonnet separated from Teach, he took Herriott to be his sailing-master. Taken prisoner with Bonnet and his crew of the *Royal James* by Colonel Rhet, at Cape Fear, North Carolina, September 27th, 1718. Herriott and the boatswain, Ignatius Pell, turned King's evidence at the trial of the pirates held at Charleston. On October 25th, Bonnet and Herriott escaped from prison, in spite of the fact that the latter had turned King's evidence. Herriott was shot on Sullivan Island a few days later.

HEWETT, WILLIAM, or HEWET, or HEWIT.
  Of Jamaica.
One of Major Stede Bonnet's crew. Tried for piracy at Charleston in 1718, and hanged at White Point on November 8th, and buried in the marsh below low-water mark.

HIDE, DANIEL.
  Of Virginia.
One of the crew of Captain Charles Harris, who, with Captain Low, played havoc on the shipping off the American coast from New York to Charleston. Hanged at Newport, Rhode Island, in July, 1723, at the age of 23.

HILL, CORPORAL JOHN.
In charge of the guard at Fort Royal, Falmouth, Maine, which all deserted one night, and went to sea with the pirate Captain Pound. Killed at Tarpaulin Cove in 1689.

HILLIARD, JOHN.
Was "chief man" of the company of Captain Bartholomew Sharp on his "dangerous voyage" to the South Seas. Died on January 2nd, 1681, of dropsy; buried at sea with the usual buccaneers' honours.

HINCHER, DR. JOHN.
  Of Edinburgh University.
Tried for piracy in July, 1723, at Newport, Rhode Island, but acquitted. This young doctor, his age

was only 22, was taken off a prize by Captain Low
against his will, to act as ship's surgeon with the
pirates.

HIND, ISRAEL, or HYNDE.
Of Bristol.

One of Captain Roberts's crew. Hanged at Cape
Coast Castle in 1722, at the age of 30.

HINGSON, JOHN.

One of Wafer's party left behind and lost in the
forest when Dampier crossed the Isthmus of Darien
on foot in 1681.

HITCHENS, ROBERT.
A Devonshire man, born in the year 1515.

Took to piracy early in life. Sailed with the pirate
Captain Heidon, and was wrecked on Alderney in the
year 1564. Arrested and tried for piracy, and was
hanged in chains at low-water mark at St. Martin's
Point, Guernsey, in 1564, at the age of 50.

HOLDING, ANTHONY.

One of John Quelch's crew of the brigantine *Charles*.
Tried for piracy at Boston in 1704.

HOLFORD, CAPTAIN. Buccaneer.
Of Jamaica.

An old friend of the notorious pirate Vane. In
1718 he happened to arrive in his ship at a small
uninhabited island in the Bay of Honduras to find
Vane on shore and destitute. Vane thought he would
be saved by Holford, but the latter was quite frank
in refusing, saying: "I shan't trust you aboard my
ship unless I carry you a prisoner, for I shall have
you caballing with my men, knock me on the head,
and run away with my ship a-pyrating." It was

owing to Holford that Vane was eventually taken a prisoner to Jamaica and there hanged.

HOLLAND, Captain Richard.

An Irishman.

Commanded a Spanish pirate vessel in the West Indies in 1724. The crew consisted of sixty Spaniards, eighteen French, and eighteen English sailors. Holland had originally belonged to the Royal Navy, but deserted from the *Suffolk* at Naples, and took shelter in a convent in that city. In August, 1724, Holland's ship took as prizes the *John and Mary*, the *Prudent Hannah of Boston*, and the *Dolphin*, of Topsham, all on their way to Virginia. From out of the *John and Mary* he took thirty-six men slaves, some gold dust, the captain's clothes, four great guns and small arms, and 400 gallons of rum.

HOPKINS, Mr.   Buccaneer and apothecary.

First lieutenant to Captain Dover (a doctor of physic) on board the *Duchess* privateer, of Bristol. Mr. Hopkins was an apothecary by profession, not a sailor, but being a kinsman to the captain, no doubt was given promotion. He sailed from Bristol on August 2nd, 1708.

HORE, Captain.

About 1650 Hore turned from a privateer into a pirate, and was very active and successful in taking prizes between New York and Newport, occasionally sailing to Madagascar to waylay ships of the East India Company.

HORNIGOLD, Captain Benjamin.

Commanded a sloop in 1716 and cruised off the Guinea coast with Teach, taking a big French Guinea ship. He then sailed to the Bahama Islands, where,

in 1718, Woodes Rogers had just arrived with the
offer of a pardon to all pirates who surrendered themselves. Teach went off again "on the account," but
Hornigold surrendered. Shortly afterwards Hornigold was wrecked on a reef and drowned.

HOW, THOMAS.
A native of Barnstaple in Devon.

One of Captain Bartholomew Roberts's crew. Condemned to death for piracy, but reprieved and sold to
the Royal African Company to work on their plantations for seven years.

HOWARD, THOMAS.
Born in London, the son of a Thames lighterman.
Sailing to Jamaica, he deserted his ship and, with
some companions of a like mind, stole a canoe and set
off to the Grand Cayman Islands, and there met with
some 200 buccaneers and pirates. Joining with these,
they took several vessels, lastly a well-armed Spanish
ship. In her they cruised off the coast of Virginia,
taking a large New England brigantine, of which
Howard was appointed quartermaster. Their next
prize was a fine Virginian galley, twenty-four guns,
crowded with convicts being transplanted to America.
These passengers were only too willing to join the
pirates.

Next, they sailed away to Guinea, where they took
numerous prizes. Here they were attacked by a
big Portuguese ship of thirty-six guns, which they
defeated. Having by now got together a well appointed pirate fleet, they sailed round the Cape of
Good Hope to Madagascar, the happy home of the
South Sea pirates. Their ship, the *Alexander*, was
wrecked and lost on a reef, and Howard, together with
the English and Dutch members of the crew, seized
the treasure, and drove off the Portuguese and Spanish

sailors and also the captain, and got to shore in a boat. They then broke up their ship, and lived for a while by fishing and hunting. On one of these hunting parties, the men ran away and left Howard behind.

Howard was found by the King of Anquala, who took care of him until he was picked up by a ship. Later on, Howard became captain of a fine vessel, the *Prosperous*, thirty-six guns, which he and some other pirates had seized at Madagascar. In her, Howard went cruising, eventually in company with Captain Bowen, attacking a Moorish fleet off St. John's Island. Howard followed the Moorish ships up a river, and, after a fierce fight, seized the largest and richest prize, a ship containing upward of a million dollars worth of goods. Howard, having now made a considerable fortune, retired from the piratical life and went to India, and there married a native woman and settled down. Howard, who was a morose, sour kind of man, ill-treated his wife, and he was at length murdered by some of her relations.

HUGGIT, Thomas.
Of London.

Hanged at Newport, Rhode Island, in July, 1723. Age 30.

HULL, Captain Edward.

Commanded the *Swallow* "frigott" in which he sailed from Boston in 1653, and captured several French and Dutch ships. He afterwards sold his vessels and went with his share of the plunder to England, where he settled down.

HUNTER, Andrew.

One of Captain Lowther's crew. Hanged at St. Kitts on March 11th, 1722.

HUSK, JOHN.

One of Blackbeard's crew in the *Queen Ann's Revenge*. Killed off North Carolina in 1718.

HUTNOT, JOSEPH.

One of the crew of the notorious brigantine *Charles*, commanded by Captain Quelch. Tried for piracy at the Star Tavern, Boston, in 1704.

HUTT, CAPTAIN GEORGE, or HOUT. Buccaneer.

An Englishman who succeeded Captain Townley when the latter was killed during a gallant fight with three Spanish galleons in 1686 near Panama.

INGRAM, GUNNER WILLIAM.

Was one of Captain Anstis's crew in the *Good Fortune* when that pirate took the *Morning Star*. After the prize had been converted to the pirates' use, Ingram was appointed gunner. Later, when Ingram came to be tried for piracy, evidence was produced to prove that he had joined the pirates of his own free will, and, in fact, had on all occasions been one of the forwardest in any action, and altogether "a very resolute hardened Fellow." He was hanged.

IRELAND, JOHN. Pirate.

" A wicked and ill-disposed person," according to the royal warrant of King William III. granted to " our truly and dearly beloved Captain William Kidd " to go in the year 1695 to seize this and other pirates who were doing great mischief to the ships trading off the coast of North America.

IRVINE, CAPTAIN.

One of the last pirates in the Atlantic. Very active in the early part of the nineteenth century.

JACKMAN, Captain. Buccaneer.

In 1665 took part with Morris and Morgan in a very successful raid on Central America, ascending the river Tabasco in the province of Campeachy with only 107 men.   Led by Indians by a detour of 300 miles, they surprised and sacked the town of Villa de Mosa. Dampier describes this small town as "standing on the starboard side of the river, inhabited chiefly by Indians, with some Spaniards."   On their return to the mouth of the river, Jackman's party found the Spaniards had seized their ship, and some three hundred of them attacked the pirates, but the Spaniards were easily beaten off.

The freebooters next attacked Rio Garta, and took it with only thirty men, crossed the Gulf of Honduras to rest on the Island of Roatan, and then proceeded to the Port of Truxillo, which they plundered.   They next sailed down the Mosquito coast, burning and pillaging as they went.

Anchoring in Monkey Bay, they ascended the San Juan River in canoes one hundred miles to Lake Nicaragua.   The pirates described the Lake of Nicaragua as being a veritable paradise, which, indeed, it must have been prior to their visit.   Hiding by day amongst the many islands and rowing by night, on the fifth night they landed near the city of Granada, just one year after Mansfield's visit.   The buccaneers marched right into the central square of the city without being observed by the Spaniards, who were taken completely by surprise, so that the English were soon masters of the city, and for sixteen hours they plundered it.   Some 1,000 Indians, driven to rebellion by the cruelty and oppression of the Spaniards, accompanied the marauders and wanted to massacre the prisoners, particularly "the religious," but when they understood that the buccaneers were not remaining in Granada, they thought better of it, having, no doubt, a shrewd inkling of what to expect in the future when their rescuers had left.

JACKSON, Captain William.   Buccaneer.

In 1642 he gathered together a crew of more than a thousand buccaneers in the Islands of St. Kitts and Barbadoes, and sailed with these in three ships to the Spanish Main, plundering Maracaibo and Truxillo.

On March 25th, 1643, Jackson's little fleet dropped anchor in the harbour, what was afterwards to be known as Kingston, in the Island of Jamaica, which was then still in the possession of Spain.   Landing 500 of his men, he attacked the town of St. Jago de la Vega, which he took after a hard fight and with the loss of some forty of his men.   For sparing the town from fire he received ransom from the Spaniards of 200 beeves, 10,000 pounds of cassava bread, and 7,000 pieces of eight.   The English sailors were so delighted by the beauty of the island that in one night twenty-three of them deserted to the Spaniards.

JACKSON, Nathaniel.

One of Captain Edward Teach's crew.   Killed at North Carolina in 1718.

JAMES, Captain.   Buccaneer.

Belonged to Jamaica and Tortuga.   In 1663 was in command of a frigate, the *American* (six guns, crew of seventy men).

JAMES, Captain.

A buccaneer captain who was in 1640 temporarily appointed " President " of Tortuga Island by the Providence Company, while their regular Governor, Captain Flood, was in London, clearing himself of charges preferred against him by the planters.

JAMES, Captain.

About 1709 commanded a pirate brigantine off Madagascar. Sailed for some time in company with a New York pirate called Ort Van Tyle.

JAMES, Charles.

One of Captain John Quelch's crew taken in the *Larimore* galley at Salem. Tried for piracy at Boston in 1704.

JAMISON, *alias* Monacre Nickola.

Born at Greenock in Scotland, the son of a rich cloth merchant, he received a polite education, spoke several languages, and was described as being of gentlemanly deportment.

He served as sailing-master to Captain Jonnia when he took the schooner *Exertion*. The captain and crew were eventually saved by Nickola. Years afterwards Nickola went to Boston, and lived with Captain Lincoln of the *Exertion,* and made a living by fishing for mackerel in the warm season, and during the winter by teaching navigation to young gentlemen.

JANQUAIS, Captain.
A French filibuster of San Domingo.

His ship, *La Dauphine,* carried thirty guns and a crew of 180 men.

JEFFERYS, Benjamin.
Of Bristol.

Taken by Roberts in the *Norman* galley in April, 1721. Roberts allowed those of the crew who did not wish to join the pirates to return to the *Norman,* but Jefferys had made such friends on the pirate ship that he was too drunk to go, and also was abusive in his cups, telling his hosts there was not one man amongst them. For this he received six lashes with the cat-o'-nine-tails from every member of the crew, "which disordered him for some weeks." But Jefferys eventually proved himself a brisk and willing lad, and was made bos'on's mate. He was hanged a year later at the age of 21.

JENNINGS.

A Welshman who in 1613 was settled on the Barbary coast with some thirty other British pirates.

JENNINGS, CAPTAIN.

This Welsh pirate had been a man of good position, education, and property before he took to piracy, which he did for the love of the life and not from necessity. He was held in high esteem by his fellow-pirates at their stronghold in the Bahamas. When notice was brought of King George's pardon in 1717, a meeting was held of all the pirates at which Jennings presided. After much discussion, Jennings boldly gave out that he himself meant to surrender, whereupon some hundred and fifty other pirates declared their intention of doing likewise. On the new Governor's arrival from England they received their certificates, though the greater part of them soon went back to piracy, or, to quote the expressive Captain Johnson, "returned again like the Dog to the Vomit."

JOBSON, RICHARD, or COBSON or GOPSON.

His original calling was that of a druggist's assistant in London. He combined piracy with the study of divinity. He was one of Dampier's party which crossed the Isthmus of Darien in 1681, and was left behind with Wafer, who tells us in his book that Gopson "was an ingenious man and a good scholar, and had with him a Greek testament which he frequently read and would translate extempore into English to such of the company as were disposed to hear him."

After great sufferings in the tropical jungle in the wet season, Jobson and his friends reached the "North Sea" to find an English buccaneer vessel lying at anchor off the shore. On rowing out to the ship the canoe upset, and Jobson and his gun were thrown overboard, but the former was rescued, though he died a few days later on board the vessel owing to the exposure he had been subjected to. He was buried in the sand at Le Sounds Cay with full honours—that is, a volley of guns and colours flown at half-mast.

JOCARD, Le Capitaine.
   A French filibuster who in 1684 had his headquarters in San Domingo.

He commanded the *Irondelle*, a ship armed with eighteen guns and a crew of 120 men.

JOHNSON, Captain. A successful and very bloody
        pirate.
   Of Jamaica.

Immediately after the publication of peace by Sir Thomas Lynch, Governor of Jamaica in 1670, which included a general pardon to all privateers, Johnson fled from Port Royal with some ten followers, and shortly after, meeting with a Spanish ship of eighteen guns, managed to take her and kill the captain and fourteen of the crew. Gradually collecting together a party of a hundred or more English and French desperadoes he plundered many ships round the Cuban coast. Tiring of his quarrelsome French companions he sailed to Jamaica to make terms with the Governor, and anchored in Morant Bay, but his ship was blown ashore by a hurricane. Johnson was im-

mediately arrested by Governor Lynch, who ordered
Colonel Modyford to assemble the justices and to proceed to trial and immediate execution.   Lynch had
had bitter experiences of trying pirates, and knew that
the sooner they were hanged the better.   But Modyford, like many other Jamaicans, felt a strong sympathy for the pirates, and he managed to get Johnson
acquitted in spite of the fact that Johnson "confessed
enough to hang a hundred honester persons."   It is
interesting to read that half an hour after the dis-
missal of the court Johnson "came to drink with his
judges."   Governor Lynch, now thoroughly roused,
took the matter into his own hands.   He again placed
Johnson under arrest, called a meeting of the council,
from which he dismissed Colonel Modyford, and
managed to have the former judgment reversed.   The
pirate was again tried, and in order that no mistake
might happen, Lynch himself presided over the
court.   Johnson, as before, made a full confession,
but was condemned and immediately executed, and
was, writes Lynch, "as much regretted as if he had
been as pious and as innocent as one of the primitive
martyrs."   This second trial was absolutely illegal,
and Lynch was reproved by the King for his rash
and high-handed conduct.

JOHNSON, Captain Ben.

When a lad he had served as a midshipman in an
East Indiaman, the *Asia,* but having been caught red-
handed robbing the purser of brandy and wine, he
was flogged and sent to serve as a sailor before the
mast.   In 1750, while in the Red Sea, he deserted his
ship and entered the service of the Sultan of Ormus.
Finding Johnson to be a clever sailor, the Sultan
appointed him admiral of his pirate fleet of fourteen
vessels.   The young admiral became a convert to
Brahminism, and was ceremoniously blessed by the

arch-priests of the Temple.   Amongst his crew
Johnson had some two hundred other Englishmen, who
also became followers of Brahmin, each of whom was
allowed, when in port, a dancing girl from the
Temple.

Johnson proved a most capable and bloodthirsty
pirate, playing havoc with the shipping of the Red
Sea, taking also several towns on the coast, and
putting to death his prisoners, often after cruel
tortures.   His boldest exploit was to attack the fortified town of Busrah.   This he did, putting the Sheik
and most of the inhabitants to death, and taking back
to his master, the Sultan, vast plunder of diamonds,
pearls, and gold.

On another occasion Johnson landed his crews on
the Island of Omalee, at the entrance to the Persian
Gulf, a favourite place of pilgrimage, and raided the
temples of the Indian God Buddha.   Putting to death
all the two thousand priests, he cut off the noses and
slit the upper lips of seven hundred dancing girls,
only sparing a few of the best looking ones, whom he
carried away with him along with plunder worth half
a million rupees.

On their way back to the Red Sea the pirates met
with an English East Indiaman, which they took and
plundered, and Johnson, remembering his previous
sufferings in the same service, murdered the whole
crew.

Shortly afterwards Johnson and ten of his English
officers contrived to run away from their master, the
Sultan, in his best and fastest lateen vessel, with an
enormous booty.   Sailing up to the head of the Persian
Gulf, Johnson managed to reach Constantinople with
his share of the plunder, worth £800,000.   With this
as an introduction, he was hospitably received, and
was made a bashaw, and at the end of a long life of
splendour died a natural death.

JOHNSON, Captain Henry, *alias* "Henriques the Englishman."

A West Indian pirate, born in the North of Ireland.

Commanded the *Two Brothers,* a Rhode Island-built sloop, eighteen guns, crew of ninety, mostly Spaniards. On March 20th, 1730, he took the *John and Jane* (Edward Burt, master), from Jamaica, off Swan Island. The *John and Jane* was armed with eight carriage and ten swivel guns, and a crew of only twenty-five men. After a gallant resistance for five hours the pirates boarded and took the English ship. The few survivors were stripped naked, and preparations made to hang them in pairs. This was prevented by Captain Johnson and an English pirate called Echlin. There was a Mrs. Groves, a passenger, in the *John and Jane,* whose husband and the English surgeon had both been killed at the first onslaught of the pirates. This poor lady was hidden in the hold of the ship during the action, and was only informed afterwards of the death of her husband. The pirates now dragged her on deck, "stript her in a manner naked," and carried her as a prize to the Spanish captain, Pedro Poleas, who immediately took her to the "great cabin and there with horrible oaths and curses insolently assaulted her Chastity." Her loud cries of distress brought Captain Johnson into the cabin, who, seeing what was on hand, drew his pistol and threatened to blow out the brains of any man who attempted the least violence upon her. He next commanded everything belonging to Mrs. Groves to be returned to her, which was done—including her clothing. The gallant conduct of Johnson is the more surprising and pleasing since he had the reputation of being as bloody and ruthless a pirate as ever took a ship or cut an innocent throat. He only had one hand, and used to fire his piece with great skill, laying the barrel on his stump, and drawing the trigger with his right hand.

In all the American "plantations" there were rewards offered for him alive or dead.

The end of this "penny-dreadful" pirate is unrecorded, but was probably a violent one, as this type of pirate seldom, if ever, died in his bed.

JOHNSON, Isaac.

One of Captain Quelch's crew. Tried for piracy at the Star Tavern at Boston in 1704.

JOHNSON, Jacob.

Taken prisoner by Captain Roberts out of the *King Solomon*, he joined the pirates.

JOHNSON, John, or Jaynson.
Born " nigh Lancaster."

Taken out of the *King Solomon*. One of Roberts's crew. Hanged in 1722 at the age of 22.

JOHNSON, Marcus.

One of Captain Roberts's crew. Hanged in 1722. Stated in his death warrant to be a native of Smyrna. Died at the age of 21.

JOHNSON, Robert.
From Whydah in West Africa.

Tried for piracy with the rest of Captain Roberts's crew, and hanged in 1722 at the age of 32. At his trial he pleaded that he did not enter with the pirates of his own free will, and called witnesses to prove that at the time he was captured he was so very drunk that he had to be hoisted out of his own ship, the *Jeremiah and Ann,* into the pirate ship in tackles.

JOHNSTON, THOMAS.
Of Boston.

Known as "the limping privateer." Sailed with Captain Pound. Wounded in the jaw in the fight at Tarpaulin Cove. Tried for piracy at Boston, and hanged on January 27th, 1690.

JONES, CAPTAIN PAUL.

Probably few persons, even in Great Britain, would to-day call Paul Jones a pirate, but this was not always the case. In all books on pirates written shortly after the American war, Paul Jones figured as a notorious character.

This famous privateer, let us call him, was born at Kirkcudbright in Scotland in 1728, the son of Mr. Paul, head gardener to Lord Selkirk, and was christened John Paul. So much has been written about this man in books, easily procurable for reference, that little need be said about him here.

Starting life as a sailor before the mast, he quickly showed abilities which led to his promotion to the rank of mate in an English ship trading in the West India Islands, and later he was made master. On the declaration of war with America, Jones joined the rebels, and was given command of a privateer, and from 1777 he became a terror to English shipping around the British Isles.

One of his most startling exploits was his surprise visit in his ship, the *Ranger,* to his old home with the object of kidnapping his former employer, Lord Selkirk.

On September 23rd, 1779, he fought his famous

action off Scarborough against a British convoy from
the Baltic under the command of Captain Pearson, in
the *Serapis,* and Captain Piercy in the *Countess of
Scarborough.* Jones had left the *Ranger* for a frigate
called the *Bonne Homme Richard* of forty guns and a
crew of three hundred and seventy men, and had also
under his command four other ships of war.   A
furious engagement took place, the utmost bravery
being shown on either side; the English ships at last
being compelled to surrender, but not until the
enemy had themselves suffered fearful damage to both
their crews and ships.   After the conclusion of peace,
Paul Jones, once the darling of two continents, faded
into obscurity and even poverty, and died in Paris in
the year 1792 at the age of 64.

JONES. Seaman.

A mariner. " A brisk young fellow " who served
with Captain Bartholomew Roberts's crew. On one
occasion Captain Roberts had reason to think that one
of his men had spoken disrespectfully to him, so, as a
warning to the rest, he killed him. The dead man's
greatest friend was Jones, who, hearing what had
happened, had a fierce fight with Roberts. This
severe breach of discipline was punished by Jones
receiving two lashes on the back from every man on
board. Jones after this sailed with Captain Anstis in
the *Good Fortune.*

JONES, Thomas.

Found to be "not guilty" at a trial for piracy at
Newport, Rhode Island, in 1723. One of Captain
Charles Harris's crew. Age 17.

JONES, William.

Tried for piracy at Boston, 1704.

JONES, William.
Of London.
Age 28. Hanged at Rhode Island, 1723.

JONNIA, Captain.
A Spaniard.
Commanded in 1821 a fast schooner, carrying a crew of forty men, armed with muskets, cutlasses, blunderbusses, long knives, dirks, two carronades—one a twelve, the other a six-pounder. They had aboard with them three Mexican negresses. The pirates took and plundered the Boston schooner *Exertion*, on December 17th, 1821, the crew being considerably drunk at the time. The plunder they took to Principe in the Island of Cuba. The pirates took everything from their prisoners, even their clothes, but as a parting gift sent the captain a copy of the "Family Prayer Book" by the Rev. Mr. Brooks. The prisoners were marooned on a small mangrove quay, but they eventually escaped. Jonnia and some of his crew were afterwards captured by an English ship and taken to Kingston, Jamaica, and there hanged.

JOSE, Miguel.
Hanged at Kingston, Jamaica, in February, 1823. This old man's last words on the scaffold were: "No he robado, no he matado ningune, muero innocente."

JUDSON, Randall.
One of Captain Roderigo's crew. Tried for piracy at Cambridge, Massachusetts, in June, 1675, and sentenced to be hanged; "presently after the lecture," which was delivered by the Rev. Increase Mather. Afterwards pardoned, but fined and banished from the colony.

KELLWANTON.

A notorious pirate in the sixteenth century. Was captured in the Isle of Man in 1531.

KENNEDY, CAPTAIN.

Began life as a pickpocket and housebreaker in London. He was Captain Roberts's lieutenant, and was afterwards given command of a prize, the *Rover*.

Kennedy could never, even when a captain, forget his old trade. It is recorded that he stole a black suit of clothes from the captain of the *Bird* at Sierra Leone in 1718. These he put on with the captain's best wig and sword. He then swaggered about on board in these till his fellow-pirates drenched him with buckets of claret, so that he had to disrobe and throw the garments overboard.

Owing to a quarrel with Captain Roberts, Kennedy went off in his ship, the *Rover*, and sailed to Barbadoes. His first prize, a Boston ship, was a distinct novelty, being commanded by one Captain Knot, a Quaker, who lived up to the principles of his sect by allowing no pistol, sword, or cutlass, or other weapon aboard his vessel. The crew, finding Kennedy had no knowledge whatever of navigation, threatened to throw him overboard, but because he was a man of great personal courage they did not in the end carry out their threat. The crew next decided to give over piracy and to set sail for Ireland. This island they altogether missed through bad navigation, and they ran the ship ashore on the north of Scotland. The crew landed and passed themselves off as shipwrecked mariners, but owing to their drinking and rioting in each village they came to, the whole countryside was soon roused. Kennedy slipped away and reached Ireland. Having soon spent all his ill-gotten gains in Dublin, he came to

Deptford and set up a house of ill-fame, adding occasionally to his income from this source by a little highwaymanry. One of the ladies of his house at Deptford, to be revenged for some slight or other, gave information to the watch, and Kennedy was imprisoned at Marshalsea and afterwards tried for robbery and piracy. Kennedy turned King's evidence against some of his old associates, but this did not save his neck, for he was condemned and hanged at Execution Dock.

KHEYR-ED-DIN. Corsair.

Brother of the famous Barbarossa. When the latter was defeated and killed by the Spaniards, Kheyr-ed-din sent an ambassador to Constantinople, begging for help to protect Algiers. He was appointed Governor of Algiers by the Sultan of Turkey in 1519. Now greatly increased both in ships and power, he scoured the whole Mediterranean for Italian and Spanish prizes. He raided the Spanish coast and carried off slaves from the Balearic Islands. He next took and destroyed the fortress of Algiers, and employed 7,000 Christian slaves to build a new one and also a great mole to protect the harbour. Invited by Solyman the Magnificent to help him against the Christian Admiral Andria Doria, in August, 1533, he sailed from Algiers with his fleet, being joined on the way by another noted corsair, Delizuff.

A year afterwards, at the age of 73, Kheyr-ed-din set out from Constantinople with a vast fleet, sacking towns and burning all Christian ships that were so unfortunate as to fall in his way. He returned to the Bosphorus with huge spoil and 11,000 prisoners. He sacked Sardinia, then sailed to Tunis, which he vanquished.

Charles V. of Spain now began to collect a large fleet and an army of 25,000 men and sailed to Tunis.

A fierce fight followed; the Christians broke into the town, massacred the inhabitants and rescued some 20,000 Christian slaves. Kheyr-ed-din escaped with a few followers, but soon was in command of a fleet of pirate galleys once more. A terrific but undecisive naval battle took place off Prevesa between the Mohammedans and the Christians, the fleet of the latter being under the command of Andrea Doria; and Kheyr-ed-din died shortly afterwards at Constantinople at a great age.

KIDD, Captain William, sometimes Robert Kidd or Kid.

In the whole history of piracy there is no name that has so taken the world's fancy than has that of William Kidd. And yet, if he be judged by his actions as a pirate, he must be placed amongst the second- or even third-rate masters of that craft. He took but two or three ships, and these have been, after two hundred years, proved to be lawful prizes taken in his legal capacity as a privateer.

Kidd was born at Greenock in Scotland about the year 1655, and was the son of the Rev. John Kidd. Of his early life little record is left, but we know that in August, 1689, he arrived at St. Nevis in the West Indies, in command of a privateer of sixteen guns. In 1691, while Kidd was on shore, his crew ran away with his ship, which was not surprising, as most of his crew were old pirates. But that Kidd was an efficient seaman and a capable captain is shown by the number of times he was given the command of different privateer vessels, both by the Government of New York and by privateer owners.

In 1695 Kidd was in London, and on October 10th signed the articles which were to prove so fatal for him. In January, 1696, King William III. issued to his "beloved friend William Kidd" a commission to apprehend certain pirates, particularly Thomas Tew, of Rhode Island, Thomas Wake, and William Maze, of New York, John Ireland, and "all other Pirates, Free-booters, and Sea Rovers of what Nature soever."

This privateer enterprise was financed chiefly by Lord Bellomont, but the other adventurers (on shore and in safety) were the Lord Chancellor; the Earl of Orford, the First Lord of the Admiralty; the Earl of Romney and the Duke of Shrewsbury, Secretaries of State; Robert Livingston, Esq., of New York; and lastly, Captain Kidd himself.

The ship the *Adventure* galley was bought and fitted up, and Kidd sailed away in her to suppress piracy, particularly on the coast of America. Nothing was heard of him till August, 1698, when ugly rumours began to get about of piracies committed by Kidd in the Indian Ocean. In December of the same year a general pardon was offered to all pirates who should surrender themselves, with two exceptions— namely, Captain Avery and Captain Kidd. In May, 1699, Kidd suddenly appeared in a small vessel at New York, with rich booty. His chief patron, Lord Bellomont, was now Governor, and was placed in the most awkward position of having to carry out his orders and arrest Kidd for piracy and send him in chains to England in H.M.S. *Advice*, which ship had been sent specially to New York to carry back Kidd, Bradish, and other pirates to England.

The trial of Kidd proved a scandal, for someone had to suffer as scapegoat for the aristocratic company privateers, and the lot fell to the luckless Kidd. Kidd was charged with piracy and with murder. The first charge of seizing two ships of the Great Mogul could have been met by the production of two documents which Kidd had taken out of these ships, and which, he claimed, proved that the ships were sailing under commissions issued by the French East India Company, and made them perfectly lawful prizes. These commissions Kidd had most foolishly handed over to Lord Bellomont, and they could not be produced at the trial, although they had been exhibited before the House of Commons a little while previously.

It is an extraordinary and tragic fact that these two documents, so vital to Kidd, were discovered only lately in the Public Records Office—too late, by some 200 years, to save an innocent man's life.

As it happened, the charge of which Kidd was hanged for was murder, and ran thus : " Being moved and seduced by the instigations of the Devil he did make an assault in and upon William Moore upon the high seas with a certain wooden bucket, bound with iron hoops, of the value of eight pence, giving the said William Moore one mortal bruise of which the aforesaid William Moore did languish and die." This aforesaid William Moore was gunner in the *Adventure* galley, and was mutinous, and Kidd, as captain, was perfectly justified in knocking him down and even of killing him ; but as the court meant Kidd to " swing," this was quite good enough for finding him guilty. The unfortunate prisoner was executed at Wapping on May 23rd, 1701, and his body afterwards hanged in chains at Tilbury.

A popular ballad was sung to commemorate the life and death of Kidd, who, for some reason, was always called Robert Kidd by the populace. It consists of no less than twenty-four verses, and we here give fifteen of them :

THE BALLAD OF CAPTAIN KIDD

My name was Robert Kidd, when I sailed, when I sailed,
My name was Robert Kidd, when I sailed,
My name was Robert Kidd,
God's laws I did forbid,
And so wickedly I did, when I sailed.

A PIRATE BEING HANGED AT EXECUTION DOCK, WAPPING.

To face p. 182.

My parents taught me well, when I sailed, when I sailed,
   My parents taught me well, when I sailed,
      My parents taught me well,
      To shun the gates of hell,
But 'gainst them I rebelled, when I sailed.

I'd a Bible in my hand, when I sailed, when I sailed,
   I'd a Bible in my hand, when I sailed,
      I'd a Bible in my hand,
      By my father's great command,
And sunk it in the sand, when I sailed.

I murdered William Moore, as I sailed, as I sailed,
   I murdered William Moore, as I sailed,
      I murdered William Moore,
      And laid him in his gore,
Not many leagues from shore, as I sailed.

I was sick and nigh to death, when I sailed, when I sailed,
   I was sick and nigh to death, when I sailed,
      I was sick and nigh to death,
      And I vowed at every breath,
To walk in wisdom's ways, as I sailed.

I thought I was undone, as I sailed, as I sailed,
   I thought I was undone, as I sailed,
      I thought I was undone,
      And my wicked glass had run,
But health did soon return, as I sailed.

My repentance lasted not, as I sailed, as I sailed,
   My repentance lasted not, as I sailed,
      My repentance lasted not,
      My vows I soon forgot,
Damnation was my lot, as I sailed.

I spyed the ships from France, as I sailed, as I sailed,
   I spyed the ships of France, as I sailed,
      I spyed the ships from France,
      To them I did advance,
And took them all by chance, as I sailed.

I spyed the ships of Spain, as I sailed, as I sailed,
   I spyed the ships of Spain, as I sailed,
      I spyed the ships of Spain,
      I fired on them amain,
'Till most of them was slain, as I sailed.

I'd ninety bars of gold, as I sailed, as I sailed,
  I'd ninety bars of gold, as I sailed,
    I'd ninety bars of gold,
    And dollars manifold,
With riches uncontrolled, as I sailed.

Thus being o'er-taken at last, I must die, I must die,
  Thus being o'er-taken at last, I must die,
    Thus being o'er-taken at last,
    And into prison cast,
And sentence being passed, I must die.

Farewell, the raging main, I must die, I must die,
  Farewell, the raging main, I must die,
    Farewell, the raging main,
    To Turkey, France and Spain,
I shall n'er see you again, I must die.

To Execution Dock I must go, I must go,
  To Execution Dock I must go,
    To Execution Dock,
    Will many thousands flock,
But I must bear the shock, and must die.

Come all ye young and old, see me die, see me die,
  Come all ye young and old, see me die,
    Come all ye young and old,
    You're welcome to my gold,
For by it I've lost my soul, and must die.

Take warning now by me, for I must die, for I must die,
  Take warning now by me, for I must die,
    Take warning now by me,
    And shun bad company,
Lest you come to hell with me, for I die.

KILLING, James.

One of Major Stede Bonnet's crew, who gave evidence against him at his trial at Charleston in 1718.

KING, Charles.

Attempted to escape in the *Larimore* galley, but was captured and brought into Salem. Tried at Boston with the rest of Quelch's crew in June, 1704.

KING, Francis.

One of Captain Quelch's crew captured in the *Larimore* galley by Major Sewall, and brought into Salem Harbour on June 11th, 1704. Tried at Boston and condemned to be hanged. Was reprieved while standing on the gallows.

KING, John.

One of Captain Quelch's crew taken out of the *Larimore* galley. Tried at Boston in June, 1704.

KING, Matthew.
Of Jamaica.

One of Major Stede Bonnet's crew. Was hanged at Charleston, South Carolina, on November 8th, 1718, and buried in the marsh below low-water mark.

KNEEVES, Peter.
Of Exeter in Devon.

Sailed with Captain Charles Harris, and was tried for piracy with the rest of his crew at Rhode Island in 1723. Hanged at Newport at the age of 32.

KNIGHT, Captain W. Buccaneer.

In 1686 Knight was cruising off the coast of Peru and Chile with Swan, Townley, and Davis. At the end of that year, having got a fair quantity of plunder, he sailed round the Horn to the West Indies.

KNIGHT, Christopher.

One of Captain Coward's crew. Tried for piracy at Boston in January, 1690, and found guilty, but afterwards reprieved.

KNOT, Captain.

An old Massachusetts pirate who retired from the sea and was settled in Boston in 1699. His wife gave information to the Governor, the Earl of Bellomont, of the whereabouts of a pirate called Gillam, who was " wanted."

KOXINGA.   His real name was Kuo-hsing Yeh,
    Koxinga being the Portuguese version.

The son of a Chinese pirate, Cheng Chih-lung, by a Japanese mother, he was born in 1623.

From early youth Koxinga was inspired with a hatred of the Manchus, who had imprisoned his father.

The young pirate soon became so successful in his raids along the coast of China that the Emperor resorted to the extraordinary expedient of ordering the inhabitants of more than eighty seaboard towns to migrate ten miles inland, after destroying their homes.

There can be no doubt that Koxinga was a thorough-going cut-throat pirate, worked solely for his own ambitious ends and to satisfy his revengeful feelings, but the fact that he fought against the alien conquerors, the Dutch in Formosa, and defeated them, caused him to be regarded as a hero pirate.

His father was executed at Peking, which only increased his bitterness against the reigning house. Koxinga made himself what was, to all intents and purposes, the ruler of Formosa, and the island became, through him, part of the Chinese Empire.

After his death, which took place in 1662, he received official canonization.

The direct descendant of Koxinga, the pirate, is one of the very few hereditary nobles in China.

LACY, ABRAHAM.
  Of Devonshire.
  Hanged at the age of 21 at Rhode Island in 1723.

DU LAERQUERAC, CAPTAIN JOHN.

This Breton pirate was captured in 1537 by a Bristol seaman called John Wynter. Du Laerquerac, with other pirates from Brittany, had been holding up ships on their way to the great fair of St. James at Bristol. On being arrested, he denied that he had "spoiled" any English ships, but on being further pressed to confess, admitted that he had taken a few odds and ends, such as ropes, sailors' clothes, some wine, fish, a gold crown in money and eleven silver halfpence, as well as four daggers and a "couverture."

LAFITTE, CAPTAIN JEAN.

Jean and his brother first appeared in New Orleans in the year 1809. Though blacksmiths by profession, they soon took to smuggling goods brought by privateersmen and pirates. The headquarters of this trade was on the Island of Grande Terre in Barataria Bay. This island was inhabited and governed by ex-pirates; one Grambo being the acknowledged chief, until he was shot by Jean Lafitte.

In 1813, the Baratarians were denounced by the Governor of Louisiana as pirates. This made no difference to the pirate smugglers, who grew more and more rich and insolent. The Governor then secured an indictment against Jean and his brother, Pierre, who retained the very best and most expensive lawyers in the State to defend them, and they were acquitted. In 1814, war was declared with England, and Jean was invited by the English to fight on their side, with the offer of a commission in the navy and a large sum of money. He refused this, and eventually General Jackson accepted his offer of the services of himself and his Baratarians, who proved invaluable in the Battle of Orleans, serving the guns. He disappeared completely after the war until 1823, when a British sloop of war captured a pirate ship with a crew

of sixty men under the command of the famous
Lafitte, who was amongst those who fell fighting.

LAGARDE, LE CAPITAINE.

A French filibuster of San Domingo, who in 1684
commanded a small ship, *La Subtille* (crew of thirty
men and two guns).

LAMBERT, JOHN.

One of Captain John Quelch's crew. Hanged on
Charles River, Boston Side, on Friday, June 30th,
1704. In a broadside published at Boston in July of
the same year, Lambert's conduct on the gallows is
described thus : "He appeared much hardened and
pleaded much on his Innocency. He desired all men
to beware of Bad Company and seemed to be in great
Agony near his Execution."

LANDER, DANIEL.

One of Captain Pound's crew.

LANDRESSON, CAPTAIN MICHEL, *alias* BREHA.
Filibuster.

Accompanied Pain in his expedition against St.
Augustine in 1683. He was a constant source of
annoyance to the Jamaicans. His ship was called
La Trompeuse, but must not be confused with the
famous ship of that name belonging to Hamlin.
Landresson, when he had got a good booty of gold,
jewels, cocoa, etc., would go to Boston to dispose of
it to the godly merchants of New England. In 1684
a Royal proclamation was published in Massachusetts,
warning all Governors that no succour or aid was to
be given to any of the outlaws, but, in spite of this,
Landresson was received with open arms and the
proclamations in the streets torn down.

In 1684 he was at San Domingo, in command of

La Fortune (crew of 100 men and fourteen guns). At this time the filibuster was disguised under the *alias* of Le Capitaine Breha.

Captured in 1686 by the Armada de Barlorento, and hanged with several of his companions.

LANE, CAPTAIN.

In 1720 Lane was one of Captain England's crew when he took the *Mercury* off the coast of West Africa. The *Mercury* was fitted up as a pirate ship, named the *Queen Ann's Revenge,* and Lane was voted captain of her. Lane left Captain England and sailed to Brazil, where he took several Portuguese ships and did a great deal of mischief.

LARIMORE, CAPTAIN THOMAS, or LARRAMORE.

Commanded the *Larimore* galley. In 1704 was with the pirate Quelch and several other pirates, and, among other prizes, seized a Portuguese ship, the *Portugal,* from which they took gold dust, bar and coined gold, and other treasure, and at the same time "acted divers villainous Murders." For these Larimore was tried, condemned and hanged at Boston, June 11th, 1704.

LAWRENCE, NICHOLAS.

Tried for piracy with the rest of Quelch's crew at Boston in 1704.

LAWRENCE, RICHARD.

One of Captain John Quelch's crew. Tried for piracy at Boston in 1704.

LAWSON, EDWARD.
Born in the Isle of Man.

One of Captain Harris's crew. Hanged at Newport, Rhode Island, in July, 1723, at the age of 20.

L'ESCAYER. A French filibuster.

In 1685, in company with Grogniet, Davis, and Swan, sacked Paita and Guayaquil and blockaded Panama. Afterwards sailed with Townley and his English pirates and again plundered Guayaquil. Suffered a severe defeat at the hands of the Spaniards at Quibo, afterwards being rescued by Townley, with whom he and his crew of buccaneers sacked Granada in Nicaragua.

LESSONE, Captain. French filibuster.

In 1680 he joined Sharp, Coxon, and other English buccaneers in an attack on Porto Bello. Putting 300 men into canoes, they landed some sixty miles from the city and marched for four days, arriving in a weak state through hardship and lack of food, but in spite of this they took the city on February 17th, 1680.

LEVERCOTT, Sam.

Hanged in 1722 at the Island of St. Kitts, with the rest of Captain Lowther's crew.

LEVIT, John.
Of North Carolina.

One of Major Stede Bonnet's crew. Hanged at White Point, Charleston, South Carolina, on November 8th, 1723.

LEWIS, James.

After being a prisoner in France, he managed to reach Spain, and was with Avery when he seized the ship *Charles the Second*. Tried for piracy at the Old Bailey in 1696 and hanged.

LEWIS, Nicholas.

One of Captain George Lowther's crew. Hanged at St. Kitts on March 11th, 1722.

LEWIS, William.

The greatest triumph and most important exploit of this pirate was the attacking, and eventually taking, of a powerful French ship of twenty-four guns.

Lewis enjoyed a longer career than most of the brethren, and by 1717 he was already one of the leading piratical lights of Nassau, and his end did not come till ten years later. In 1726, he spent several months on the coast of South Carolina and Virginia, trading with the inhabitants the spoils he had taken from vessels in the Atlantic. He learnt his trade under the daring pirate Bannister, who was brought into Port Royal, hanging dead from his own yardarm. On this occasion, Lewis and another boy were triced up to the corvette's mizzen-peak like "two living flags."

Lewis, amongst other accomplishments, was a born linguist, and could speak with fluency in several languages, even the dialect of the Mosquito Indians. He was once captured by the Spaniards, and taken to Havana, but escaped with a few other prisoners in a canoe, seized a piragua, and with this captured a sloop employed in the turtle trade, and by gradually taking larger and larger prizes, Lewis soon found himself master of a fine ship and a crew of more than fifty men. He renamed her the *Morning Star*, and made her his flagship.

On one occasion when chasing a vessel off the Carolina coast, his fore and main topmasts were carried away. Lewis, in a frenzy of excitement, clambered up the main top, tore out a handful of his hair, which he tossed into the wind, crying: "Good devil, take this till I come." The ship, in spite of her damaged rigging, gained on the other ship, which they took. Lewis's sailors, superstitious at the best of times, considered this intimacy of their captain with Satan a little too much, and soon afterwards one of the Frenchmen aboard murdered Lewis in his sleep.

LEYTON, FRANCIS.

One of Captain Charles Harris's crew. Hanged for piracy at Newport, Rhode Island, on July 19th, 1723. Age 39.

LIMA, MANUEL.

Taken by H.M. sloop *Tyne,* and hanged at Kingston, Jamaica, in February, 1823.

LINCH, CAPTAIN. Buccaneer.

Of Port Royal, Jamaica.

In 1680 Lionel Wafer, tiring of the life of a civil surgeon at Port Royal, left Jamaica to go on a voyage with Captains Linch and Cook to the Spanish Main.

LING, CAPTAIN WILLIAM.

A notorious pirate of New Providence. Captured and hanged shortly after accepting King George's pardon of 1718.

LINISLER, THOMAS.

Of Lancashire.

One of Captain Charles Harris's crew. Hanged at Rhode Island in 1723 at the age of 21.

LITHGOW, CAPTAIN.

Famous in his day for his activities in the West Indies, this pirate had his headquarters at New Providence in the Bahamas.

LIVER, WILLIAM, *alias* EVIS.

One of Major Stede Bonnet's crew. Hanged for piracy at Charleston, South Carolina, in 1718.

LO, MRS. HON-CHO.

This Chinese woman pirate was the widow of another noted pirate who was killed in 1921. She took command after the death of her husband, and soon became a terror to the countryside about Pakhoi, carrying on the work in the best traditions of the craft, being the Admiral of some sixty ocean-going junks. Although both young and pretty, she won a reputation for being a thorough-going murderess and pirate.

During the late revolution, Mrs. Lo joined General Wong Min-Tong's forces, and received the rank of full Colonel. After the war, she resumed her piracies, occasionally for the sake of variety, surprising and sacking a village or two, and from these she usually carried away some fifty or sixty girls to sell as slaves.

Her career ended quite suddenly in October, 1922.

LODGE, THOMAS.   Poet, buccaneer, and physician.

Born about 1557, he was the son of Sir Thomas Lodge, grocer, and Lord Mayor of London in 1563. He was educated at Merchant Taylors' School and Trinity College, Oxford. The poet engaged in more than one freebooting expedition to Spanish waters between 1584 and 1590, and he tells us that he accompanied Captain Clarke in an attack on the Azores and the Canaries. "Having," he tells his friend Lord Hunsdon, "with Captain Clarke made a voyage to the Islands of Terceras and the Canaries, to beguile the time with labour, I writ this book, rough, as hatched in the storms of the ocean, and feathered in the surges of many perilous seas." On August 26th, 1591, Lodge sailed from Plymouth with Sir Thomas Cavendish in the *Desire*, a galleon of 140 tons. The freebooters sailed to Brazil and attacked the town of

Santa, while the people were at Mass. They remained there from December 15th until January 22nd, 1592. Some of the Englishmen, of whom Lodge was one, took up their quarters in the College of the Jesuits, and this literary buccaneer spent his time amongst the books in the library of the Fathers.

Leaving Brazil, the small fleet sailed south to the Straits of Magellan. While storm-bound amongst the icy cliffs of Patagonia, Lodge wrote his Arcadian romance " Margarite of America."

From the point of view of plunder, this expedition was a dismal failure, and the *Desire* returned and reached the coast of Ireland on June 11th, 1593. The crew had been reduced to sixteen, and of these only five were even in tolerable health.

At the age of 40, Lodge deserted literature and studied medicine, taking his degree of Doctor of Physics at Avignon in 1600. His last original work was a " Treatise on the Plague," published in 1603. After practising medicine with great success for many years, Thomas Lodge died, it is said, of the plague, in the year 1625, at the age of 68.

LONG, ZACHARIAH.
  Of the Province of Holland.

  One of Major Stede Bonnet's crew. Hanged at White Point, Charleston, in 1718, and buried in the marsh below low-water mark.

LOPEZ, JOHN.
  Of Oporto.

  This Portuguese pirate sailed in the *Royal James*, and was hanged with the rest of the crew at Charleston, South Carolina, on November 8th, 1718.

LORD, JOHN.

A soldier. Deserted from Fort Loyal, Falmouth, Maine. Killed at Tarpaulin Cove in 1689.

LOW, CAPTAIN EDWARD, or LOE.

Born in Westminster, he began in very early life to plunder the boys of their farthings, and as he grew bigger used to gamble with the footmen who waited in the lobby of the House of Commons. While still quite small one of his elder brothers used to carry little Edward hidden in a basket on his back, and when in a crowd the future pirate would, from above, snatch the hats and even the wigs off the heads of passing citizens and secret them in the basket and so get away with them. The Low family were the originators of this ingenious and fascinating trick, and for a time it was most successful, until the people of the city took to tying on their hats and wigs with bands to prevent their sudden removal. When he grew up, Ned went to Boston and earned an honest living as a rigger, but after a while he tired of this and sailed in a sloop to Honduras to steal log-wood. Here Low quarrelled with his captain, tried to shoot him, and then went off in an open boat with twelve other men, and the very next day they took a small vessel, in which they began their "war against all the world." Low soon happened to meet with Captain Lowther, the pirate, and the two agreed to sail in company. This partnership lasted until May 28th, 1722, when they took a prize, a brigantine from Boston, which Low went into with a crew of forty-four men. This vessel they armed with two guns, four swivels, and six quarter-casks of powder, and saying good-bye to Lowther, sailed off on their own account. A week later a prize fell into their hands, which was the first of several. Things soon became too hot for Low along the American coast and the West Indies, as several men-of-war were

searching for him; so he sailed to the Azores, taking
on his way a big French ship of thirty-four guns,
and later, in the harbour of St. Michael, he seized
several vessels which he found at anchor there. Here
they burnt the French ship, but let the crew all go,
except the cook, who, they said, "being a greasy
fellow would fry well in the fire, so the poor man was
bound to the main mast and burnt in the ship to the
no small derision of Low and his Mirmidons."

Low and his crew now began to treat their prisoners
with great brutality. However, on one occasion the
biter was bitten. It happened that one of the drunken
crew, playfully cutting at a prisoner, missed his mark
and accidentally slashed Captain Low across his lower
jaw, the sword opening his cheek and laying bare his
teeth. The surgeon was called, who at once stitched
up the wound, but Low found some fault with the
operation, as well he might, seeing that "the surgeon
was tollerably drunk" at the time. The surgeon's
professional pride was outraged by this criticism of his
skill by a layman, and he showed his annoyance in
a ready, if unprofessional, manner, by striking "Low
such a blow with his Fists, that broke out all the
Stitches, and then bid him sew up his Chops himself
and be damned, so that the captain made a very pitiful
Figure for some time after." Low took a large
number of prizes, but he was not a sympathetic figure,
and the list of his prizes and brutalities soon becomes
irksome reading. Low, still in the *Fancy*, and accompanied by Captain Harris in the *Ranger*, then
sailed back to the West Indies, and later to South
Carolina, where he took several prizes, one the
Amsterdam Merchant (Captain Willard), belonging to
New England, and as Low never missed an opportunity of showing his dislike of all New Englanders,
he sent the captain away with both his ears cut off
and with various other wounds about his body.

Low and Harris now made a most unfortunate mistake in giving chase to a ship which on close quarters proved to be not a merchant vessel, but H.M.S. *Greyhound*. After a short fight, the coward Low slipped away, and left his consort, Harris, to carry on an unequal contest until he was compelled to surrender his ship.

Low's cruelties became more and more disgusting, and there can be little doubt that he was really by this time a lunatic.

In July, 1723, Low took a new ship for himself, naming himself Admiral, and sporting a new black flag with a red skeleton upon it. He again cruised off the Azores, the Canaries, and the Guinea coast, but what the end was of this repulsive, uninteresting, and bloody pirate has never been known.

LOWTHER, Captain George.

Sailed as second mate from the Thames in the *Gambia Castle*, a ship belonging to the African Company, sixteen guns and a crew of thirty men. On board as passengers were Captain Massey and a number of soldiers. Arriving at their destination, Massey quarrelled with the merchants on shore, and, a few days later, with Lowther, seized the ship, which he renamed the *Delivery*. They now went a-pirating, their first prize being a Boston ship, and cruising about off the Island of Hispaniola, several more were taken, but nothing very rich. Lowther quarrelled with Captain Massey, who, being a soldier, wished to land on some island to plunder the French settlements, but this was not agreed to, and Massey and his followers were sent away in a sloop. Life for Lowther now became a series of successes, prizes being taken, and visits to land being occasionally made for the crew to enjoy a drunken revel.

Having met with Captain Low, for a while the two

sailed together, and took the *Greyhound,* a merchant-man, and several more rich prizes. Lowther now commanded a small pirate fleet, and styled himself Admiral, his flagship being the *Happy Delivery.* While careening their ships in the Gulf of Matigue, they were suddenly attacked by the natives, and the pirates barely escaped in a sloop with their lives. Lowther soon improved himself by seizing a brigan-tine, and in her shaped his course to the coast of South Carolina, a favourite resort for the pirates. Here he attacked an English ship, but was so roughly handled that he was glad to run his ship ashore and escape.

In 1723 he steered for Newfoundland, taking many small vessels there, and returning to the West Indies. While cleaning his ship at the Isle of Blanco, he was suddenly attacked by a South Sea Company's ship, the *Eagle,* and the pirates were compelled to sur-render. Lowther and a dozen of his crew escaped by climbing out of the cabin window, and, reaching the island, hid themselves in the woods. All were caught except Lowther and three men and a boy. He was shortly afterwards found lying dead with a pistol by his side, and was supposed to have shot himself. Three of his crew who were caught were carried to St. Christopher's, and there tried for piracy and hanged.

LUDBURY, Captain. Buccaneer.

Sailed in company with Captains Prince and Harri-son in October, 1670, ascended the San Juan River in Nicaragua with a party of 170 men, and surprised and plundered the city of Granada.

LUKE, Captain Matthew.

This Italian pirate had his headquarters at Porto Rico, and specialized in attacking English ships. In

1718 he took four of these and murdered all the crews. In May, 1722, Luke made a terrible mistake. Perceiving what he thought to be a merchant ship, he attacked her, to find out all too late that she was an English man-of-war, the *Lauceston*. Luke and his crew were taken to Jamaica and hanged. One of his crew confessed to having killed twenty English sailors with his own hands.

LUSHINGHAM, Captain.

In 1564 this pirate was at Berehaven in the South of Ireland, having just sold a cargo of wine out of a Spanish prize to the Lord O'Sullivan, when some of Queen Elizabeth's ships arrived in the bay in search of pirates. By Lord O'Sullivan's help the pirates escaped, but Lushingham was killed " by a piece of ordnance " as he was in the act of waving his cap towards the Queen's ships.

LUSSAN, Le Sieur Raveneau de.

This French filibuster was a man of much better birth and education than the usual buccaneer. Also, he was the author of a most entertaining book recording his adventures and exploits as a buccaneer, called "Journal du Voyage fait a la Mer de sud avec les Flibustiers de l'Amerique en 1684."

Pressure from his creditors drove de Lussan into buccaneering, as being a rapid method of gaining enough money to satisfy them and to enable him to return to the fashionable life he loved so well in Paris. De Lussan was, according to his own account, a man of the highest principles, and very religious. He never allowed his crew to molest priests, nuns, or churches. After taking a Spanish town, the fighting being over, he would lead his crew of pirates to attend Mass in the church, and when this was done—

and not until then—would he allow the plundering and looting to begin.

De Lussan was surprised and grieved to find that his Spanish prisoners had a most exaggerated idea of the brutality of the buccaneers, and on one occasion when he was conducting a fair young Spanish lady, a prisoner, to a place of safety, he was overwhelmed when he discovered that the reason of her terror was that she believed she was shortly to be eaten by him and his crew. To remedy this erroneous impression, it was the custom of the French commander to gather together all his prisoners into the church or the plaza, and there to give them a lecture on the true life and character of the buccaneers.

The student who wishes to learn more about the adventures of de Lussan can do so in his book. There he will read, amongst other interesting events, particulars about the filibuster's surprising and romantic affair with the beautiful and wealthy Spanish widow who fell so violently in love with him.

It happened on one occasion that Raveneau and his crew, having taken a town on the West Coast of South America after a somewhat bloody battle, had, as usual, attended Mass in the Cathedral, before setting out to plunder the place.

Entering one of the chief houses in the town, de Lussan discovered the widow of the late town treasurer dissolved in tears, upon which the tender buccaneer hastened, with profound apologies, discreetly to withdraw, but calling again next day to offer his sympathy he found the widow had forgotten all about the late treasurer, for she had fallen violently in love with her gallant, handsome, and fashionably dressed visitor.

After various adventures, de Lussan arrived safely back in Paris with ample means in his possession not only to satisfy his creditors, but also to enable him to live there as a gentleman of fortune and fashion.

MACHAULY, Daniel, or Maccawly, or McCawley.

A Scotch pirate. One of Captain Gow's crew. Hanged at Execution Dock at Wapping on June 11th, 1725.

MACKDONALD, Edward.

One of Captain George Lowther's crew in the *Happy Delivery*. Hanged at St. Kitts on March 11th, 1722.

MACKET, Captain, or Maggott.

On March 23rd, 1679, Macket, who commanded a small vessel of fourteen tons, with a crew of twenty men, was at Boca del Toro with Coxon, Hawkins, and other famous buccaneers, having just returned from the sacking of Porto Bello.

Shortly afterwards the fleet sailed to Golden Island, off the coast of Darien, and from thence set out to attack Santa Maria and Panama.

MACKINTOSH, William.

Of Canterbury in Kent.

One of Captain Roberts's crew. Hanged at Cape Coast Castle in 1722 at the age of 21.

MAGNES, William, or Magnus.

Born at Minehead in Somersetshire in 1687. Quartermaster of the *Royal Fortune* (Captain Bartholomew Roberts). Tried for piracy at Cape Coast Castle, and hanged in chains in 1718, for taking and plundering the *King Solomon*.

MAIN, William.

One of Captain Roberts's crew. Hanged in April, 1722, at the age of 28 years.

MAIN, WILLIAM.

Boatswain to Captain Bartholomew Roberts in the *Royal Fortune*. Was blown up, the explosion being caused by one of the crew firing his pistol into some gunpowder when the ship was taken by H.M.S. *Swallow* in 1722.

MAINTENON, MARQUIS DE.

Arrived in the West Indies from France in 1676. In 1678 commanded *La Sorcière,* a frigate, and, in company with other French filibusters from Tortuga Island, cruised off the coast of Caracas. He ravaged the islands of Margarita and Trinidad. He met with but little success, and soon afterwards his fleet scattered.

MAINWARING, CAPTAIN HENRY.

A notorious Newfoundland pirate.

On June 4th, 1614, when off the coast of that island, in command of eight vessels, he plundered the fishing fleet, stealing what provisions and stores he was in need of, also taking away with him all the carpenters and mariners he wanted for his own fleet.

It was his custom, when taking seamen, to pick one out of every six. In all he took 400 men, some of whom joined him willingly, while others were " performen." Sailing across the Atlantic to the coast of Spain, Mainwaring took a Portuguese ship and stole from out of her a good store of wine, and out of a French prize 10,000 dried fish. A few years later this pirate was pardoned and placed in command of a squadron and sent to the Barbary coast in an unsuccessful attempt to drive out the pirates who were settled there. Here he may well have met with his old friend Captain Peter Easton, who had also been a Newfoundland pirate, but in 1613 had joined the Barbary corsairs.

EL MAJORCAM, CAPTAIN ANTONIO.

At one time an officer in the Spanish Navy. Became a notorious West Indian pirate, but about 1824 he retired from the sea to become a highwayman on shore.

MANSFIELD, Jo.

One of Captain Bartholomew Roberts's men. Must not be confused with Edward Mansfield, the famous buccaneer.

A native of the Orkney Islands. At one time was a highwayman. Later on deserted from the *Rose,* man-of-war. Volunteered to join the pirates at the island of Dominica, and was always keen to do any mischief. He was a bully and a drunkard.

When Roberts's ship was attacked by H.M.S. *Swallow* and had surrendered after a sharp fight, Mansfield, who had been below all the while, very drunk, came staggering and swearing up on deck, with a drawn cutlass in his hand, crying out to know who would go on board the prize with him, and it was some time before his friends could persuade him of the true condition of things.

At his trial at Cape Coast Castle he said little in his defence, but pleaded that the cause of his backsliding was drunkenness. Hanged in the year 1722 at the age of 30.

MANSFIELD, CAPTAIN EDWARD, or MANSVELT.
A Dutchman born in the Island of Curacao.

He was the chief of the buccaneers, and at his death was succeeded by Henry Morgan. He was the first buccaneer to cross the Isthmus of Darien to the Pacific Ocean. Noted for his charm of manner, he was very popular with the buccaneers of all nationalities. In 1663 he commanded a brigantine carrying

four guns and a crew of sixty men. Was chosen
admiral of the fleet of buccaneers that gathered at
Bleufields Bay in Jamaica in November, 1665, at
the invitation of Modyford, the Governor, when he
appointed young Henry Morgan to be his vice-
admiral. This fleet was to sail and attempt to seize
the Island of Curacao, and consisted of fifteen ships
and a mixed crew of 500 buccaneers. On the way
there they landed in Cuba, although England was at
peace with Spain, and marched forty miles inland, to
surprise and sack the town of Sancti Spiritus, from
which they took a rich booty.

Mansfield, "being resolved never to face the
Governor of Jamaica until he had done some service
to the King," next made a very daring attack on the
Island of Old Providence, which the Spaniards had
fortified and used as a penal settlement. This was
successful, and Mansfield, with great humanity,
landed all the prisoners on the mainland of America.
For a long while it had been Mansfield's dream to
make this island a permanent home of the buccaneers,
as it was close to the Spanish Main, with the towns of
Porto Bello and Vera Cruz, and on the trade route of
the Spanish galleons, taking their rich cargoes to
Spain.

Mansfield's next exploit was to ascend the San Juan
River and to sack Granada, the capital of Nicaragua.
From there he coasted south along Costa Rica, burning plantations, smashing the images in the churches,
ham-stringing cows and mules, and cutting down
fruit-trees.

He returned in June, 1665, to Port Royal, with a
rich booty. For this inexcusable attack on a country
at peace with England, Governor Modyford mildly
reproved him !

Mansfield, now an old man, died suddenly at the

Island of Tortuga, off Hispaniola, when on a visit to
the French pirates there. Another account says that
he was captured by the Spaniards and taken by them
to Porto Bello, and there put to death.

MARTEEN, CAPTAIN DAVID. Buccaneer.
In 1665 he had his headquarters in Jamaica.

MARTEL, CAPTAIN JOHN.
An old Jamaican privateer. After the Peace of
Utrecht, being out of employment, he took to piracy.
His career as a pirate was very successful so long as
it lasted. Cruising off Jamaica, Cuba, and other
islands, he continued taking ship after ship, with one
particularly rich prize, a West African ship containing gold-dust, elephants' teeth, and slaves. His
original command was a sloop of eight guns and a
crew of eighty men, but after a short while he commanded a small fleet consisting of two ships (each
armed with twenty guns), three sloops, and several
armed prizes. With these Martel entered a bay in a
small island called Santa Cruz, near Porto Rico, to
careen and refit. This was in December, 1716, but
news had leaked out of the pirate's whereabouts, and
soon there arrived on the scene Captain Hume, of
H.M.S. *Scarborough*. Martel tried to escape, but his
ship ran aground, and many of the pirates were
killed, but a few, with Martel, got ashore and hid on
the island. None of them were heard of again except
Martel, and it was supposed that they had died of
hunger. In the space of three months Martel took
and plundered thirteen vessels, all of considerable
size. Two years later he was back in New Providence
Island, when Governor Rogers arrived with King
George's offer of pardon to the pirates, and Martel
was one of those who surrendered.

MARTIN, John.

Hanged in Virginia in 1718 with the rest of Black-beard's crew.

MASSEY, Captain John.

As a lieutenant, he " served with great applause " in the army in Flanders, under the command of the Duke of Marlborough.

He afterwards sailed from the Thames in the *Gambia Castle*, a ship of the African Company, in command of a company of soldiers which was being sent to garrison the fort. The merchants of Gambia were supposed to victual this garrison, but the rations supplied were considered by Massey to be quite insufficient. He quarrelled with the Governor and merchants, and took his soldiers back on board the ship, and with Lowther, the second mate, seized the ship and turned pirate. Lowther and Massey eventually quarrelled, for the latter, being a soldier, " was solicitous to move in his own sphere "—that is, he wanted to land his troops and plunder the French West Indian settlements. In the end Massey and a few followers were permitted to go off in a captured sloop, and in this sailed for Port Royal, Jamaica. Arrived there, " with a bold countenance he went to the Governor " and told a long and plausible tale of how he had managed to escape from the pirates at the first opportunity. He deceived the sympathetic Governor, and was sent with Captain Laws to hunt for Lowther. Returning to Jamaica without finding Lowther, he was granted a " certificate of his surrender," and came to England as a passenger.

On reaching London, he wrote a narrative of the whole affair—or as much as he deemed wise—to the African Company, who, receiving the story with far less credulity than the Governor of Jamaica, returned him answer " that he should be fairly hanged," and very shortly afterwards he was, at Tyburn on July 26th, 1723.

MAY, WILLIAM.

A London mariner. One of Captain Avery's crew, left behind in Madagascar very sick. A negro, hearing that an Englishman was there, came to him and nursed and fed him. This negro spoke good English, having lived at Bethnal Green.

May was promoted afterwards to be captain of a ship in the Red Sea. He was described by a shipmate as being " a true cock of the Game and an old sportsman." Hanged at London in 1696.

MAZE, CAPTAIN WILLIAM, or MACE, or MAISE.

A notorious pirate; particularly mentioned in the royal warrant authorizing Captain Kidd to go and capture certain " wicked and ill-disposed persons."

Arrived in command of a big ship at New York in 1699, loaded with booty taken in the Red Sea.

McCARTHY, CAPTAIN DENNIS.

Of New Providence, Bahama Islands.

This pirate and prize-fighter was one of those who refused King George's pardon in 1717, and was eventually hanged by his late fellow-pirates. On the gallows he made the following dying speech :

" Some friends of mine have often said I should die in my shoes, but I would rather make them liars." And so, kicking off his shoes, he was hanged.

MEGHLYN, HANS VAN.

A pirate of Antwerp, who owned a vessel of forty-five tons, painted black with pitch, and carried a crew of thirty. In 1539 he was cruising off Whitstable, on the lookout for vessels entering or leaving the

Thames. Cromwell had been warned by Vaughan
to look out for this pirate ship.

DE MELTON.

A well-known pirate in the sixteenth century. Was
with Kellwanton when he was captured in the Isle of
Man in 1531, but de Melton managed to escape with
some of the crew and get away in their ship to
Grimsby.

MELVIN, WILLIAM.

This Scotch pirate was hanged, with other members
of Gow's crew, at Wapping in June, 1725.

MENDOZA, ANTONIO.
A Spaniard from San Domingo.

Mention is made of this unlucky mariner in a very
interesting document which Mr. A. Hyatt Verrill was
fortunate enough to acquire quite recently in the
island of St. Kitts. It runs as follows:
" An assize and generall Gaole delivrie held at St.
Christophers Colonie from ye nineteenthe daye of
Maye to ye 22n. daye off ye same Monthe 1701
Captaine Josias Pendringhame Magustrate &c. The
Jurye of our Soveraigne Lord the Kinge Doe presente
Antonio Mendoza of Hispaniola and a subjecte of ye
Kinge of Spain for that ye said on or about ye 11
Daye of Apryl 1701 feloneousely delibyrately and
malliciousley and encontrarye to ye laws off Almightie
God and our Soveraigne Lord the Kinge did in his
cuppes saucely and arrogantyly speak of the Governour and Lord the Kinge and bye force and armies
into ye tavernne of John Wilkes Esq. did entre and
there did Horrible sware and cursse and did felono-
slye use threatteninge words and did strike and cutte
most murtherouslye severalle subjects of our Soveraigne Lord the Kinge. Of w'h Indictment he

pleadeth not Guiltie butte onne presente Master
Samuel Dunscombe mariner did sware that said
Antonio Mendoza was of his knowenge a Blood-
thirste piratte and Guiltie of diabolicalle practises &
ye Grande Inquest findinge yt a trewe bill to be tryd
by God and ye Countrye w'h beinge a Jurie of 12 men
sworne finde him Guiltie & for the same he be adjuged
to be carryd to ye Fort Prison to have both his earres
cutt close by his head and be burnet throughe ye
tongue with an Hot iron and to be caste chained in
ye Dungon to awaitte ye plesyure of God and Our
Soveraigne Lord the Kinge.''

MEYEURS.

A South Sea pirate, killed when taking part with
Captain Williams in a raid against an Arab settlement at Bayu.

MICHEL, CAPITAINE. Filibuster.

His ship, *La Mutine*, was armed with forty-four
guns and carried a crew of 200 men.

MICHEL LE BASQUE. A French filibuster.

In company with the butcher L'Onnais and 650
other buccaneers, he pillaged the town of Maracaibo
in Venezuela, in the year 1667. A very successful
but ruthless buccaneer.

DON MIGUEL.

In 1830 commanded a squadron of small pirate
vessels off the Azores. After seizing a Sardinian
brig off St. Michael's, was himself captured by a
British frigate.

MIGUEL, FRANCESCO.

Hanged at Kingston, Jamaica, in 1823.

MILLER, John.

One of Captain John Quelch's crew. Hanged at Boston on June 30th, 1704. A broadsheet published at the time, describing the scenes at the execution, tells us that Miller "seemed much concerned, and complained of a great Burden of Sins to answer for, expressing often : ' Lord, what shall I do to be Saved?' "

MILLER, Thomas.

Quartermaster on the pirate ship *Queen Ann's Revenge,* and killed on November 22nd, 1718.

MISNIL, Sieur du.

A French filibuster who commanded a ship, *La Trompeuse* (one hundred men and fourteen guns).

MISSON, Captain.

This unique pirate came of an ancient French family of Provence. He was the youngest of a large family, and received a good education. At the age of 15 he had already shown unusual distinction in the subjects of humanity and logic, and had passed quite tolerably in mathematics. Deciding to carve a fortune for himself with his sword, he was sent to the Academy at Angiers for a year, and at the conclusion of his military studies his father would have bought him a commission in a regiment of musketeers. But young Misson had been reading books of travel, and begged so earnestly to be allowed to go to sea that his father got him admitted as a volunteer on the French man-of-war *Victoire,* commanded by Monsieur Fourbin. Joining his ship at Marseilles, they cruised in the Mediterranean, and the young volunteer soon showed great keenness in his duties, and lost no opportunity of learning all he could about navigation and the construction of ships, even parting with his pocket-money to the boatswain and the carpenter to receive special instruction from them.

Arriving one day at Naples, Misson obtained permission from the captain to visit Rome, a visit that eventually changed his whole career.

It happened that while in Rome the young sailor met a priest, a Signor Caraccioli, a Dominican, who held most unclerical views about the priesthood; and, indeed, his ideas on life in general were, to say the least, unorthodox. A great friendship was struck up between these two, which at length led the priest to throw off his habit and join the crew of the *Victoire*. Two days out from port they met and fought a desperate hand-to-hand engagement with a Sallee pirate, in which the ex-priest and Misson both distinguished themselves by their bravery. Misson's next voyage was in a privateer, the *Triumph*, and, meeting one day an English ship, the *Mayflower*, between Guernsey and Start Point, the merchantman was defeated after a gallant resistance.

Rejoining the *Victoire*, Misson sailed from Rochelle to the West Indies, and Caraccioli lost no opportunity of preaching to young Misson the gospel of atheism and communism, and with such success that the willing convert soon held views as extreme as those of his teacher. These two apostles now began to talk to the crew, and their views, particularly on the rights of private property, were soon held by almost all on board. A fortunate event happened just then to help the new "cause." Meeting with an English man-of-war, the *Winchester*, off the island of Martinique, a smart engagement took place between the two ships, at the very commencement of which Captain Fourbin and three of the officers on the French ship were killed. The fight ended by the English ship blowing up, and an era of speech-making may be said to have now begun.

Firstly, Signor Caraccioli, stepping forward, made a long and eloquent address to Misson, inviting him to become captain of the *Victoire*, and calling upon him to follow the example of Alexander the Great with the Persians, and that of the Kings Henry IV. and VII. of England, reminding him how Mahomet, with but a few camel-drivers, founded the Ottoman Empire, also how Darius, with a handful of companions, got possession of Persia. Inflamed by this speech, young Misson showed what he could do, when, calling all hands up on deck, he made his first, but, as events proved, by far from last, speech. The result was a triumph of oratory, the excited French sailors crying out : " Vive le Capitaine Misson et son Lieutenant le Scavant Caraccioli !" Misson, returning thanks in a few graceful words, promised to do his utmost as their commander for their new marine republic. The newly elected officers retiring to the great cabin, a friendly discussion began as to their future arrangements. The first question that arose was to choose what colours they should sail under. The newly elected boatswain, Mathew le Tondu, a brave but simple mariner, advised a black one, as being the most terrifying. This brought down a full blast of eloquence from Caraccioli, the new lieutenant, who objected that "they were no pirates, but men who were resolved to affect the Liberty which God and Nature gave them," with a great deal about "guardians of the Peoples Rights and Liberties," etc., and, gradually becoming worked up, gave the wretched boatswain, who must have regretted his unfortunate remark, a heated lecture on the soul, on shaking "the Yoak of Tyranny " off their necks, on "Oppression and Poverty " and the miseries of life under these conditions as compared to those of

" Pomp and Dignity." In the end he showed that
their policy was not to be one of piracy, for pirates
were men of no principle and led dissolute lives; but
their lives were to be brave, just, and innocent, and
their cause the cause of Liberty ; and therefore, instead
of a black flag, they should live under a white ensign,
with the motto " For God and Liberty " embroidered
upon it.

The simple sailors, debarred from these councils,
had gathered outside the cabin, but were able to over-
hear this speech, and at its conclusion, carried away
by enthusiasm, loud cries went up of "Liberty!
Liberty ! We are free men ! Vive the brave Captain
Misson and the noble Lieutenant Caraccioli !" Alas !
it is impossible in the space of this work to do justice
to the perfectly wonderful and idealistic conditions of
this pirate crew. Their speeches and their kind acts
follow each other in fascinating profusion. We can
only recommend those who feel disposed to follow
more closely the history of these delightful pirates, to
read the account printed in English in 1726, if they
are fortunate enough to come by a copy.

The first prize taken by these pirates under the
white flag was an English sloop commanded by one
Captain Thomas Butler, only a day's sail out from
St. Kitts. After helping themselves to a couple of
puncheons of rum and a few other articles which the
pirates needed, but without doing any unkindness to
the crew, nor stripping them, as was the usual custom
of pirates on such occasions, they let them go, greatly
to the surprise of Captain Butler, who handsomely
admitted that he had never before met with so much
"candour " in any similar situation, and to further
express his gratitude he ordered his crew to man ship,
and at parting called for three rousing British cheers
for the good pirate and his men, which were en-
thusiastically given.

Sailing to the coast of Africa, Misson took a Dutch ship, the *Nieuwstadt,* of Amsterdam. The cargo was found to consist of gold dust and seventeen slaves. In the latter Captain Misson recognized a good text for one of his little sermons to his crew, so, calling all hands on deck, he made the following observations on the vile trade of slavery, telling his men :

" That the Trading for those of our own Species, cou'd never be agreeable to the Eyes of divine Justice. That no Man had Power of the Liberty of another; and while those who profess a more enlightened Knowledge of the Deity, sold Men like Beasts; they prov'd that their Religion was no more than Grimace, and that they differ'd from the Barbarians in Name only, since their Practice was in nothing more humane. For his Part, and he hop'd he spoke the Sentiments of all his brave Companions, he had not exempted his Neck from the galling Yoak of Slavery, and asserted his own Liberty, to enslave others. That however, these Men, were distinguished from the Europeans by their Colour, Customs, or religious Rites, they were the Work of the same omnipotent Being, and endued with equal Reason. Wherefore, he desired they might be treated like Freemen (for he wou'd banish even the Name of Slavery from among them) and be divided into Messes among them, to the end they might the sooner learn their language, be sensible of the Obligations they had to them, and more capable and zealous to defend that Liberty they owed to their Justice and Humanity." This speech was met with general applause, and once again the good ship *Victoire* rang with cries of " Vive le Capitaine Misson !" The negroes were freed of their irons, dressed up in the clothes of their late Dutch masters, and it is gratifying to read that " by their Gesticulations, they shew'd they were gratefully sensible of their being delivered from their Chains." But

alas ! a sad cloud was creeping insidiously over the
fair reputation of these super-pirates.   Out of the last
slave ship they had taken, a number of Dutch sailors
had volunteered to serve with Misson and had come
aboard as members of his crew.   Hitherto no swear-
word was ever heard, no loose or profane expression
had pained the ears of Captain Misson or his ex-
priestly lieutenant.   But the Dutch mariners began
to lead the crew into ways of swearing and drunkenness, which, coming to the captain's notice, he
thought best to nip these weeds in the bud ; so, calling
both French and Dutch upon deck, and desiring the
Dutch captain to translate his remarks into the Dutch
language, he told them that—

"Before he had the Misfortune of having them on
Board, his Ears were never grated with hearing the
Name of the great Creator profaned, tho' he, to his
Sorrow, had often since heard his own Men guilty
of that Sin, which administer'd neither Profit nor
Pleasure, and might draw upon them a severe Punish-
ment :   That if they had a just Idea of that great
Being, they wou'd never mention him, but they wou'd
immediately reflect on his Purity, and their own Vile-
ness.   That we so easily took Impression from our
Company, that the Spanish Proverb says : 'Let a
Hermit and a Thief live together, the Thief wou'd
become Hermit, or the Hermit thief ' :   That he saw
this verified in his ship, for he cou'd attribute the
Oaths and Curses he had heard among his brave
Companions, to nothing but the odious Example of
the Dutch :   That this was not the only Vice they
had introduced, for before they were on Board, his
Men were Men, but he found by their beastly Pattern
they were degenerated into Brutes, by drowning that
only Faculty, which distinguishes between Man and
Beast, Reason.   That as he had the Honour to command them, he could not see them run into these

odious Vices without a sincere Concern, as he had a
paternal Affection for them, and he should reproach
himself as neglectful of the common Good, if he did
not admonish them; and as by the Post which they
had honour'd him, he was obliged to have a watchful
Eye over their general Interest; he was obliged to tell
them his Sentiments were, that the Dutch allured
them to a dissolute Way of Life, that they might take
some Advantage over them :   Wherefore, as his brave
Companions, he was assured, wou'd be guided by
reason, he gave the Dutch Notice, that the first whom
he catch'd either with an Oath in his Mouth or Liquor
in his Head, should be brought to the Geers, whipped
and pickled, for an Example to the rest of his Nation :
As to his Friends, his Companions, his Children,
those gallant, those generous, noble and heroick Souls
he had the Honour to command, he entreated them to
allow a small Time for Reflection, and to consider
how little Pleasure, and how much Danger, might
flow from imitating the Vices of their Enemies; and
that they would among themselves, make a Law for
the Suppression of what would otherwise estrange
them from the Source of Life, and consequently leave
them destitute of his Protection.''

This speech had the desired effect, and ever afterwards, when any one of the crew had reason to
mention the name of his captain, he never failed to
add the epithet " Good " before it.

These chaste pirates soon took and plundered many
rich merchant ships, but always in the most gentlemanly manner, so that none failed to be "not a
little surprised at the Regularity, Tranquillity and
Humanity of these new-fashioned Pyrates." From
out of one of these, an English vessel, they took a
sum of £60,000, but during the engagement the
captain was killed. Poor Captain Misson was broken-
hearted over this unfortunate mishap, and to show as

best he could his regret, he buried the body on shore, and, finding that one of his men was by trade a stone-cutter, raised a monument over the grave with, en-graved upon it, the words : " Here lies a gallant English Man." And at the conclusion of a very moving burial service he paid a final tribute by " a triple Discharge of 50 small Arms and fired Minute Guns."

Misson now sailed to the Island of Johanna in the Indian Ocean, which became his future home. Misson married the sister of the local dusky queen, and his lieutenant led to the altar her niece, while many of the crew also were joined in holy wedlock to one or more ladies of more humble social standing.

Already Misson has received more space than he is entitled to in a work of reference of this kind, but his career is so full of charming incidents that one is tempted to continue to unseemly length. Let it suffice to say that for some years Misson made speeches, robbed ships, and now and again, when unavoidably driven to it, would reluctantly slaughter his enemies.

Finally, Misson took his followers to a sheltered bay in Madagascar, and on landing there made a little speech, telling them that here they could settle down, build a town, that here, in fact, " they might have some Place to call their own ; and a Receptacle, when Age or Wounds had render'd them incapable of Hardship, where they might enjoy the Fruits of their Labour, and go to their Graves in Peace."

This ideal colony was called Libertatia, and was run on strictly Socialistic lines, for no one owned any individual property ; all money was kept in a common treasury, and no hedges bounded any man's particular plot of land. Docks were made and fortifications set up. Soon Misson had two ships built, called the *Childhood* and the *Liberty*, and these were sent for a

voyage round the island, to map and chart the coast,
and to train the released slaves to be efficient sailors.
A Session House was built, and a form of Government arranged.   At the first meeting Misson was
elected Lord Conservator, as they called the President, for a term of three years, and during that period
he was to have " all the Ensigns of Royalty to attend
him." Captain Tew, the English pirate, was elected
Admiral of the Fleet of Libertatia, Caraccioli became
Secretary of State, while the Council was formed of
the ablest amongst the pirates, without distinction
of nation or colour.   The difficulty of language, as
French, English, Portuguese, and Dutch were equally
spoken, was overcome by the invention of a new
language, a kind of Esperanto, which was built up of
words from all four.   For many years this ideally
successful and happy pirate Utopia flourished; but at
length misfortunes came, one on top of the other,
and a sudden and unexpected attack by the hitherto
friendly natives finally drove Misson and a few other
survivors to seek safety at sea, but, overtaken by a
hurricane, their vessel foundered, and Misson and all
his crew were drowned; and thus ended the era of
what may be called " piracy without tears."

> He was the mildest-manner'd man
> That ever scuttled ship or cut a throat.
>
> BYRON.

MITCHELL, CAPTAIN.

An English buccaneer of Jamaica, who flourished
in 1663.

MITCHELL, JOHN.

Of Shadwell Parish, London.

One of the crew of the *Ranger*.   Condemned to
death, but reprieved and sold to the Royal African
Company.

M'KINLIE, PETER. Irish pirate.

Boatswain in a merchant ship which sailed from
the Canaries to England in the year 1765. On board
were three passengers, the adventurous Captain Glass
and his wife and daughter. One night M'Kinlie and
four other mutineers murdered the commander of the
vessel, Captain Cockeran, and Captain Glass and his
family, as well as all the crew except two cabin-boys.
After throwing their bodies overboard, M'Kinlie
steered for the coast of Ireland, and on December 3rd
arrived in the neighbourhood of the harbour of Ross.
Filling the long-boat with dollars, weighing some
two tons, they rowed ashore, after killing the two boys
and scuttling the ship. On landing, the pirates found
they had much more booty than they could carry, so
they buried 250 bags of dollars in the sand, and took
what they could with them to a village called Fisher-
town. Here they regaled themselves, while one of the
villagers relieved them of a bag containing 1,200
dollars. Next day they walked into Ross, and there
sold another bag of dollars, and with the proceeds
each man bought a pair of pistols and a horse and
rode to Dublin. In the meanwhile the ship, instead
of sinking, was washed up on the shore. Strong
suspicion being roused in the countryside, messengers
were sent post-haste to inform the Lords of the
Regency at Dublin that the supposed pirates were
in the city. Three of them were arrested in the Black
Bull Inn in Thomas Street, but M'Kinlie and another
pirate, who had already taken a post-chaise for Cork,
intending to embark there on a vessel for England,
were arrested on the way.

The five pirates were tried in Dublin, condemned
and executed, their bodies being hung in chains, on
December 19th, 1765.

MONTBARS, The Exterminator.

A native of Languedoc. He joined the buccaneers after reading a book which recorded the cruelty of the Spaniards to the American natives, and this story inspired him with such a hatred of all Spaniards that he determined to go to the West Indies, throw in his lot with the buccaneers, and to devote his whole life and energies to punishing the Spaniards. He carried out his resolve most thoroughly, and treated all Spaniards who came into his power with such cruelty that he became known all up and down the Spanish Main as the Exterminator. Eventually Montbars became a notorious and successful buccaneer or pirate chief, having his headquarters at St. Bartholomew, one of the Virgin Islands, to which he used to bring all his prisoners and spoils taken out of Spanish ships and towns.

MONTENEGRO.

A Columbian. One of Captain Gilbert's crew in the pirate schooner *Panda*. Hanged at Boston in 1835.

DE MONT, Francis.

Captured in South Carolina in 1717. Tried at Charleston, and convicted of taking the *Turtle Dove* and other vessels in the previous July. Hanged in June, 1717.

MOODY, Captain Christopher.

A notorious pirate. Very active off the coast of Carolina, 1717, with two ships under his command. In 1722 was with Roberts on board the *Royal Fortune*, being one of his chief men or "Lords." Taken prisoner, and tried at Cape Coast Castle, and hanged in chains at the age of 28.

MOORE. Gunner.

A gunner aboard Captain Kidd's ship the *Adventure*. When Kidd's mutinous crew were all for attacking a Dutch ship, Kidd refused to allow them to, and Moore threatened the captain, who seized a bucket and struck Moore on the head with it, the blow killing him. Kidd was perfectly justified in killing this mutinous sailor, but eventually it was for this act that he was hanged in London.

MORGAN, CAPTAIN.

This pirate must not be confused with the buccaneer, Sir Henry Morgan. Little is known about him except that he was with Hamlin, the French pirate, in 1683, off the coast of West Africa, and helped to take several Danish and English ships. Soon the pirates quarrelled over the division of their plunder and separated into two companies, the English following Captain Morgan in one of the prizes.

MORGAN, COLONEL BLODRE, or BLEDRY.

This buccaneer was probably a relation of Sir Henry Morgan. He was an important person in Jamaica between 1660 and 1670. At the taking of Panama by Henry Morgan in 1670 the Colonel commanded the rearguard of 300 men. In May, 1671, he was appointed to act as Deputy Governor of Providence Island by Sir James Modyford.

MORGAN, LIEUT.-COLONEL EDWARD. Buccaneer.
Uncle and father-in-law of Sir Henry Morgan.

In 1665, when war had been declared on Holland, the Governor of Jamaica issued commissions to several pirates and buccaneers to sail to and attack the Dutch islands of St. Eustatius, Saba, and

Curacao. Morgan was put in command of ten ships
and some 500 men; most of them were "reformed
prisoners," while some were condemned pirates who
had been pardoned in order to let them join the
expedition.

Before leaving Jamaica the crews mutinied, but
were pacified by the promise of an equal share of all
the spoils that should be taken. Three ships out of
the fleet slipped away on the voyage, but the rest
arrived at St. Kitts, landed, and took the fort.
Colonel Morgan, who was an old and corpulent man,
died of the heat and exertion during the campaign.

MORGAN, Lieut.-Colonel Thomas.

Sailed with Colonel Edward Morgan to attack
St. Eustatius and Saba Islands, and after these were
surrendered by the Dutch, Thomas Morgan was left
in charge.

In 1686 he sailed in command of a company of
buccaneers to assist Governor Wells, of St. Kitts,
against the French. The defence of the island was
disgraceful, and Morgan's company was the only one
which displayed any courage or discipline, and most
of them were killed or wounded, Colonel Morgan
himself being shot in both legs.

Often these buccaneer leaders altered their titles
from colonel to captain, to suit the particular enterprise on which they were engaged, according if it
took place on sea or land.

MORGAN, Sir Henry. Buccaneer.

This, the greatest of all the "brethren of the
coast," was a Welshman, born at Llanrhymmy in
Monmouthshire in the year 1635. The son of a well-
to-do farmer, Robert Morgan, he early took to the
seafaring life. When quite a young man Morgan

went to Barbadoes, but afterwards he settled at
Jamaica, which was his home for the rest of his
life.

Morgan may have been induced to go to the West
Indies by his uncle, Colonel Morgan, who was for a
time Deputy Governor of Jamaica, a post Sir Henry
Morgan afterwards held.

Morgan was a man of great energy, and must have
possessed great power of winning his own way with
people. That he could be absolutely unscrupulous
when it suited his ends there can be little doubt. He
was cruel at times, but was not the inhuman monster
that he is made out to be by Esquemeling in his
"History of the Bucaniers." This was largely
proved by the evidence given in the suit for libel
brought and won by Morgan against the publishers,
although Morgan was, if possible, more indignant
over the statement in the same book that he had been
kidnapped in Wales and sold, as a boy, and sent to be
a slave in Barbadoes. That he could descend to rank
dishonesty was shown when, returning from his extraordinary and successful assault on the city of Panama
in 1670, to Chagres, he left most of his faithful
followers behind, without ships or food, while he
slipped off in the night with most of the booty to
Jamaica. No doubt, young Morgan came to Jamaica
with good credentials from his uncle, the Colonel, for
the latter was held in high esteem by Modyford, then
Governor of Barbadoes, who describes Colonel Morgan
as " that honest privateer."

Colonel Morgan did not live to see his nephew reach
the pinnacle of his success, for in the year 1665 he
was sent at the head of an expedition to attack the
Dutch stronghold at St. Eustatius Island, but he was
too old to stand the hardships of such an expedition
and died shortly afterwards.

By this time Morgan had made his name as

a successful and resolute buccaneer by returning to Port Royal from a raiding expedition in Central America with a huge booty.

In 1665 Morgan, with two other buccaneers, Jackman and Morris, plundered the province of Campeachy, and then, acting as Vice-Admiral to the most famous buccaneer of the day, Captain Mansfield, plundered Cuba, captured Providence Island, sacked Granada, burnt and plundered the coast of Costa Rica, bringing back another booty of almost fabulous wealth to Jamaica. In this year Morgan married a daughter of his uncle, Colonel Morgan.

In 1668, when 33 years of age, Morgan was commissioned by the Jamaican Government to collect together the privateers, and by 1669 he was in command of a big fleet, when he was almost killed by a great explosion in the *Oxford*, which happened while Morgan was giving a banquet to his captains. About this time Morgan calmly took a fine ship, the *Cour Volant*, from a French pirate, and made her his own flagship, christening her the *Satisfaction*.

In 1670 the greatest event of Morgan's life took place—the sacking of Panama. First landing a party which took the Castle of San Lorenzo at the mouth of the Chagres River, Morgan left a strong garrison there to cover his retreat and pushed on with 1,400 men in a fleet of canoes up the river on January 9th, 1671. The journey across the isthmus, through the tropical jungle, was very hard on the men, particularly as they had depended on finding provisions to supply their wants on the way, and carried no food with them. They practically starved until the sixth day, when they found a barn full of maize, which the fleeing Spaniards had neglected to destroy. On the evening of the ninth day a scout reported he had seen the steeple of a church in Panama. Morgan, with that touch of genius which so often brought him

success, attacked the city from a direction the
Spaniards had not thought possible, so that their
guns were all placed where they were useless, and
they were compelled to do just what the buccaneer
leader wanted them to do—namely, to come out of
their fortifications and fight him in the open. The
battle raged fiercely for two hours between the
brave Spanish defenders and the equally brave but
almost exhausted buccaneers. When at last the
Spaniards turned and ran, the buccaneers were too
tired to immediately follow up their success, but
after resting they advanced, and at the end of three
hours' street fighting the city was theirs. The first
thing Morgan now did was to assemble all his men
and strictly forbid them to drink any wine, telling
them that he had secret information that the wine had
been poisoned by the Spaniards before they left the
city. This was, of course, a scheme of Morgan's to
stop his men from becoming drunk, when they would
be at the mercy of the enemy, as had happened in
many a previous buccaneer assault.

Morgan now set about plundering the city, a large
part of which was burnt to the ground, though
whether this was done by his orders or by the
Spanish Governor has never been decided. After
three weeks the buccaneers started back on their
journey to San Lorenzo, with a troop of 200 pack-
mules laden with gold, silver, and goods of all sorts,
together with a large number of prisoners. The
rearguard on the march was under the command
of a kinsman of the Admiral, Colonel Bledry
Morgan.

On their arrival at Chagres the spoils were divided,
amidst a great deal of quarrelling, and in March,
1671, Morgan sailed off to Port Royal with a few
friends and the greater part of the plunder, leaving
his faithful followers behind without ships or pro-

visions, and with but £10 apiece as their share of the spoils.

On May 31st, 1671, the Council of Jamaica passed a vote of thanks to Morgan for his successful expedition, and this in spite of the fact that in July, a year before, a treaty had been concluded at Madrid between Spain and England for "restraining depredations and establishing peace" in the New World.

In April, 1672, Morgan was carried to England as a prisoner in the *Welcome* frigate. But he was too popular to be convicted, and after being acquitted was appointed Deputy Governor of Jamaica, and in November, 1674, he was knighted and returned to the West Indies. In 1672 Major-General Banister, who was Commander-in-Chief of the troops in Jamaica, writing to Lord Arlington about Morgan, said : " He (Morgan) is a well deserving person, and one of great courage and conduct, who may, with His Majesty's pleasure, perform good public service at home, or be very advantageous to this island if war should again break forth with the Spaniards."

While Morgan was in England he brought an action for libel against William Crooke, the publisher of the "History of the Bucaniers of America." The result of this trial was that Crooke paid £200 damages to Morgan and published a long and grovelling apology.

Morgan was essentially a man of action, and a regular life on shore proved irksome to him, for we learn from a report sent home by Lord Vaughan in 1674 that Morgan "frequented the taverns of Port Royal, drinking and gambling in unseemly fashion," but nevertheless the Jamaican Assembly had voted the Lieutenant-Governor a sum of £600 special salary. In 1676 Vaughan brought definite charges against Morgan and another member of the Council, Robert Byndloss, of giving aid to certain Jamaica pirates.

Morgan made a spirited defence and, no doubt largely owing to his popularity, got off, and in 1678 was granted a commission to be a captain of a company of 100 men.

The Governor to succeed Vaughan was Lord Carlisle, who seems to have liked Morgan, in spite of his jovial "goings on" with his old buccaneer friends in the taverns of Port Royal, and in some of his letters speaks of Morgan's "generous manner," and hints that whatever allowances are made to him "he will be a beggar."

In 1681 Sir Thomas Lynch was appointed to be Governor, and trouble at once began between him and his deputy. Amongst the charges the former brought against Morgan was one of his having been overheard to say, "God damn the Assembly!" for which he was suspended from that body.

In April, 1688, the King, at the urgent request of the Duke of Albemarle, ordered Morgan to be re-instated in the Assembly, but Morgan did not live long to enjoy his restored honours, for he died on August 25th, 1688.

An extract from the journal of Captain Lawrence Wright, commander of H.M.S. *Assistance*, dated August, 1688, describes the ceremonies held at Port Royal at the burial of Morgan, and shows how important and popular a man he was thought to be. It runs :

"Saturday 25. This day about eleven hours noone Sir Henry Morgan died, & the 26th was brought over from Passage-fort to the King's house at Port Royall, from thence to the Church, & after a sermon was carried to the Pallisadoes & there buried. All the forts fired an equal number of guns, wee fired two & twenty & after wee & the Drake had fired, all the merchant men fired."

Morgan was buried in Jamaica, and his will, which

was filed in the Record Office at Spanish Town, makes provision for his wife and near relations.

MORRICE, HUMPHREY.
Of New Providence, Bahama Islands.

Hanged at New Providence in 1718 by his lately reformed fellow-pirates, and on the gallows taxed them with " pusillanimity and cowardice " because they did not rescue him and his fellow-sufferers.

MORRIS, CAPTAIN JOHN.
Of Jamaica.

A privateer until 1665, he afterwards became a buccaneer with Mansfield. Took part in successful raids in Central America, plundering Vildemo in the Bay of Campeachy ; he also sacked Truxillo, and then, after a journey by canoe up the San Juan River to take Nicaragua, surprised and plundered the city of Granada in March, 1666.

MORRIS, CAPTAIN THOMAS.

One of the pirates of New Providence, Bahamas, who, on pardon being offered by King George in 1717, escaped, and for a while carried on piracy in the West Indian Islands. Caught and hanged a few years afterwards.

MORRIS, JOHN.

One of Captain Bartholomew Roberts's crew. When the *Royal Fortune* surrendered to H.M.S. *Swallow*, Morris fired his pistol into the gunpowder in the steerage and caused an explosion that killed or maimed many of the pirates.

MORRISON, CAPTAIN.

A Scotch pirate, who lived on Prince Edward Island.

For an account of his career, see Captain NELSON.

MORRISON, William.

Of Jamaica.

One of Major Stede Bonnet's crew. Hanged at White Point, Charleston, South Carolina, on November 8th, 1718, and buried in the marsh below low-water mark.

MORTON, Philip.

Gunner on board " Blackbeard's " ship, the *Queen Ann's Revenge*. Killed on November 22nd, 1718, in North Carolina, during the fight with Lieutenant Maynard.

MULLET, James, *alias* Millet.

Of London.

One of the crew of the *Royal James,* in which vessel Major Stede Bonnet played havoc with the shipping along the coasts of South Carolina and New England. Hanged at Charleston in 1718.

MULLINS, Darby.

This Irish pirate was born in the north of Ireland, not many miles from Londonderry. Being left an orphan at the age of 18, he was sold to a planter in the West Indies for a term of four years.

After the great earthquake at Jamaica in 1691, Mullins built himself a house at Kingston and ran it as a punch-house—often a very profitable business when the buccaneers returned to Port Royal with good plunder. This business failing, he went to New York, where he met Captain Kidd, and was, according to his own story, persuaded to engage in piracy, it being urged that the robbing only of infidels, the enemies of Christianity, was an act, not only lawful, but one highly meritorious.

At his trial later on in London his judges did not agree with this view of the rights of property, and Mullins was hanged at Execution Dock on May 23rd, 1701.

MUMPER, THOMAS.
An Indian of Mather's Vineyard, New England.

Tried for piracy with Captain Charles Harris and his men, but found to be " not guilty."

MUNDON, STEPHEN.
Of London.

Hanged for piracy at Newport, Rhode Island, on July 19th, 1723, at the age of 20.

MUSTAPHA.   Turkish pirate.

In 1558 he sailed, with a fleet of 140 vessels, to the Island of Minorca.   Landed, and besieged the forti-fied town of Ciudadda, which at length surrendered. The Turks slew great numbers of the inhabitants, taking the rest away as slaves.

NAU, CAPTAIN JEAN DAVID, alias FRANCIS L'OLLO-NAIS.
A Frenchman born at Les Sables d'Ollone.

In his youth he was transported as an indented labourer to the French Island of Dominica in the West Indies.   Having served his time L'Ollonais went to the Island of Hispaniola, and joined the buccaneers there, living by hunting wild cattle and drying the flesh or boucan.

He then sailed for a few voyages as a sailor before the mast, and acted with such ability and courage that the Governor of Tortuga Island, Monsieur de la

Place, gave him the command of a vessel and sent him out to seek his fortune.

At first the young buccaneer was very successful, and he took many Spanish ships, but owing to his ferocious treatment of his prisoners he soon won a name for cruelty which has never been surpassed. But at the height of this success his ship was wrecked in a storm, and, although most of the pirates got ashore, they were at once attacked by a party of Spaniards, and all but L'Ollonais were killed. The captain escaped, after being wounded, by smearing blood and sand over his face and hiding himself amongst his dead companions. Disguised as a Spaniard he entered the city of Campeachy, where bonfires and other manifestations of public relief were being held, to express the joy of the citizens at the news of the death of their terror, L'Ollonais.

Meeting with some French slaves, the fugitive planned with them to escape in the night in a canoe, this being successfully carried out, they eventually arrived back at Tortuga, the pirate stronghold. Here the enterprising captain stole a small vessel, and again started off "on the account," plundering a village called De los Cagos in Cuba. The Governor of Havana receiving word of the notorious and apparently resurrected pirate's arrival sent a well-armed ship to take him, adding to the ship's company a negro executioner, with orders to hang all the pirate crew with the exception of L'Ollonais, who was to be brought back to Havana alive and in chains.

Instead of the Spaniards taking the Frenchman, the opposite happened, and everyone of them was murdered, including the negro hangman, with the exception of one man, who was sent with a written message to the Governor to tell him that in future L'Ollonais would kill every Spaniard he met with.

Joining with a famous filibuster, Michael de Basco,

L'Ollonais soon organized a more important expedition, consisting of a fleet of eight vessels and
400 men.   Sailing to the Gulf of Venezuela in 1667,
they entered the lake, destroying the fort that stood to
guard the entrance.   Thence sailing to the city of
Maracaibo they found all the inhabitants had fled in
terror.   The filibusters caught many of the inhabitants hiding in the neighbouring woods, and killed
numbers of them in their attempts to force from the
rest the hiding-places of their treasure.   They next
marched upon and attacked the town of Gibraltar,
which was valiantly defended by the Spaniards, until
the evening, when, having lost 500 men killed, they
surrendered.   For four weeks this town was pillaged,
the inhabitants murdered, while torture and rape were
daily occurrences.   At last, to the relief of the wretched
inhabitants, the buccaneers, with a huge booty, sailed
away to Corso Island, a place of rendezvous of the
French buccaneers.   Here they divided their spoil,
which totalled the great sum of 260,000 pieces of eight,
which, when divided amongst them, gave each man
above one hundred pieces of eight, as well as his
share of plate, silk, and jewels.

Also, a share was allotted for the next-of-kin of each
man killed, and extra rewards for those pirates who
had lost a limb or an eye.   L'Ollonais had now
become most famous amongst the " Brethren of the
Coast," and began to make arrangements for an
even more daring expedition to attack and plunder the
coast of Nicaragua.   Here he burnt and pillaged
ruthlessly, committing the most revolting cruelties
on the Spanish inhabitants.   One example of this
monster's inhuman deeds will more than suffice to tell
of.   It happened that during an attack on the town of
San Pedros the buccaneers had been caught in an
ambuscade and many of them killed, although the
Spaniards had at last turned and fled.   The pirates

killed most of their prisoners, but kept a few to be
questioned by L'Ollonais so as to find some other
way to the town. As he could get no information out
of these men, the Frenchman drew his cutlass and,
with it cut open the breast of one of the Spaniards,
and pulling out his still beating heart he began to bite
and gnaw it witl. his teeth like a ravenous wolf,
saying to the other prisoners, "I will serve you all
alike, if you show me not another way."

Shortly after this, many of the buccaneers broke
away from L'Ollonais and sailed under the command of Moses van Vin, the second in command.
L'Ollonais, in his big ship, sailed to the coast of
Honduras, but ran his vessel on a sand-bank and lost
her. While building a new but small craft on one of
the Las Pertas Islands, they cultivated beans and
other vegetables, and also wheat, for which they baked
bread in portable ovens which these French buccaneers
carried about with them. It took them six months to
build their long-boat, and when it was finished it
would not carry more than half the number of
buccaneers. Lots were drawn to settle who should
sail and who remain behind. L'Ollonais steered the
boat towards Cartagena, but was caught by the
Indians, as described by Esquemeling. "Here suddenly his ill-fortune assailed him, which of a long
time had been reserved for him as a punishment due
to the multitude of horrible crimes, which in his
licentious and wicked life he had committed. For God
Almighty, the time of His divine justice being now
already come, had appointed the Indians of Darien to
be the instruments and executioners thereof."

These "instruments of God," having caught
L'Ollonais, tore him in pieces alive, throwing his
body limb by limb into the fire and his ashes into the
air, to the intent " no trace nor memory might remain
of such an infamous inhuman creature."

Thus died a monster of cruelty, who would, had he lived to-day, have been confined in an asylum for lunatics.

NEAL.

A fisherman of Cork.

Mutinied in a French ship sailing from Cork to Nantes in 1721, and, under the leadership of Philip Roche, murdered the captain and many of the crew and became a pirate.

NEFF, WILLIAM.

Born at Haverhill, Massachusetts, in 1667.

A soldier, one of the guard at Fort Loyal, Falmouth, Maine. Deserted in 1689 and went to sea with the pirate Captain Pound.

NELSON, CAPTAIN.

Born on Prince Edward Island, where his father had a grant of land for services rendered in the American war. He was a wealthy man, a member of the Council and a Colonel of the Militia. In order to set his son up in life he bought him a captaincy in the Militia and a fine farm, where young Nelson married and settled down. Buying a schooner, he used to sail to Halifax with cargoes of potatoes and fruit. He seems to have liked these trips in which he combined business with pleasure, for we learn that on these visits to Halifax he " was very wild, and drank and intrigued with the girls in an extravagant manner." Getting into disgrace on Prince Edward Island, and losing his commission, he went to live near Halifax, and became a lieutenant in the Nova Scotia Fencibles, while his wife remained on the island to look after his estates, which brought him in £300 a year. Meeting with a Scotchman called Morrison, together they bought a " pretty little New York battleship," mounting ten guns. Manning this dangerous toy with a crew of ninety desperate characters, the partners went "on the account," and began well by taking a brig belonging to Mr. Hill, of Rotherhithe, which they took to New York, and there sold both ship and cargo.

They next cruised in the West Indies, taking several English and Dutch ships, the crews of which they treated with the greatest brutality.

Landing on St. Kitts Island, they burnt and plundered two Dutch plantations, murdering the owners and slaves. Sailing north to Newfoundland they took ten more vessels, which they sold in New York. After further successful voyages in the West Indies and off the coast of Brazil, Nelson felt the call of home ties becoming so strong that he ventured to return to Prince Edward Island to visit his wife and family, where no one dared to molest him.

By this time Nelson had been a pirate for three years and had, by his industry, won for himself a fortune worth £150,000, but his Scotch partner, Morrison, being a frugal soul, had in the meantime saved an even larger sum. Eventually their ship was wrecked in a fog on a small barren island near Prince Edward Island, and Morrison and most of the crew were drowned, but Nelson and a few others were saved. At last he reached New York, where he lived the rest of his life in peaceful happiness with his wife and family.

NICHOLLS, THOMAS, *alias* NICHOLAS.
Of London.

One of Major Stede Bonnet's crew in the *Royal James*. Tried for piracy at Charleston on November 8th, 1718, and found " not guilty."

NONDRE, PEDRO.
Hanged at Kingston, Jamaica, in February, 1823. At the time of execution it was observed that he was

covered with the marks of deep wounds. On the scaffold he wept bitterly. An immensely heavy man, he broke the rope, and had to be hanged a second time.

NORMAN, Captain. Buccaneer.

Served under Morgan in 1670, and after the fall of Chagres Fort, Norman was left in charge with 500 men to hold it, while Morgan crossed the isthmus to attack Panama. Norman soon " sent forth to sea two boats to exercise piracy." These hoisted Spanish colours and met a big Spanish merchant ship on the same day. They chased the ship, which fled for safety into the Chagres River, only to be caught there by Norman. She proved a valuable prize, being loaded with all kinds of provisions, of which the garrison was in sore need.

NORTH, Captain Nathaniel.

Born in Bermuda, and by profession a lawyer, Captain North was a man of remarkable ability, and in his later calling of piracy he gained great notoriety, and was a born leader of men. His history has been written fully, and is well worth reading. He had many ups and downs in his early seafaring life in the West Indies; being no less than three times taken by the pressgang, each time escaping. He served in Dutch and Spanish privateers, and eventually rose to being a pirate captain, making his headquarters in Madagascar. From here he sailed out to the East Indies, and preyed on the ships of the East India Company. Several times he was wrecked, once he was the only survivor, and swam ashore at Madagascar stark naked. The unusual sight of a naked Englishman spread terror amongst the natives who were on the beach, and they all fled into the jungle except one, a woman, who from previous personal ex-

perience knew that this was but a human being and not
a sea devil. She supplied him with clothes, of a sort,
and led him to the nearest pirate settlement, some six
miles away. On another occasion when the pirates were
having a jollification ashore, having left their Moorish
prisoners on the ship at anchor, North gave the
prisoners a hint to clear off in the night with the ship,
otherwise they would all be made slaves. This
friendly hint was acted upon, and in the morning both
ship and prisoners had vanished. The pirates having
lost their ship took to the peaceful and harmless life of
planters, with North as their ruler. He won the con-
fidence of the natives, who abided by his decision in
all quarrels and misunderstandings. Occasionally
North and his men would join forces with a neighbouring friendly tribe and go to war, North leading
the combined army, and victory always resulted. The
call of piracy was too strong in his bones to resist, and
after three years planting he was back to sea and the
Jolly Roger once more. On one occasion he seized
the opportunity, when in the neighbourhood of the
Mascarenhas Islands, to go ashore and visit the
Catholic priest and confess, and at the same time
made suitable arrangements for his children to be
educated by the Church. North evidently truly re-
pented his former sins, for he returned to resume his
simple life on his plantation. On arriving home he
found the settlement in an uproar. He soon settled
all the disputes, appeased the natives, and before long
had this garden-city of pirates back in its previous
peaceful and happy state. Beyond an occasional little
voyage, taking a ship or two, or burning an Arab
village, North's career as a pirate may be considered
to have terminated, as, indeed, his life was shortly
afterwards, being murdered in his bed by a treacherous
native. North's friends the pirates, shocked at this
cold-blooded murder, waged a ruthless war on the

natives for seven years : thus in their simple way thinking to revenge the loss of this estimable man, who had always been the natives' best friend.

NORTON, George.

One of Captain John Quelch's crew. Tried for piracy in June, 1704, at the Star Tavern at Boston.

NUTT, John.

One of Captain John Phillip's original crew of five pirates in the *Revenge* in 1723. Nutt was made master or navigator.

OCHALI.   Barbary renegade.

In 1511 he sailed from Algiers with a fleet of twenty-two vessels and 1,700 men to raid Majorca. The Moors landed at Soller and pillaged it. Before they could get back to their ship, the pirates were attacked by the Majorcans, headed by Miguel Angelats, and completely routed, 500 of them being killed.

ODELL, Samuel.

Taken prisoner by the pirate Captain Teach on November 21st, 1718, and on the very next day re-taken by Lieutenant Maynard. Odell received no less than seventy wounds in the fight, but recovered, and was carried to Virginia to stand his trial for piracy, and was acquitted.

OUGHTERLAUNEY, Thomas.

Acted as pilot in the *Royal Fortune*. Took an active part in taking and plundering the *King Solomon* on the West Coast of Africa in 1721.

Was tried for piracy with the rest of Roberts's crew, when one witness, Captain Trahern, deposed that the prisoner dressed himself up in the captain's best suit of clothes, his new tye wig, and called loudly for a bottle of wine, and then, very arrogantly, gave orders as to the steering of the captured ship.

Hanged at Cape Coast Castle in 1722.

PAIN, Captain.

A Bahaman privateer who in 1683 turned pirate and attacked St. Augustine in Florida under French colours. Being driven off by the Spaniards, he had to content himself with looting some neighbouring settlements. On returning to New Providence, the Governor attempted, but without success, to arrest Pain and his crew. Pain afterwards appeared in Rhode Island, and when the authorities tried to seize him and his ship, he got off by exhibiting an old commission to hunt for pirates given him a long while before by Sir Thomas Lynch. When the West Indies became too hot for him, Pain made the coast of Carolina his headquarters.

PAINE, Captain Peter, alias Le Pain. A French buccaneer.

He brought into Port Royal in 1684 a merchant ship, *La Trompeuse*. Pretending to be the owner, he sold both ship and cargo, which brought about great trouble afterwards between the French and English Governments, because he had stolen the ship on the high seas. He was sent from Jamaica under arrest to France the same year, to answer for his crimes.

PAINTER, Peter.

This Carolina pirate retired and lived at Charleston. In August, 1710, he was recommended for the position of public powder-receiver, but was rejected by the Upper House. "Mr. Painter Having committed Piracy, and not having his Majesties Pardon for the same, Its resolved he is not fit for that Trust." Which only goes to show how hard it was for a man to live down a thing like piracy.

PARDAL, Captain Manuel Rivero.

Known to the Jamaicans as " the vapouring admiral of St. Jago," because in July, 1670, he had nailed a piece of canvas to a tree on the Jamaican coast with this curious challenge written both in English and Spanish :

" I, Captain Manuel Rivero Pardal, to the chief of the squadron of privateers in Jamaica. I am he who this year have done that which follows. I went on shore at Caimanos, and burnt 20 houses and fought with Captain Ary, and took from him a catch laden with provisions and a canoe. And I am he who took Captain Baines and did carry the prize to Cartagena, and now am arrived to this coast, and have burnt it. And I come to seek General Morgan, with 2 ships of 20 guns, and having seen this, I crave he would come out upon the coast and seek me, that he might see the valour of the Spaniards. And because I had no time I did not come to the mouth of Port Royal to speak by word of mouth in the name of my king, whom God preserve. Dated the 5th of July, 1670."

PARKER, Captain William. Buccaneer.

Just after the city of Porto Bello had been made, as the Spanish thought, impregnable, by the building of the massive stone fort of San Jerome, the daring Parker, with but 200 English desperadoes, took the place by storm, burning part of the town and getting quickly and safely away with a huge amount of booty.

PARKINS, BENJAMIN.

One of Captain John Quelch's crew in the brigantine *Charles*. Tried at Boston for piracy in 1704.

PARROT, JAMES.

One of Quelch's crew, who turned King's evidence at the trial at Boston in 1704, and thus escaped hanging.

PATTERSON, NEAL.
Of Aberdeen.

One of Major Stede Bonnet's crew in the *Royal James*. Hanged at Charleston, South Carolina, on November 8th, 1718, and buried in the marsh.

PATTISON, JAMES.

Tried for piracy at Boston in 1704.

PEASE, CAPTAIN.

A low down, latter-day South Sea pirate. Arrived in an armed ship with a Malay crew at Apia in Samoa in June, 1870, and rescued the pirate Bully Hayes, who was under arrest of the English Consul. He pleased the British inhabitants of the island by his display of loyalty to Queen Victoria by firing a salute of twenty-one guns on her Majesty's birthday.

PELL, IGNATIUS.

Boatswain of the *Royal James*, Major Stede Bonnet's ship. Turned King's evidence at trial of Bonnet and his crew at Charleston, Carolina, in 1718.

PENNER, MAJOR.

We have been able to find out nothing of this pirate except that he was at New Providence Island in 1718

and took the King's pardon for pirates. He seems to
have returned to the old life and was killed soon after,
though how this came about is not recorded.

PERKINS, Benjamin.

One of Quelch's crew. Captured at Marblehead in
1704.

PERRY, Daniel.
Of Guernsey.

Tried for piracy in 1718 at Charleston, South Carolina, and found guilty. Hanged on November 8th at
White Point. Buried in the marsh below low-water
mark.

PETERSON, Captain.
Of Newport, Rhode Island.

In 1688 he arrived at Newport in a "barkalonga"
armed with ten guns and seventy men. The Governor
prosecuted him for piracy, but the grand jury, which
consisted of friends and neighbours of Peterson, threw
out the bill. Among other charges, Peterson was
accused of selling some hides and elephants' teeth to
a Boston merchant for £57, being part of the booty
he had previously taken out of prizes in the West
Indies.

PETERSON, Erasmus.

Tried for piracy with the rest of Captain Quelch's
crew at Boston. Was hanged there on June 30th,
1704. When standing on the gallows "He cryed of
injustice done him and said, 'It is very hard for so
many lives to be taken away for a little Gold.' He
said his peace was made with God, yet he found it
extremely hard to forgive those who had wronged
him. He told the Executioner ' he was a strong man

and Prayed to be put out of his misery as soon as possible.' "

PETERSON, John.

A Swedish pirate, one of Gow's crew. He was hanged at Wapping in June, 1725.

PETIT, Captain. French filibuster.
Of San Domingo.

In 1634 was in command of *Le Ruze,* crew of forty men and four guns.

PETTY, William.
Born at Deptford.

A sailmaker in Captain Roberts's *Royal Fortune* when the *King Solomon* was taken and plundered in West Africa. Petty, as sailmaker, had to see that all the sails and canvas aboard the prizes were removed to the pirate ship. Hanged at the age of 30.

PHELIPP, Captain William.

In 1533 a Portuguese merchant, Peter Alves, engaged Phelipp to pilot his ship, the *Santa Maria Desaie,* from Tenby to Bastabill Haven. Off the Welsh coast the ship was attacked by a pirate vessel called the *Furtuskewys,* with a crew of thirty-five pirates. Alves was put ashore on the Welsh coast, and the two ships then sailed to Cork, where the ship and her cargo were sold to the mayor for 1,524 crowns.

Alves complained to the King of England, and orders were sent to the Mayor of Cork, Richard Gowllys, to give up the ship, which he refused to do, but by way of excusing his actions he explained that he thought the ship was a Scotch one and not a Portuguese.

PHILLIPS, Captain.

In 1723 this noted pirate took a sloop, the *Dolphin*, of Cape Ann, on the Banks of Newfoundland. The crew of the *Dolphin* were compelled by Phillips to join the pirates. Amongst the prisoners was a fisherman, John Fillmore. Finding no opportunity to escape, Fillmore with another sailor, Edward Cheesman, and an Indian, suddenly seized and killed Phillips and the two other chief pirates. The rest of the crew agreeing, the ship was taken to Boston.

PHILIPS, James.
Of the Island of Antigua.

Formerly of the *Revenge*, and afterwards in the *Royal Fortune* (Captain Roberts). When the *Royal Fortune* surrendered in 1722 to H.M.S. *Swallow*, Philips seized a lighted match and attempted to blow up the ship, swearing he would " send them all to Hell together," but was prevented by the master, Glasby. Hanged at the age of 35.

PHILLIPS, John.

A carpenter by trade, he sailed from the West Country for Newfoundland in a ship that was captured by the pirate Anstis in the *Good Fortune*. Phillips soon became reconciled to the life of a pirate, and, being a brisk fellow, he was appointed carpenter to the ship. Returning to England he soon found it necessary to quit the country again, and he shipped himself on board a vessel at Topsham for Newfoundland. On arriving at Peter Harbour he ran away, and hired himself as a splitter to the Newfoundland cod fishery.

On the night of August 29th, 1723, with four others, he stole a vessel in the harbour and sailed away. Phillips was chosen captain. Articles were now drawn up and were sworn to upon a hatchet, because no Bible could be found on board. Amongst other laws was the punishment of " 40 stripes lacking one, known as Moses's law, to be afflicted for striking a fellow-pirate." The last law of the nine casts a curious light on these murderers; it runs : " If at any time you meet with a prudent Woman, that Man that offers to meddle with her, without her Consent, shall suffer present Death." The pirates, fortified by these laws, met with instant success, taking several fishing vessels, from which they augmented their small crew by the addition of several likely and brisk seamen. Amongst these they had the good fortune to take prisoner an old pirate called John Rose Archer, who had served his pirate apprenticeship under the able tuition of the famous Blackbeard, and who they at once promoted to be quartermaster. This quick promotion caused trouble afterwards, for some of the original crew, particularly carpenter Fern, resented it. The pirates next sailed to Barbadoes, that happy hunting ground, but for three months never a sail did they meet with, so that they were almost starving for want of provisions, being reduced to a pound of dried meat a day amongst ten of them.

At last they met with a French vessel, a Martinico ship, of twelve guns, and hunger drove them to attack even so big a ship as this, but the sight of the Black flag so terrified the French crew that they surrendered without firing a shot. After this, they took several vessels, and matters began to look much brighter. Phillips quickly developed into a most accomplished and bloody pirate, butchering his prisoners on very little or on no provocation whatever. But even this desperate pirate had an occasional "qualm of conscience come athwart his stomach," for when he captured a Newfoundland vessel and was about to scuttle her, he found out that she was the property of a Mr. Minors of that island, from whom they stole the original vessel in which they went a-pirating, so Phillips, telling his companions " We have done him enough injury already," ordered the vessel to be repaired and returned to the owner. On another occasion, they took a ship, the master of which was a " Saint " of New England, by name Dependance Ellery, who gave them a pretty chase before being overhauled, and so, as a punishment, the " Saint " was compelled to dance the deck until he fell down exhausted.

This pirate's career ended with a mutiny of his unruly crew, Phillips being tripped up and then thrown overboard to drown off Newfoundland in April, 1724.

During the nine months of Phillips's command as a pirate captain, he accounted for more than thirty ships.

PHILLIPS, JOSEPH.

One of Teach's crew. Hanged in Virginia in 1718.

PHILLIPS, WILLIAM.

Born at Lower Shadwell.

Boatswain in the *King Solomon,* a Guinea merchant ship. This ship, while lying at anchor in January, 1721, was attacked by a boatful of pirates from Bartholomew Roberts's ship, the *Royal Fortune.* The captain of the *King Solomon* fired a musket at the approaching boat, and called upon his crew to do the same, but Phillips called for quarter and persuaded the rest of the crew to lay down their arms and surrender the ship. Phillips eagerly joined the pirates and signed the articles, and was "very forward and brisk " in helping to rob his own ship of provisions and stores.

At his trial at Cape Coast Castle, he pleaded, as nearly all the prisoners did, that he was compelled to sign the pirates' articles, which were offered to him on a dish, on which lay a loaded pistol beside the copy of the articles.

Found guilty and hanged in April, 1722, within the flood marks at Cape Coast Castle, in his 29th year.

PHIPS, RICHARD.

An English soldier who deserted from Fort Loyal, Falmouth, Maine, in 1689. Wounded by a bullet in the head at Tarpaulin Cove. Taken to Boston Prison, where he died.

PICKERING, CAPTAIN CHARLES.

Commanded the *Cinque Ports* galley, sixteen guns, crew of sixty-three men, and accompanied Dampier on his voyage in 1703. Died off the coast of Brazil in the same year.

PIERSE, GEORGE.

Tried for piracy along with the rest of the crew of the brigantine *Charles*, at Boston, in 1704.

PITMAN, JOHN.

One of Captain Quelch's crew. Tried for piracy at Boston in 1704.

POLEAS, PEDRO. Spanish pirate.

Co-commander with Captain Johnson of a pirate sloop, the *Two Brothers*. In March, 1731, took a ship, the *John and Jane* (Edward Burt, master), south of Jamaica, on board of which was a passenger, John Cockburn, who afterwards wrote a book relating his adventures on a journey on foot of 240 miles on the mainland of America.

PORTER, CAPTAIN.

A West Indian pirate, who commanded a sloop, and, in company with a Captain Tuckerman in another sloop, came one day into Bennet's Key in Hispaniola.

The two captains were but beginners at piracy, and finding the great Bartholomew Roberts in the bay, paid him a polite visit, hoping to pick up a few wrinkles from the "master." This scene is described by Captain Johnson, in his "Lives of the Pirates," when Porter and his friend "addressed the Pyrate, as the Queen of Sheba did Solomon, to wit, That having heard of his Fame and Achievements, they had put in there to learn his Art and Wisdom in the Business of pyrating, being Vessels on the same honourable Design with himself; and hoped with the Communication of his Knowledge, they should also receive his Charity, being in want of Necessaries for such Adventures. Roberts was won upon by the Peculiarity and Bluntness of these two Men and gave them Powder, Arms, and what ever else they had Occasion for, spent two or three merry Nights with them, and at parting, said, he hoped the L—— would Prosper their handy Works."

POUND, CAPTAIN THOMAS.

On August 8th, 1689, this pirate, with five men and a boy, sailed out of Boston Harbour as passengers in a small vessel. When off Lovell's Island, five other armed men joined them. Pound now seized the craft and took command, and declared his intention of going on a piratical cruise. The first vessel they met with they decided to take. It was a fishing boat. Pound ran his craft alongside, but at the last moment his heart failed him, and he merely bought eight penn'o'th of mackerel from the surprised fishermen.

He then sailed to Falmouth, Maine, where the corporal and soldiers of the guard at the fort deserted in the night and sailed off with Pound and his crew. Fortified by this addition to his crew, the pirate attacked a sloop, the *Good Speed,* off Cape Cod, and a brigantine, the *Merrimack,* and several other prizes.

By this time, the Governor at Boston had heard of Pound's escapades, and sent an armed sloop, the *Mary*, to search for him. The pirate was discovered in Tarpaulin Cove, and a fierce and bloody fight took place before the pirates struck their " Red flagg." The prisoners were cast into Boston Gaol to await their trial. Pound had been wounded, being shot in the arm and side. The trial took place on January 13th, 1690. Pound was found guilty, but reprieved, and was sent to England, but was later on liberated. Afterwards he got command of a ship. He died in England in 1703.

POWELL, THOMAS.
   Of Connecticut, New England.

One of Captain Charles Harris's crew. Hanged at Newport, Rhode Island, on July 19th, 1723, at the age of 21.

POWER, JOHN.
   Born in the West of England.

Served in a slave vessel, the *Polly* (Captain Fox, commander), on a voyage to the coast of West Africa. While the captain was on shore, the crew ran away with the ship, turned pirates, called their vessel the *Bravo,* and elected Power to be captain and sailed to the West Indies. Arrived there, he tried to sell his cargo of slaves, but being suspected of having stolen them, he thought it best to sail to New York. Here the pirates got ashore, but the ship's surgeon informed the authorities, and Power was arrested and sent to England, where he was tried, and hanged at Execution Dock on March 10th, 1768.

PRICE, THOMAS.
   Of Bristol.

Hanged at Charleston, South Carolina, on November 8th, 1718. One of Major Stede Bonnet's crew.

PRIMER, Matthew.

One of Captain Quelch's crew. Turned King's evidence at the trial for piracy held at the Star Tavern, Boston, in June, 1704.

PRINCE, Captain Lawrence.

In 1760 this buccaneer sacked the city of Granada in company with Captains Harris and Ludbury. Late in the same year, Prince, with the rank of Lieut.-Colonel, led the vanguard in the attack on Panama.

PRO, Captain.

This Dutch South Sea pirate owned a small plantation in Madagascar, and was joined there by the pirate Williams after he had escaped from slavery. Both were taken prisoner by an English frigate. In a fight with the natives, the pirate crew was defeated, but Pro and Williams managed to escape and to reach some friendly natives. Procuring a boat, they sailed away to join some other pirates at Methulage in Madagascar.

PROWSE, Captain Lawrence.

A Devon man, a noted sea captain, and a terror to the Spaniards. Was imprisoned by King James I. at the instance of the King of Spain for piracy and was to have been executed, but English public feeling ran so high that Prowse was discharged.

PULLING, Captain John.

Commanded the *Fame*, which set out in 1703 in company with Dampier in the *St. George* on a plundering expedition to the South Seas. Their commissions were to attack only Spanish and French

ships. The two captains quarrelled at the very beginning of the voyage, while lying off the Downs, and
Pulling slipped away by himself to go a-pirating
amongst the Canary Islands.

PURSSER, Captain.

In the sixteenth century this pirate became notorious
for his piracies off the coast of Wales, and with Calles
and Clinton, two other pirates, "grew famous, till
Queene Elizabeth of blessed memory, hanged them at
Wapping."

QUELCH, Captain John.
A native of Massachusetts Colony.

In 1703 was one of the crew of the brigantine
Charles, eighty tons, owned by some leading citizens
of Boston, and fitted out to go privateering off the
coasts of Arcadia and Newfoundland. On leaving
Marblehead the crew mutinied, locked the captain in
his cabin, and elected Quelch their commander. They
sailed to the south, and shortly afterwards threw the
captain overboard. They hoisted a flag, the "Old
Roger," described as having "in the middle of it an
Anatomy with an Hourglars in one hand and a dart
in the Heart with three drops of Blood proceeding from
it in the other." They took nine Portuguese vessels
off the coast of Brazil, out of which they took plunder
of very great value.

Quelch now had the audacity to sail back to Marblehead, where his crew landed and quickly scattered
with their plunder. Within a week Quelch was in
gaol, and was taken to Boston, where his trial began
on June 17th, 1704, and he was found guilty. The
days between the sentence and the execution must have,
indeed, been trying for the prisoner. We read in a
pamphlet published at the time: "The Ministers of

the Town used more than ordinary Endeavours to Instruct the Prisoners and bring them to Repentance. There were Sermons Preached in their hearing Every Day, and Prayer daily made with them. And they were Catechised, and they had many occasional Exhortations. And nothing was left that could be done for their Good."

On Friday, June 30th, 1704, Quelch and his companions marched on foot through the town of Boston to Scarlil's Wharf with a strong armed guard of musketeers, accompanied by various officials and two ministers, while in front was carried a silver oar, the emblem of a pirate's execution. Before the last act the minister gave a long and fervent harangue to the wretched culprits, in all of whom were observed suitable signs of repentance except Quelch, who, stepping forward on the platform, his hat in his hand, and bowing left and right to the spectators, gave a short address, in which he warned them "They should take care how they brought Money into New England to be Hanged for it."

QUITTANCE, John.

One of Captain Quelch's crew of the brigantine *Charles*. Tried with the rest of that crew at the Star Tavern at Boston in June, 1704.

RACKAM, Captain John, *alias* Calico Jack.

Served as quartermaster in Captain Vane's company. On one occasion Vane refused to fight a big French ship, and in consequence was dismissed his ship and marooned on an uninhabited island off the coast of America, while the crew elected Rackam to be their captain in his place. This was on November 24th, 1718, and on the very first day of his command he had the good fortune to take and plunder several small vessels.

Off the Island of Jamaica they took a Madeira ship, and found an old friend on board as a passenger—a Mr. Hosea Tisdell, who kept a tavern in the island, and they treated him with great respect.

Christmas Day coming, the pirates landed on a small island to celebrate this festival in a thorough manner, carousing and drinking as long as the liquor lasted, when they sailed away to seek more. Their next prize was a strange one. On coming alongside a ship, she surrendered, and the pirates boarding her to examine her cargo, found it to consist of thieves from Newgate on their way to the plantations. Taking two more vessels, Rackam sailed to the Bahama Islands, but the Governor, Captain Woodes Rogers, sent a sloop, which took away their prizes.

Rackam now sailed his ship to a snug little cove he knew of in Cuba, where he had more than one lady acquaintance. Here the pirates were very happy until all their provisions and money was spent. Just as they were about to sail, in comes a Spanish Guarda del Costa with a small English sloop which they had recently taken. Rackam was now in a very awkward position, being unable to get past the Spaniard, and all he could do was to hide behind a small island. Night came on, and when it was dark Rackam put all his crew into a boat, rowed quietly up to the sloop, clambered aboard, threatening instant death to the Spanish guards if they cried out, then cut the cables and sailed out of the bay. As soon as it was light the Spanish ship commenced a furious bombardment of Rackam's empty vessel, thinking he was still aboard her.

In the summer of 1720 he took numbers of small vessels and fishing boats, but nothing very rich, and was not above stealing the fishermen's nets and landing and taking cattle. In October Rackam was chased near Nigril Bay by a Government sloop com-

manded by a Captain Barret. After a short fight
Rackam surrendered, and was carried a prisoner to
Port Royal.

On November 16th Rackam and his crew were
tried at St. Jago de la Vega, convicted and sentenced
to death. Amongst the crew were two women dressed
as men, Anne Bonny and Mary Read. The former
was married, in pirate fashion, to Rackam.

On the morning of his execution Rackam was
allowed, as a special favour, to visit his Anne, but all
the comfort he got from her was " that she was sorry
to see him there, but if he had fought like a man, he
need not have been hanged like a Dog."

Rackam was hanged on November 17th, 1720, at
Gallows Point, at Port Royal, Jamaica.

RAPHAELINA, CAPTAIN.

Much dreaded by the merchant sailors navigating
the South Atlantic. In 1822 he controlled a fleet of
pirate vessels in the vicinity of Cape Antonio.

RAYNER, CAPTAIN.

In a letter to the Lords of Trade, dated from Philadelphia, February 28th, 1701, William Penn mentions
that several of Captain Kidd's men had settled as
planters in Carolina with Rayner as their captain.

RAYNOR, WILLIAM.

One of Captain John Quelch's crew. Tried at
Boston in 1704.

READ, CAPTAIN.

Commanded a brigantine which had its headquarters at Madagascar. Rescued the pirate Thomas
White. Read died at sea.

READ, MARY. Woman pirate.

Born in London of obscure parentage; all that is known for certain is that her mother was a "young and airy widow." Mary was brought up as a boy, and at the age of 13 was engaged as a footboy to wait on a French lady. Having a roving spirit, Mary ran away and entered herself on board a man-of-war. Deserting a few years later, she enlisted in a regiment of foot and fought in Flanders, showing on all occasions great bravery, but quitted the service to enlist in a regiment of horse. Her particular comrade in this regiment was a Fleming, with whom she fell in love and disclosed to him the secret of her sex. She now dressed as a woman, and the two troopers were married, "which made a great noise," and several of her officers attended the nuptials. She and her husband got their discharge and kept an eating house or ordinary, the Three Horseshoes, near the Castle of Breda. The husband died, and Mary once again donned male attire and enlisted in a regiment in Holland. Soon tiring of this, she deserted, and shipped herself aboard a vessel bound for the West Indies. This ship was taken by an English pirate, Captain Rackam, and Mary joined his crew as a seaman.

She was at New Providence Island, Bahama, when Woodes Rogers came there with the royal pardon to all pirates, and she shipped herself aboard a privateer sent out by Rogers to cruise against the Spaniards. The crew mutinied and again became pirates. She now sailed under Captain Rackam, who had with him another woman pirate, Anne Bonny. They took a large number of ships belonging to Jamaica, and out of one of these took prisoner "a young fellow of engaging behaviour" with whom Mary fell deeply in love. This young fellow had a quarrel with one of the pirates, and as the ship lay at anchor they were to go to fight it out on shore according to pirate law. Mary, to save her lover, picked a quarrel with the same pirate, and managed to have her duel at once, and fighting with sword and pistol killed him on the spot.

She now married the young man "of engaging behaviour," and not long after was taken prisoner with Captain Rackam and the rest of the crew to Jamaica. She was tried at St. Jago de la Vega in Jamaica, and on November 28th, 1720, was convicted, but died in prison soon after of a violent fever.

That Mary Read was a woman of great spirit is shown by her reply to Captain Rackam, who had asked her (thinking she was a young man) what pleasure she could find in a life continually in danger of death by fire, sword, or else by hanging; to which Mary replied "that as to hanging, she thought it no great Hardship, for were it not for that, every cowardly Fellow would turn Pirate and so unfit the Seas, that Men of Courage must starve."

READ, ROBERT.

Tried for piracy with Gow's crew at Newgate in 1725, and acquitted.

READ, WILLIAM.
Of Londonderry, Ireland.

One of Captain Harris's crew. Was hanged at Newport, Rhode Island, in 1723, at the age of 35.

READHEAD, PHILIP.

One of Captain Heidon's crew of the pirate ship *John of Sandwich*, wrecked on Alderney Island in 1564. Was arrested and hanged at St. Martin's Point, Guernsey, in the same year.

ANN BONNY AND MARY READ, CONVICTED OF PIRACY, NOVEMBER 28, 1720, AT A COURT OF
VICE-ADMIRALTY HELD AT ST. JAGO DE LA VEGA IN THE ISLAND OF JAMAICA.

To face p. 256.

RHOADE, CAPTAIN JOHN.

A Dutch coasting pilot of Boston.

In 1674 appointed chief pilot to the Curacao privateer *Flying Horse,* and sailed along the coast of Maine and as far north as the St. John River. Afterwards attacked and plundered several small English craft occupied in bartering furs with the Indians. Condemned to be hanged at Cambridge, Massachusetts, in June, 1675.

RICE, DAVID. Welsh pirate.

Of Bristol.

Taken out of the *Cornwall* galley by Captain Roberts, he served in the *Royal Fortune.* Tried and found guilty of piracy and condemned to death, but was reprieved and sold to the Royal African Company to serve for seven years in their plantations.

RICE, OWEN. Welsh pirate.

Of South Wales.

Hanged at the age of 27 at Rhode Island in 1723. One of Captain Charles Harris's crew.

RICHARDS, LIEUTENANT.

Lieutenant to Blackbeard on board the *Queen Ann's Revenge.* Cruised in the West Indies and along the coast of Carolina and Virginia.

In 1717 Teach blockaded the harbour at Charleston and sent Richards with a party of pirates to the Governor to demand a medicine chest and all necessary medical supplies, with a threat that if these were not forthcoming he would cut the throats of all his prisoners, many of them the leading merchants of the town. While waiting for the Governor's reply, Richards and his companions scandalized the townsfolk of Charleston by their outrageous and swaggering conduct.

RICHARDSON, JOHN.

His father was a goldsmith at New York. John, tiring of the trade of cooper, to which he was apprenticed, ran away to sea. For many years he served both in men-of-war and in merchant ships. Although an unmitigated blackguard, he did not commit piracy nor murder until some years later, when, being at Ancona, he met a Captain Benjamin Hartley, who had come there with a loading of pilchards. Richardson was taken on board to serve as ship's carpenter, and sailed for Leghorn. With another sailor called Coyle, Richardson concocted a mutiny, murdered the captain in the most brutal manner, and was appointed mate in the pirate ship. As a pirate Richardson was beneath contempt. His life ended on the gallows at Execution Dock on January 25th, 1738.

RICHARDSON, NICHOLAS.

One of Captain Quelch's crew. Taken out of the brigantine *Charles,* and tried for piracy at Boston in 1704.

RIDGE, JOHN.
Of London.

One of Major Stede Bonnet's crew. Hanged in 1718 at Charleston, South Carolina.

RINGROSE, BASIL. Buccaneer, pirate, and author.

Sailed in 1679 to the West Indies. A year later Ringrose had joined the buccaneers at their rendezvous in the Gulf of Darien, where they were preparing for a bold enterprise on the Spanish Main. They landed and marched to the town of Santa Maria,

which they plundered and burnt.   Thence they
travelled in canoes down the river to the Bay of
Panama.   After attacking the Spanish fleet and
laying siege to the city, the buccaneers cruised up
and down the West Coast of South America for
eighteen months, sacking towns and attacking
Spanish ships.   All this while Ringrose kept a very
full and graphic journal, in which he recorded not
only their exploits, but also their hardships and
quarrels, and gave descriptions as well of the various
natives and their customs, and drew charts and
sketches.

In 1681 Ringrose was still with Captain Sharp, and
sailed through the Straits of Magellan, and on January 30th of the same year anchored off Antigua.   Here
he got a passage in a ship to England, landing safely
at Dartmouth on March 26th.

A year later he published an account of his voyage,
as a second volume to Esquemeling's, " Bucaniers of
America."   In 1684 he went to sea again in the
Cygnet (Captain Swan), to traffic with the Spanish
colonies.   But the Spaniards refused to trade with
them.   In October, 1684, they met the famous Captain Edward Davis at that favourite haunt of the
buccaneers, the Isle of Plate.   The two captains
agreed to join forces and to go together "on the
account," so all the cargo was thrown overboard the
Cygnet, and the ships set out to make war on any
Spanish ships they might meet with.

In February, 1686, Ringrose with one hundred men
took the town of Santiago in Mexico, but while returning with the plunder to their ship were caught by
the Spaniards in an ambush, and Ringrose was killed.

Ringrose never attained any rank among the
buccaneers beyond occasionally being put in charge of
a boat or a small company on shore, but as a recorder
of the doings of his companions he proved both care-

ful and painstaking. Dampier had a great regard for
him, and in his book he writes: " My ingenious
friend Ringrose had no mind to this voyage, but was
necessitated to engage in it or starve."

The title of Ringrose's book, first published in
1685, is " The Dangerous Voyage and Bold Assaults
of Captain Bartholomew Sharp and Others."

Written by Mr. Basil Ringrose.

Printed for William Crooke, 1685.

ROACH, PETER.

When Captain Quelch was captured with his crew,
Roach escaped near the Cape by Snake Island. He
was afterwards captured and thrown into the gaol at
Salem. Tried for piracy at the Star Tavern at
Boston, and on June 30th, 1704, was hanged. At the
place of execution Roach disappointed the onlooking
crowd, as, instead of the expected and hoped-for re-
pentant speech, " he seemed little concerned, and said
but little or nothing at all."

ROB, ALEXANDER.

One of Captain Gow's crew. Hanged at Execution
Dock, Wapping, in June, 1724. He was not one of
the original crew of the *George* galley, but was taken
out of a prize and joined the pirates of his own free-
will.

ROBBINS, JAMES.

Hanged in Virginia in 1718 along with the rest of
Captain Teach's crew.

ROBBINS, JAMES.
Of London.

One of the crew of the *Royal James*. Hanged in
1718 at Charleston, South Carolina.

ROBERTS, Captain Bartholomew. Welsh pirate.
  Born 1682. Died 1722.

If a pirate is to be reckoned by the amount of
damage he does and the number of ships he takes
there can be no doubt that Captain Roberts should
be placed at the very head of his profession, for he is
said to have taken over 400 vessels. The only man
who can be said to rival him is Sir Henry Morgan,
but Morgan, although in some ways an unmitigated
blackguard, was a man of much greater breadth of
outlook than Roberts ever was, and, moreover, was a
buccaneer rather than a pirate.

Roberts, like many other successful pirates, was
born in Wales, not far from Haverfordwest. He
is described as being "a tall black man," and was
about 40 years of age at the time of his death. He
was remarkable, even among his remarkable companions, for several things. First of all, he only
drank tea—thus being the only total abstainer known
to the fraternity. Also he was a strict disciplinarian,
and on board his ships all lights had to be extinguished
by 8 p.m., any of the crew who wished to continue
drinking after that hour had to do so on the open
deck. But try as he would this ardent apostle of ab-
stemiousness was unable to put down drinking. If
Roberts had lived to-day, no doubt he would have
been on the council of the local vigilance committee.
He would allow no women aboard his ships, in fact
he made it a law that any man who brought a woman
on board disguised as a man was to suffer death.
Roberts allowed no games at cards or dice to be
played for money, as he strongly disapproved of
gambling. He was a strict Sabbatarian, and allowed
the musicians to have a rest on the seventh day. This
was as well, for the post of musician on a pirate ship
was no sinecure, as every pirate had the right to
demand a tune at any hour of the day or night. He

used to place a guard to protect all his women
prisoners, and it is sadly suspicious that there was
always the greatest competition amongst the worst
characters in the ship to be appointed sentinel over a
good-looking woman prisoner. All quarrels had to
be settled on shore, pirate fashion, the duellists
standing back to back armed with pistol and cutlass.
Roberts would have no fighting among the crew on
board his ship.

Bartholomew must have looked the very part of a
pirate when dressed for action. A tall, dark man, he
used to wear a rich damask waistcoat and breeches, a
red feather in his cap, a gold chain round his neck
with a large diamond cross dangling from it, a sword
in his hand, and two pairs of pistols hanging at the
end of a silk sling flung over his shoulders.

We first hear of Roberts as sailing, in honest
employ, as master of the *Princess* (Captain Plumb),
from London in November, 1719, bound for the coast
of Guinea to pick up a cargo of " black ivory " at
Anamaboe. Here his ship was taken by the Welsh
pirate Howel Davis. At first Roberts was disinclined
for the pirate life, but soon changed his mind.

On the death of Davis there were several candidates
for the post of commander, all brisk and lively men,
distinguished by the title of " Lords," such as Sympson, Ashplant, Anstis, and others. One of these
" Lords," Dennis, concluded an eloquent harangue
over a bowl of punch with a strong appeal for Roberts
to be the new chief. This proposal was acclaimed
with but one dissenting voice, that of " Lord " Sympson, who had hopes of being elected himself, and who
sullenly left the meeting swearing " he did not care
who they chose captain so it was not a papist." So
Roberts was elected after being a pirate only six
weeks; thus was true merit quickly appreciated and
rewarded amongst them.

CAPTAIN BARTHOLOMEW ROBERTS.

To face p. 262.

Roberts's speech to his fellow-pirates was short but to the point, saying "that since he had dipped his hands in muddy water, and must be a pyrate, it was better being a commander than a common man," not perhaps a graceful nor grateful way of expressing his thanks, but one which was no doubt understood by his audience.

Roberts began his career in a bright manner, for to revenge the perfectly justifiable death of their late captain he seized and razed the fort, bombarded the town, and setting on fire two Portuguese ships so as to act as torches, sailed away the same night. Sailing to Brazil they found in the Bay of Bahia a fleet of forty-two Portuguese ships ready laden and on the point of leaving for Lisbon, and Roberts, with the most astounding boldness, sailed right in amongst them until he found the deepest laden, which he attacked and boarded, although his was a much smaller ship. He sailed away with his prize from the harbour. This prize, amongst the merchandise, contained 40,000 moidors and a cross of diamonds designed for the King of Portugal.

He then took a Dutch ship, and two days later an English one, and sailed back to Brazil, refitting and cleaning at the Island of Ferdinando.

In a work such as this is, it is impossible to recount all, or even a few, of the daring adventures, or the piratical ups and downs of one pirate. Roberts sailed to the West Indies devastating the commerce of Jamaica and Barbadoes. When things grew too hot there, he went north to Newfoundland, and played the very devil with the English and French fishing fleets and settlements.

His first ship he called the *Fortune*, his next, a bigger ship, the *Royal Fortune*, another the *Good Fortune*.

On two occasions Roberts had been very roughly

handled, once by a ship from Barbadoes and once by
the inhabitants of Martinica, so when he designed his
new flag, he portrayed on it a huge figure of himself
standing sword in hand upon two skulls, and under
these were the letters A.B.H. and A.M.H., signi-
fying a Barbadian's and a Martinican's head.

In April, 1721, Roberts was back again on the
Guinea Coast, burning and plundering. Amongst
the prisoners he took out of one of his prizes was a
clergyman. The captain dearly wished to have a
chaplain on board his ship to administer to the
spiritual welfare of his crew, and tried all he could to
persuade the parson to sign on, promising him that
his only duties should be to say prayers and make
punch. But the prelate begged to be excused, and was
at length allowed to go with all his belongings, except
three prayer-books and a corkscrew—articles which
were sorely needed aboard the *Royal Fortune*.

The end of Roberts's career was now in sight. A
King's ship, the *Swallow* (Captain Chaloner Ogle),
discovered Roberts's ships at Parrot Island, and, pretending to fly from them, was followed out to sea by
one of the pirates. A fight took place, and after two
hours the pirates struck, flinging overboard their
black flag "that it might not rise in Judgement over
them." The *Swallow* returned in a few days to
Parrot Island to look for Roberts in the *Royal
Fortune*. Roberts being at breakfast, enjoying a
savoury dish of solomongundy, was informed of the
approach of the ship, but refused to take any notice of
it. At last, thoroughly alarmed, he cut his cables and
sailed out, but most of his crew being drunk, even at
this early hour, the pirates did not make as good a
resistance as if they had been sober. Early in the
engagement Roberts was hit in the throat by a
grape-shot and killed; this being on February 10th,
1722. His body, fully dressed, with his arms and

ornaments, was thrown overboard according to his repeated request made during his lifetime. Thus the arch-pirate died, as he always said he wished to die, fighting. His motto had always been " A short life and a merry one." One good word can be said for Roberts, that he never forced a man to become a pirate against his wish.

ROBERTS, OWEN. Welsh pirate.

Carpenter in the *Queen Ann's Revenge,* and killed on November 22nd, 1718, off the North Carolina Coast.

ROBINSON, EDWARD.
Of Newcastle-upon-Tyne.
Hanged at Charleston, South Carolina, in 1718.

ROCHE, CAPTAIN PHILIP, *alias* JOHN EUSTACE.

In company with three other mariners—Cullen, Wife, and Neale—this Irish pirate shipped himself on board a French snow at Cork in November, 1721, for a passage to Nantes. Owing to Roche's briskness, genteel manners, and knowledge of navigation, the master used occasionally to place him in charge of the vessel. One night a few days out a pre-arranged mutiny took place, the French crew being butchered and thrown overboard. The captain, who pleaded for mercy, was also thrown into the sea. Driven by bad weather to Dartmouth, the new captain, Roche, had the ship repainted and disguised, and renamed her the *Mary.* Then sailing to Rotterdam he sold the cargo of beef and took on a fresh cargo with the owner, Mr. Annesly. The first night out of port they threw Mr. Annesly overboard, and he swam alongside for some while pleading to be taken in. On going into a French port, and hearing that an enquiry was being made about his ship, Roche ran away. The crew took the ship to Scotland, and there landed and disappeared, and the ship was seized and taken to the Thames.

Later on Roche was arrested in London and committed to Newgate Prison, found guilty of piracy, and hanged on August 5th, 1723, at Execution Dock, at the age of 30. The hanging was not, from the public spectators point of view, a complete success, for the culprit " was so ill at the time that he could not make any public declaration of his abhorrence of the crime for which he suffered."

RODERIGO, Peter.

A " Flanderkin."

Commanded a Dutch vessel, the *Edward and Thomas,* that sailed from Boston in 1674, and took several small English vessels along the coast of Maine. Tried for piracy at Cambridge, Massachusetts, and condemned to be hanged, but was afterwards pardoned.

ROGERS, Captain Thomas.

Commanded a ship, the *Forlorn.* Routed the Spaniards at Venta Cruz in 1671. One of Morgan's captains in his attack on Panama.

ROGERS, Captain Woodes.

As the life of this famous navigator and privateer is, very justly, treated fully in the "Dictionary of National Biography " it is unnecessary to mention more than a few incidents in his adventurous career. Woodes Rogers was not only a good navigator, for on many occasions he showed a remarkable gift for commanding mutinous crews in spite of having many

officers on whom he could place little reliance. On
leaving Cork in 1708, after an incompetent pilot had
almost run his ship on two rocks off Kinsale called
" The Sovereigne's Bollacks," Rogers describes his
crew thus : " A third were foreigners, while of Her
Majestie's subjects many were taylors, tinkers, pedlars, fiddlers, and hay-makers, with ten boys and one
negro." It was with crews such as these that many of
the boldest and most remarkable early voyages were
made, and they required a man of Woodes Rogers
stamp to knock them into sailors. Rogers had a gift
for inspiring friendship wherever he went. On
arriving at the coast of Brazil, his boat was fired on
when trying to land at Angre de Reys. This settlement had but lately received several hostile visitors in
the way of French pirates. But before a week was
passed Woodes Rogers had so won the hearts of the
Portuguese Governor and the settlers that he and his
" musick " were invited to take part in an important
religious function, or " entertainment," as Rogers
calls it, " where," he says, " we waited on the
Governour, Signior Raphael de Silva Lagos, in a
body, being ten of us, with two trumpets and a
hautboy, which he desir'd might play us to church,
where our musick did the office of an organ, but
separate from the singing, which was by the fathers
well perform'd. Our musick played ' Hey, boys, up
go we !' and all manner of noisy paltry tunes. And
after service, our musicians, who were by that time
more than half drunk, march'd at the head of the company ; next to them an old father and two fryars carrying lamps of incense, then an image dressed with
flowers and wax candles, then about forty priests,
fryars, etc., followed by the Governor of the town,
myself, and Capt. Courtney, with each of us a long
wax candle lighted. The ceremony held about two
hours ; after which we were splendidly entertained by

the fathers of the Convent, and then by the Governour.
They unanimously told us they expected nothing from
us but our Company, and they had no more but our
musick.''

What a delightful picture this calls to the mind—
the little Brazilian town, the tropical foliage, the Holy
Procession, " wax figure '' and priests, followed by
the Governor with an English buccaneer on either
side, and headed by a crew of drunken Protestant
English sailors playing " Hey, boys, up go we !''

Rogers, not to be outdone in hospitality, next day
entertained the Governor and fathers on board the
Duke, " when,'' he says, " they were very merry,
and in their cups propos'd the Pope's health to us.
But we were quits with 'em by toasting the Arch-
bishop of Canterbury ; and to keep up the humour, we
also proposed William Pen's health, and they liked
the liquor so well, that they refused neither.'' Alas !
the good Governor and the fathers were not in a fit
state to leave the ship when the end came to the entertainment, so slept on board, being put ashore in the
morning, " when we saluted 'em with a huzza from
each ship, because,'' as Rogers says, " we were not
overstocked with powder.''

It was in March, 1710, that Rogers brought his
little fleet into the harbour of Guam, one of the
Ladrone Islands. Although at war with Spain, the
captain soon became on his usual friendly terms with
the Governor of this Spanish colony, and gave an
entertainment on board his ship to him and four other
Spanish gentlemen, making them " as welcome as
time and place would afford, with musick and our
sailors dancing.'' The Governor gave a return party
on shore, to which Rogers and all his brother officers
were invited, partaking of " sixty dishes of various
sorts.'' After this feast Rogers gave his host a

present, consisting of "two negro boys dress'd in liveries." One other instance of Woodes Rogers adaptability must suffice. In the year 1717 he was appointed Governor to the Bahama Islands, at New Providence, now called Nassau. His chief duty was to stamp out the West India pirates who had made this island their headquarters for many years, and were in complete power there, and numbered more than 2,000 desperadoes, including such famous men as Vane and Teach. Rogers's only weapon, besides the man-of-war he arrived in, was a royal proclamation from King George offering free pardon to all pirates or buccaneers who would surrender at once to the new Governor. At first the pirates were inclined to resist his landing, but in the end the tactful Rogers got his own way, and not only landed, but was received by an armed guard of honour, and passed between two lines of pirates who fired salutes with their muskets.

Most of the pirates surrendered and received their pardons, but some, who reverted shortly afterwards to piracy and were captured and brought back to New Providence, were tried and actually hanged by Rogers's late buccaneer subjects.

Woodes Rogers eventually died in Nassau in the year 1729.

He was the author of a delightful book entitled " A Cruising Voyage Round the World, begun in 1708 and finish'd in 1711, by Captain Woodes Rogers, Commander-in-Chief on this Expedition, with the ships *Duke* and *Duchess* of Bristol."

This was published in London in 1712.

ROLLSON, PETER.

Captain Gow's gunner in the *Revenge*. Hanged at Execution Dock, Wapping, in June, 1725.

ROSS, George, or Rose.
  Of Glasgow.

One of Major Stede Bonnet's crew of the *Royal James*. Was hanged at Charleston, South Carolina, on November 8th, 1718, and buried in the marsh below low-water mark.

ROSSOE, Francis.

In June, 1717, in company with four other Carolina pirates, was placed on trial for his life. Convicted with De Cossey, De Mont, and Ernandos, of piratically taking the vessels the *Turtle Dove*, the *Penelope*, and the *Virgin Queen* in July of the previous year, and, after being sentenced to death by Judge Trott, Rossoe and his fellow-pirates were promptly executed.

ROUNDSIVEL, Captain George.
  Of the Bahama Islands.

He refused to avail himself of King George's pardon to all pirates in 1717, and went off again on the " main chance " till captured.

ROW, Captain. Buccaneer.

In 1679, at the Boca del Toro, was with the buccaneer fleet that attacked and sacked Santa Maria. Row commanded a small vessel of twenty tons, a crew of twenty-five men, and no guns.

RUIZ.

One of Captain Gilbert's crew in the pirate schooner *Panda*, which plundered the Salem brig *Mexican* in 1834. Tried in Boston and condemned to be hanged. Pleading insanity, he was respited for sixty days and then hanged on September 12th, 1835.

RUPERT. Prince of the Rhine.

After an adventurous life as a soldier on the Continent, he sailed from Ireland in 1648 with seven ships. His own ship was the *Swallow*. He was a man of boundless energy, who was never happy if not engaged in some enterprise, and as legitimate warfare gave him few opportunities he turned pirate. He spent five years at sea, largely in the West Indies, meeting with every kind of adventure.

In 1653 he was caught in a storm in the Virgin Islands, and his fleet was wrecked. His brother, Prince Maurice, was lost with his ship, the *Defiance*, the only ship saved being the *Swallow*. Prince Rupert returned in the *Swallow* to France in the same year. Hitherto the prince had been a restless, clever man, " very sparkish in his dress," but this catastrophe to his fleet and the loss of his brother broke his spirit, and he retired to England, where he died in his bed in 1682 at Spring Gardens.

LE SAGE, CAPTAIN. French filibuster.

In 1684 was at San Domingo, in command ot the *Tigre*, carrying thirty guns and a crew of 130 men.

SALTER, EDWARD.

Hanged in Virginia in 1718 with the rest of Captain Teach's crew.

SAMPLE, CAPTAIN RICHARD. Buccaneer.

Was at New Providence Island in 1718, and received the royal pardon from King George, offered to those pirates who surrendered themselves to Governor Woodes Rogers. Like many another, he fell again into his former wicked ways, and ended his life by being hanged.

SAMPLE, Captain Robert.

One of England's crew in the *Royal James*. In 1720 they took a prize, the *Elizabeth and Katherine*, off the coast of West Africa. Fitting her out for a pirate, they named her the *Flying King*, and Sample was put in command. In company with Captain Low, he sailed to Brazil and did much mischief amongst the Portuguese shipping. In November of the same year the two pirate ships were attacked by a very powerful man-of-war. Lane got away, but Sample was compelled to run his ship ashore on the coast. Of his crew of seventy men, twelve were killed and the rest taken prisoners, of whom the Portuguese hanged thirty-eight. Of these, thirty-two were English, three Dutch, two French, and one Portuguese.

SANDERS, Thomas.

An Elizabethan mariner who was taken prisoner by the Moors. He wrote a narrative of his life as a slave on a Barbary pirate galley.

"I and six more of my fellowes," he wrote, "together with four-score Italians and Spaniards, were sent foorth in a Galeot to take a Greekish Carmosell, which came into Africa to steale Negroes. We were chained three and three to an oare, and we rowed naked above the girdle, and the Boteswaine of the Galley walked abaft the masts, and his Mate afore the maste . . . and when their develish choller rose, they would strike the Christians for no cause. And they allowed us but halfe a pound of bread a man in a day without any other kind of sustenance, water excepted. . . . We were then so cruelly manackled in such sort, that we could not put our hands the length of one foote asunder the one from the other, and every night they searched our chains three times, to see if they were fast riveted."

SAWKINS, Captain Richard. Buccaneer.

We know little of the early career of this remarkable buccaneer. He was loved by his crew, and had
great influence over them. It is recorded that one
Sunday morning, finding some of his men gambling,
he threw the dice overboard, saying " he would have
no gambling aboard his ship."

We know that on one occasion he was caught in his
vessel by H.M.S. *Success* and brought to Port Royal,
Jamaica, and that on December 1st, 1679, he was in
prison awaiting trial for piracy. Apparently he got
off, for this brilliant young buccaneer is soon afterwards heard of as commanding a small vessel of
sixteen tons, armed with but one gun and a crew of
thirty-five men. He was one of a party of 330 buccaneers who, under the leadership of Coxon and
Sharp, landed on the coast of Darien and marched
through the jungle to attack and plunder the town of
Santa Maria. The remainder of the journey across
the isthmus was done in canoes, in which the pirates
travelled down the Santa Maria River until they found
themselves in the Pacific. On this expedition each
captain had his company and had his own colours,
Sawkins's flag being a red one with yellow stripes.
Arrived at the sea, they captured two small Spanish
vessels, and, the rest of the company being in the
canoes, they boldly sailed towards Panama City.
Meeting with the Spanish fleet of eight ships, the
buccaneers attacked it, and, after a most furious
battle, came off victorious. This was one of the most
gallant episodes in the whole history of the " brethren
of the coast," and was afterwards known as the Battle
of Perico. Sawkins fought in the most brave and
desperate manner, and took a large share in the successful enterprise. After this action some quarrelling
took place, which ended by Captain Coxon going off
with some seventy men, to return across the isthmus

on foot. The company that remained in the Pacific
elected Sawkins to be their leader, as Captain Sharp,
a much older man, was away in his ship.

The buccaneers, ever since they defeated the
Spanish fleet, had blockaded the harbour, and a
correspondence took place between the Governor of
Panama and Sawkins, the former wishing to know
what the pirates had come there for. To this message
Sawkins sent back answer "that we came to assist
the King of Darien, who was the true Lord of Panama
and all the country thereabouts. And that since we
were come so far, there was no reason but that we
should have some satisfaction. So that if he pleased
to send us five hundred pieces of eight for each man,
and one thousand for each commander, and not any
farther to annoy the Indians, but suffer them to use
their own power and liberty, as became the true and
natural lords of the country, that then we would desist
from all further hostilities, and go away peaceably;
otherwise that we should stay there, and get what we
could, causing to them what damage was possible."

This message was just bluff on Sawkins's part, but
having heard that the Bishop of Santa Martha was in
the city, Sawkins sent him two loaves of sugar as a
present, and reminded the prelate that he had been
his prisoner five years before, when Sawkins took
that town. Further messengers returned from Panama
next day, bringing a gold ring for Sawkins from
the well-disposed Bishop, and a message from the
Governor, in which he inquired "from whom we had
our commission and to whom he ought to complain
for the damage we had already done them?" To this
Sawkins sent back answer "that as yet all his company were not come together; but that when they
were come up we would come and visit him at
Panama, and bring our commissions on the muzzles
of our guns, at which time he should read them

as plain as the flame of gunpowder could make them."

After lying off Panama for some while without meeting with any plunder, and their victuals running short, the crews began to grumble, and persuaded Sawkins to sail south along the coast. This he did, and, arriving off the town of Puebla Nueva on May 22nd, 1679, Sawkins landed a party of sixty men and led them against the town. But the Spaniards had been warned in time, and had built up three strong breastworks.

Sawkins, who never knew what fear meant, stormed the town at the head of his men, but was killed by a musket-ball.

Basil Ringrose, the buccaneer who wrote the narrative of this voyage, describes Sawkins as being " a man who was as valiant and courageous as any man could be, and the best beloved of all our company "; and on another occasion he speaks of him as " a man whom nothing on earth could terrifie."

SAWNEY, Captain.

A pirate of New Providence Island in the Bahamas. In this pirate republic this old man lived in the best hut, and was playfully known as " Governor Sawney."

de SAYAS, Francisco.

A Spanish pirate hanged at Kingston, Jamaica, in 1823.

SCOT, Lewis.

Distinguished as being the first pirate to carry on the trade on land as well as at sea. Before this time pirates were never known to be anything but harmless drunkards when on shore, whatever they might be on board their ships. Scot changed all this when he sacked and pillaged the city of Campeachy. So successful was he that his example was quickly followed by Mansfield, John Davis, and other pirates.

SCOT, ROGER.
Born at Bristol.

One of Captain Roberts's crew. Tried for piracy in April, 1722, at Cape Coast Castle, West Africa, after the great defeat of the pirates by H.M.S. *Swallow*. On this occasion no less than 267 pirates were accounted for. The finding of the Honourable the President and Judges of the Court of Admiralty for trying of pirates was as follows :

Acquitted - - - - -	74
Executed - - - - -	52
Respited - - - - -	2
To Servitude - - -	20
To the Marshallsea - -	17 for tryal

The rest were accounted for as follows :

Killed { In the *Ranger* -	-	10
In the *Fortune* -	-	3
Dy'd { In the passage to Cape Corso		15
Afterwards in the castle	-	4
Negroes in both ships -	-	70
		267

A number of the prisoners signed a " humble petition " begging that, as they, being " unhappily and unwisely drawn into that wretched and detestable Crime of Piracy," they might be permitted to serve in the Royal African Company in the country for seven years, in remission of their crimes. This clemency was granted to twenty of the prisoners, of which Scot was one.

A very impressive indenture was drawn up, according to which the prisoners were to become the slaves of the Company for seven years, and this was signed by the prisoners and by the President.

SCOTT, WILLIAM.

One of Major Stede Bonnet's crew in the *Royal James*. Tried for piracy in 1718 at Charleston, South Carolina, and hanged at White Point on November 8th.

SCUDAMORE, CHRISTOPHER.

One of Captain John Quelch's crew. Tried for piracy at the Star Tavern in Hanover Street, Boston, in 1704, and hanged on Charles River, Boston Side, on June 30th. A report of the trial and execution of these pirates, describing Scudamore's conduct on the gallows, says : " He appeared very Penitent since his Condemnation, was very diligent to improve his time going to, and at the place of Execution."

SCUDAMORE, PETER.
Belonging to Bristol.

Surgeon in the *Mercy* galley, and taken by Captain Roberts in 1721. It was a rule on all pirate vessels for the surgeon to be excused from signing the ship's articles. When the next prize was taken, if she carried a surgeon, he was taken in place of their present one, if the latter wished to leave. But when Scudamore came on board the *Royal Fortune* he insisted on signing the pirate articles and boasted that he was the first surgeon that had ever done so, and he hoped, he said, to prove as great a rogue as any of them.

When the African Company's Guinea ship, the *King Solomon*, was taken, Scudamore came aboard and helped himself to their surgeon's instruments and medicines. He also took a fancy for a backgammon board, but only kept it after a violent quarrel with another pirate. It came out at his trial that on a voyage from the Island of St. Thomas, in a prize, the *Fortune,* in which was a cargo of slaves, Scudamore had tried to bring about a mutiny of the blacks to kill the prize crew which was on board, and he was detected in the night going about amongst the negroes, talking to them in the Angolan language. He said that he knew enough about navigation to sail the ship himself, and he was heard to say that " this were better than to be taken to Cape Corso to be hanged and sun dried."

The same witness told how he had approached the prisoner when he was trying to persuade a wounded pirate, one James Harris, to join him in his scheme, but fearing to be overheard, Scudamore turned the conversation to horse-racing.

Scudamore was condemned to death, but allowed three days' grace before being hanged, which he spent in incessant prayers and reading of the Scriptures. On the gallows he sang, solo, the Thirty-first Psalm. Died at the age of 35.

SEARLES, CAPTAIN ROBERT.

In 1664 he brought in two Spanish prizes to Port Royal, but as orders had only lately come from England to the Governor to do all in his power to promote friendly relations with the Spanish islands, these prizes were returned to their owners. To prevent Searle's doing such things again, he was deprived of his ship's rudder and sails. In 1666, Searle, in company with a Captain Stedman and a party of only eighty men, took the Island of Tobago, near Trinidad, from the Dutch, destroying everything they could not carry away.

SELKIRK, ALEXANDER. The original Robinson
    Crusoe.

Born in 1676 at Largo in Fifeshire, he was the
seventh son of John Selcraig, a shoemaker. In 1695
he was cited to appear before the Session for "indecent conduct in church," but ran away to sea. In
1701 he was back again in Largo, and was rebuked
in the face of the congregation for quarrelling with
his brothers. A year later Selkirk sailed to England,
and in 1703 joined Dampier's expedition to the South
Seas. Appointed sailing-master to the *Cinque Ports,*
commanded by Captain Stradling.

In September, 1704, he arrived at the uninhabited
island of Juan Fernandez, in the South Pacific.
Selkirk, having quarrelled with the captain, insisted
on being landed on the island with all his belongings.
He lived alone here for nearly four years, building
himself two cabins, hunting the goats which abounded,
and taming young goats and cats to be his companions.

On the night of January 31st, 1709, seeing two
ships, Selkirk lit a fire, and a boat was sent ashore.
These ships were the *Duke* and *Duchess* of Bristol,
under the command of Captain Woodes Rogers, while
his old friend Dampier was acting as pilot. Selkirk
was at once appointed sailing-master of the *Duchess,*
and eventually arrived back in the Thames on
October 14th, 1711, with booty worth £800, having
been away from England for eight years. While in
England he met Steele, who described Selkirk as a
"man of good sense, with strong but cheerful expression." Whether Selkirk ever met Defoe is uncertain, though the character of Robinson Crusoe
was certainly founded on his adventures in Juan
Fernandez. In 1712 he returned to Largo, living the
life of a recluse, and we must be forgiven for suspect-
ing that he rather acted up to the part, since it is

recorded that he made a cave in his father's garden in which to meditate. This life of meditation in an artificial cave was soon rudely interrupted by the appearance of a certain Miss Sophia Bonce, with whom Selkirk fell violently in love, and they eloped together to Bristol, which must have proved indeed a sad scandal to the elders and other godly citizens of Largo. Beyond the fact that he was charged at Bristol with assaulting one Richard Nettle, a shipwright, we hear no more of Selkirk until his first will was drawn up in 1717, in which he leaves his fortune and house to "my loving friend Sophia Bonce, of the Pall Mall, London, Spinster." Shortly after this, Alexander basely deserted his loving friend and married a widow, one Mrs. Francis Candis, at Oarston in Devon.

In 1720 he was appointed mate to H.M.S. *Weymouth*, on board of which he died a year later at the age of 45.

Selkirk is immortalized in literature, not only by Defoe, but by Cowper in his "Lines on Solitude," beginning : "I am monarch of all I survey."

SHARP, ROWLAND.

Of Bath Town in North Carolina.

One of Major Stede Bonnet's crew. Tried for piracy at Charleston in 1718 and found "not guilty."

SHASTER, ROGER.

One of Captain Heidon's crew of the pirate ship *John of Sandwich*, which was wrecked on the coast of Alderney. Shaster was arrested and hanged at St. Martin's Point, Guernsey, in 1564.

SHAW, JOHN.

One of Captain Lowther's crew. Hanged at St. Kitts on March 11th, 1722.

SHERGALL, Henry, or Sherral. Buccaneer.

A seaman with Captain Bartholomew Sharp in his South Sea voyage. One October day he fell into the sea while going into the spritsail-top and was drowned. "This incident several of our company interpreted as a bad omen, which proved not so, through the providence of the Almighty."

SHIRLEY, Sir Anthony.

In January, 1597, headed an expedition to the Island of Jamaica. He met with little opposition from the Spaniards, and seized and plundered St. Jago de la Vega.

SHIVERS, Captain.

This South Sea pirate cruised in company with Culliford and Nathaniel North in the Red Sea, preying principally on Moorish ships, and also sailed about the Indian Ocean as far as the Malacca Islands. He accepted the royal pardon to pirates, which was brought out to Madagascar by Commodore Littleton, and apparently gave up his wicked ways thereafter.

SHUTFIELD, William.
Of Lancaster.

Hanged at Rhode Island in July, 1723, at the age of 40.

SICCADAM, John.
Of Boston.

One of Captain Pound's crew. Found guilty of piracy, but pardoned.

SIMMS, Henry, alias "Gentleman Harry." Pickpocket, highwayman, pirate, and Old Etonian.
Born in 1716 at St. Martin's-in-the-Fields. Sent

while quite young to school at Eton, where he "shewed an early inclination to vice," and at the age of 14 was taken from school and apprenticed to a breeches-maker. No Old Etonian, either then or now, would stand that kind of treatment, so Simms ran away, becoming a pickpocket and later a highwayman. After numerous adventures and escapes from prison, he was pressed on board H.M.S. *Rye,* but he deserted his ship at Leith. After an "affair" at Croydon, Simms was transplanted with other convicts to Maryland, in the *Italian Merchant.* On the voyage he attempted, but without success, to raise a mutiny. On his arrival in America he was sold to the master of the *Two Sisters,* which was taken a few days out from Maryland by a Bayonne pirate. Carried to Spain, Simms got to Oporto, and there was pressed on board H.M.S. *King Fisher.* Eventually he reached Bristol, where he bought, with his share of booty, a horse and two pistols, with which to go on the highway.

Hanged on June 17th, 1747, for stealing an old silver watch and 5s. from Mr. Francis Sleep at Dunstable.

SKIPTON, CAPTAIN.

Commanded a pirate ship, in which he sailed in company with Captain Spriggs. Being chased by H.M.S. *Diamond* off the coast of Cuba, Skipton ran his sloop on to the Florida Reef. Escaping with his crew to an island, they were attacked by the Indians, and many of them were captured and eaten. The survivors, embarking in a canoe, were caught by the man-of-war and taken prisoner.

SKYRM, CAPTAIN JAMES. Welsh pirate.

Hanged at the advanced age—for a pirate—of 44.

Commanded the *Ranger,* one of Captain Roberts's ships that cruised in 1721 and 1722 off the West Coast of Africa. In the fight with the King's ship that took him he was very active with a drawn sword in his hand, with which he beat any of his crew who were at all backward. One of his legs was shot away in this action, but he refused to leave the deck and go below as long as the action lasted. He was condemned to death and hanged in chains.

SMITH, GEORGE. Welsh pirate.

One of Captain Roberts's pirates. Hanged at the age of 25.

SMITH, JOHN.

One of the mutinous crew of the *Antonio*. Hanged at Boston in 1672.

SMITH, JOHN WILLIAMS.
Of Charleston, Carolina.

Hanged in 1718 for piracy, at Charleston.

SMITH, MAJOR SAMUEL. Buccaneer.

At one time a buccaneer with the famous Mansfield.

In 1641 he was sent, by the Governor of Jamaica, with a party to reinforce the troops which under Mansfield had recaptured the New Providence Island from the Spanish. In 1660 he was taken prisoner by the Spanish and carried to Panama and there kept in chains in a dungeon for seventeen months.

DE SOTO, BERNADO.

One of the crew of the schooner *Panda* that took and plundered the Salem brig *Mexican*. The crew of the *Panda* were captured by an English man-of-war and taken to Boston. De Soto was condemned to death, but eventually fully pardoned owing to his heroic conduct in rescuing the crew of an American vessel some time previously.

DE SOTO, CAPTAIN BENITO.

A Portuguese.

A most notorious pirate in and about 1830.

In 1827 he shipped at Buenos Ayres as mate in a slaver, named the *Defenser de Pedro,* and plotted to seize the ship off the African coast. The pirates took the cargo of slaves to the West Indies, where they sold them. De Soto plundered many vessels in the Caribbean Sea, then sailed to the South Atlantic, naming his ship the *Black Joke.* The fear of the *Black Joke* became so great amongst the East India-men homeward bound that they used to make up convoys at St. Helena before heading north.

In 1832 de Soto attacked the *Morning Star,* an East Indiaman, and took her, when he plundered the ship and murdered the captain. After taking several more ships, de Soto lost his own on the rocky coast of Spain, near Cadiz. His crew, although pretending to be honest shipwrecked sailors, were arrested, but de Soto managed to escape to Gibraltar. Here he was recognized by a soldier who had seen de Soto when he took the *Morning Star,* in which he had been a passenger. The pirate was arrested, and tried before Sir George Don, the Governor of Gibraltar, and sentenced to death. He was sent to Cadiz to be hanged with the rest of his crew. The gallows was erected at the water's edge, and de Soto, with his coffin, was conveyed there in a cart. He died bravely, arranging the noose around his own neck, stepping up into his coffin to do so; then, crying out, " Adios todos," he threw himself off the cart.

This man must not be confused with one Bernado de Soto, who was tried for piracy at Boston in 1834.

SOUND, JOSEPH.

Of the city of Westminster.

Hanged, at the age of 28, at Newport, Rhode Island, in 1723.

SPARKS, James.

A Newfoundland fisherman.

In August, 1723, with John Phillips and three others, ran away with a vessel to go "on the account." Sparks was appointed gunner.

SPARKES, John.

A member of Captain Avery's crew, and described by one of his shipmates as being "a true cock of the game." A thief, he robbed his fellow-shipmates, and from one, Philip Middleton, he stole 270 pieces of gold.

Hanged at Execution Dock in 1696.

SPRATLIN, Robert.

Was one of Dampier's party which in 1681 crossed the Isthmus of Darien, when he was left behind in the jungle with Wafer. Spratlin was lost when the little party attempted to ford the swollen Chagres River. He afterwards rejoined Wafer.

SPRIGGS, Captain Francis Farrington.

An uninteresting and bloody pirate without one single redeeming character.

He learnt his art with the pirate Captain Lowther, afterwards serving as quartermaster with Captain Low and taking an active part in all the barbarities committed by the latter.

About 1720 Low took a prize, a man-of-war called the *Squirrel*. This he handed over to some of the crew, who elected Spriggs their captain. The ship they renamed the *Delight*, and in the night altered their course and left Low. They made a flag, bearing upon it a white skeleton, holding in one hand a dart striking a bleeding heart, and in the other an hourglass. Sailing to the West Indies, Spriggs took several prizes, treating the crews with abominable cruelty. On one occasion the pirates chased what they believed to be a Spanish ship, and after a long while they came alongside and fired a broadside into her. The ship immediately surrendered, and turned out to be a vessel the pirate had plundered only a few days previously. This infuriated Spriggs and his crew, who showed their disappointment by half murdering the captain. After a narrow escape from being captured by a French man-of-war near the Island of St. Kitts, Spriggs sailed north to the Summer Isles, or Bermudas. Taking a ship coming from Rhode Island, they found her cargo to consist of horses. Several of the pirates mounted these and galloped up and down the deck until they were thrown. While plundering several small vessels of their cargo of logwood in the Bay of Honduras, Spriggs was surprised and attacked by an English man-of-war, and the pirates only escaped by using their sweeps. Spriggs now went for a cruise off the coast of South Carolina, returning again to Honduras. This was a rash proceeding on Spriggs's part, for as he was sailing off the west end of Cuba he again met the man-of-war which had so nearly caught him before in the bay. Spriggs clapped on all sail, but ran his ship on Rattan Island, where she was burnt by the *Spence*, while Captain Spriggs and his crew escaped to the woods.

SPRINGER, CAPTAIN.

He fought gallantly with Sawkins and Ringrose in the Battle of Perico off Panama on St. George's Day in 1680. He gave his name to Springer's Cay, one of the Samballoes Islands. This was the rendezvous chosen by the pirates, where Dampier and his party found the French pirate ship that rescued them after their famous trudge across the Isthmus of Darien.

STANLEY, CAPTAIN. Buccaneer.

With a few other buccaneers in their stronghold at New Providence Island in 1660, withstood an attack by a Spanish fleet for five days. The three English captains, Stanley, Sir Thomas Whetstone, and Major Smith, were carried to Panama and there cast into a dungeon and bound in irons for seventeen months.

STEDMAN, CAPTAIN.   Buccaneer.

In 1666, with Captain Searle and a party of only eighty men, he took and plundered the Dutch island of Tobago. Later on, after the outbreak of war with France, he was captured by a French frigate off the Island of Guadeloupe. Stedman had a small vessel and a crew of only 100 men, and found himself becalmed and unable to escape, so he boldly boarded the Frenchman and fought for two hours, being finally overcome.

STEPHENS, WILLIAM.

Died on January 14th, 1682, on board of Captain Sharp's ship a few days before their return to the Barbadoes from the South Seas. His death was supposed to have been caused by indulging too freely in mancanilla while ashore at Golfo Dulce. " Next morning we threw overboard our dead man and gave him two French vollies and one English one."

STEPHENSON, JOHN.

Sailed as an honest seaman in the *Onslow* (Captain Gee) from Sestos. Taken in May, 1721, by the pirate Captain Roberts, he willingly joined the pirates. When Roberts was killed on board the *Royal Fortune*, Stephenson burst into tears, and declared that he wished the next shot might kill him. Hanged in 1722.

STILES, RICHARD.

Hanged in Virginia in 1718 with the rest of Captain Teach's crew.

STOREY, THOMAS.

One of William Coward's crew which stole the ketch *Elinor* in Boston Harbour. Condemned to be hanged on January 27th, 1690, but afterwards reprieved.

ST. QUINTIN, RICHARD.
A native of Yorkshire.

One of M'Kinlie's crew that murdered Captain Glass and his family in the Canary ship. Afterwards arrested at Cork and hanged in chains near Dublin on March 19th, 1765.

STURGES, CAPTAIN.

An Elizabethan pirate, who had his headquarters at Rochelle. In company with the notorious pirate Calles, he in one year pillaged two Portuguese, one French, one Spanish, and also a Scotch ship. His end is not known.

O'SULLIVAN, LORD.   Receiver of pirate plunder.
The Sulivan Bere, of Berehaven in Ireland.

A notorious friend of the English pirates, he bought their spoils, which he stored in his castle. He helped to fit out pirate captains for their cruises, and protected them when Queen Elizabeth sent ships to try and arrest them.

SUTTON, THOMAS.
Born at Berwick in 1699.

Gunner in Roberts's ship the *Royal Fortune*. At his trial he was proved to have been particularly active in helping to take a Dutch merchantman, the *Gertruycht*. Hanged in chains at Cape Coast Castle in April, 1722, at the age of 23.

SWAN, Captain.

Commanded the *Nicholas*, and met Dampier when in the *Batchelor's Delight* at the Island of Juan Fernandez in 1684. The two captains cruised together off the west coast of South America, the *Nicholas* leaving Dampier, who returned to England by way of the East Indies.

SWAN, Captain. Buccaneer.

Of the *Cygnet*. Left England as an honest trader. Rounded the Horn and sailed up to the Bay of Nicoya, there taking on a crew of buccaneers who had crossed the Isthmus of Darien on foot. Dampier was appointed pilot or quartermaster to the *Cygnet*, a post analogous to that of a navigating officer on a modern man-of-war, while Ringrose was appointed supercargo. Swan had an adventurous and chequered voyage, sometimes meeting with successes, but often with reverses. Eventually he sailed to the Philippine Islands, where the crew mutinied and left Swan and thirty-six of the crew behind. After various adventures the *Cygnet*, by now in a very crazy state, just managed to reach Madagascar, where she sank at her anchorage.

SWITZER, Joseph.

Of Boston in New England.

Tried for piracy at Rhode Island in 1723, but found to be "not guilty."

SYMPSON, David.

Born at North Berwick.

One of Roberts's crew. Tried and hanged at Cape Coast Castle in 1722. On the day of execution Sympson was among the first six prisoners to be brought up from the ship's hold to have their fetters knocked off and to be fitted with halters, and it was observed that none of the culprits appeared in the least dejected, except Sympson, who "spoke a little faint, but this was rather imputed to a Flux that had seized him two or three days before, than Fear." There being no clergyman in the colony, a kindly surgeon tried to take on the duties of the ordinary, but with ill-success, the hardened ruffians being quite unmoved by his attempts at exhortation. In fact, the spectators were considerably shocked, as indeed they well might be, by Sympson, suddenly recognizing among the crowd a woman whom he knew, calling out " he had lain with that B——h three times, and now she was come to see him hanged."

Sympson died at the age of 36, which was considerably above the average age to which a pirate might expect to live.

TAYLOR, Captain.

This formidable South Sea pirate must indeed have looked, as well as acted, the part, since his appearance is described by Captain Johnson as follows: " A Fellow with a terrible pair of Whiskers, and a wooden Leg, being stuck round with Pistols, like the Man in the Almanack with Darts."

This man Taylor it was who stirred up the crew of the *Victory* to turn out and maroon Captain England, and elect himself in his place. He was a villain of the deepest dye, and burnt ships and houses and tortured his prisoners.

The pirates sailed down the West Coast of India from Goa to Cochin, and returned to Mauritius. Thence sailing to the Island of Mascarine they found a big Portuguese ship, which they took. In her they discovered the Conde de Eviceira, Viceroy of Goa, and, even better, four million dollars worth of diamonds.

Taylor, now sailing in the *Cassandra*, heard that there were four men-of-war on his tracks, so he sailed to Delagoa Bay and spent the winter of the year 1722 there. It was now decided that as they had a huge amount of plunder they had better give up piracy, so they sailed away to the West Indies and surrendered themselves to the Governor of Porto Bello. The crew broke up and each man, with a bag of diamonds, went whither he would; but Captain Taylor joined the Spanish service, and was put in command of a man-of-war, which was sent to attack the English logwood cutters in the Bay of Honduras.

TAYLOR, WILLIAM.

One of Captain Phillips's crew. Wounded in the leg while attempting to desert. There being no surgeon on board, a consultation was held over the patient by the whole crew, and these learned men were unanimous in agreeing that the leg should be amputated. Some dispute then arose as to who should act the part of surgeon, and at length the carpenter was chosen as the most proper person. "Upon which he fetch'd up the biggest saw, and taking the limb under his Arm, fell to Work, and separated it from the Body of the Patient in as little Time as he could have cut a Deal Board in two." This surgeon-carpenter evidently appreciated the importance of aseptics, for, "after that he had heated his Ax red hot in the Fire, cauteriz'd the Wound but not with so much Art as he perform'd the other Part for he so burnt the Flesh distant from the Place of Amputation that it had like to have mortify'd." Taylor was tried and condemned to death at Boston on May 12th, 1714, but for some reason not explained was reprieved.

TEACH, CAPTAIN EDWARD, or THATCH, or THACH, alias DRUMMOND, alias BLACKBEARD. Arch-pirate.

A Bristol man who settled in Jamaica, sailing in privateers, but not in the capacity of an officer.

In 1716, Teach took to piracy, being put in command of a sloop by the pirate Benjamin Hornigold. In 1717, Hornigold and Teach sailed together from Providence towards the American coast, taking a billop from Havana and several other prizes. After careening their vessels on the coast of Virginia, the pirates took a fine French Guineaman bound to Martinico; this ship they armed with forty guns, named her the *Queen Ann's Revenge,* and Blackbeard went aboard as captain. Teach now had a ship that allowed him to go for larger prizes, and he began by taking a big ship called the *Great Allen,* which he plundered and then set fire to. A few days later, Teach was attacked by H.M.S. *Scarborough,* of thirty guns, but after a sharp engagement lasting some hours, the pirate was able to drive off the King's ship.

The next ship he met with was the sloop of that amateur pirate and landsman, Major Stede Bonnet. Teach and Bonnet became friends and sailed together for a few days, when Teach, finding that Bonnet was quite ignorant of maritime matters, ordered the Major, in the most high-handed way, to come aboard his ship, while he put another officer in command of Bonnet's vessel. Teach now took ship after ship, one of which, with the curious name of the *Protestant Cæsar,* the pirates burnt out of spite, not because of her name, but because she belonged to Boston, where there had lately been a hanging of pirates.

Blackbeard now sailed north along the American coast, arriving off Charleston, South Carolina. Here he lay off the bar for several days, seizing every vessel that attempted to enter or leave the port, "striking great Terror to the whole Province of Carolina," the more so since the colony was scarcely recovered from a recent visit by another pirate, Vane.

Being in want of medicines, Teach sent his lieutenant, Richards, on shore with a letter to the

Governor demanding that he should instantly send
off a medicine chest, or else Teach would murder all
his prisoners, and threatening to send their heads to
Government House; many of these prisoners being
the chief persons of the colony.

Teach, who was unprincipled, even for a pirate,
now commanded three vessels, and he wanted to get
rid of his crews and keep all the booty for himself and
a few chosen friends. To do this, he contrived to
wreck his own vessel and one of his sloops. Then
with his friends and all the booty he sailed off, leaving
the rest marooned on a small sandy island. Teach
next sailed to North Carolina, and with the greatest
coolness surrendered with twenty of his men to the
Governor, Charles Eden, and received the Royal
pardon. The ex-pirate spent the next few weeks in
cultivating an intimate friendship with the Governor,
who, no doubt, shared Teach's booty with him.

A romantic episode took place at this time at Bath
Town. The pirate fell in love, not by any means for
the first time, with a young lady of 16 years of age.
To show his delight at this charming union, the
Governor himself married the happy pair, this being
the captain's fourteenth wife; though certain Bath
Town gossips were heard to say that there were no
fewer than twelve Mrs. Teach still alive at different
ports up and down the West India Islands.

In June, 1718, the bridegroom felt that the call of
duty must be obeyed, so kissing good-bye to the new
Mrs. Teach, he sailed away to the Bermudas, meeting
on his way half a dozen ships, which he plundered,
and then hurried back to share the spoils with the
Governor of North Carolina and his secretary, Mr.
Knight.

For several months, Blackbeard remained in the
river, exacting a toll from all the shipping, often
going ashore to make merry at the expense of the

planters. At length, things became so unbearable
that the citizens and planters sent a request to the
Governor of the neighbouring colony of Virginia for
help to rid them of the presence of Teach. The
Governor, Spotswood, an energetic man, at once made
plans for taking the pirate, and commissioned a
gallant young naval officer, Lieutenant Robert Maynard, of H.M.S. *Pearl,* to go in a sloop, the *Ranger,*
in search of him. On November 17, 1718, the lieutenant sailed for Kicquetan in the James River, and on
the 21st arrived at the mouth of Okerecock Inlet,
where he discovered the pirate he was in search of.
Blackbeard would have been caught unprepared had
not his friend, Mr. Secretary Knight, hearing what
was on foot, sent a letter warning him to be on his
guard, and also any of Teach's crew whom he could find
in the taverns of Bath Town. Maynard lost no time
in attacking the pirate's ship, which had run aground.
The fight was furious, Teach boarding the sloop and
a terrific hand-to-hand struggle taking place, the
lieutenant and Teach fighting with swords and pistols.
Teach was wounded in twenty-five places before he fell
dead, while the lieutenant escaped with nothing worse
than a cut over the fingers.

  Maynard now returned in triumph in his sloop to
Bath Town, with the head of Blackbeard hung up to
the bolt-spit end, and received a tremendous ovation
from the inhabitants.

  During his meteoric career as a pirate, the name of
Blackbeard was one that created terror up and down
the coast of America from Newfoundland to Trinidad.
This was not only due to the number of ships Teach
took, but in no small measure to his alarming appearance. Teach was a tall, powerful man, with a fierce
expression, which was increased by a long, black
beard which grew from below his eyes and hung down
to a great length. This he plaited into many tails,

each one tied with a coloured ribbon and turned back over his ears. When going into action, Teach wore a sling on his shoulders with three pairs of pistols, and struck lighted matches under the brim of his hat. These so added to his fearful appearance as to strike terror into all beholders. Teach had a peculiar sense of humour, and one that could at times cause much uneasiness amongst his friends. Thus we are told that one day on the deck of his ship, being at the time a little flushed with wine, Blackbeard addressed his crew, saying : " Come let us make a Hell of our own, and try how long we can bear it," whereupon Teach, with several others, descended to the hold, shut themselves in, and then set fire to several pots of brimstone. For a while they stood it, choking and gasping, but at length had to escape to save themselves from being asphyxiated, but the last to give up was the captain, who was wont to boast afterwards that he had outlasted all the rest.

Then there was that little affair in the cabin, when Teach blew out the candle and in the dark fired his pistols under the table, severely wounding one of his guests in the knee, for no other reason, as he explained to them afterwards, than " if he did not shoot one or two of them now and then they'd forget who he was."

Teach kept a log or journal, which unfortunately is lost, but the entries for two days have been preserved, and are worth giving, and seem to smack of Robert Louis Stevenson in " Treasure Island." The entries, written in Teach's handwriting, run as follows :

" 1718. Rum all out—Our Company somewhat sober—A damn'd Confusion amongst us !—Rogues a plotting—great Talk of Separation—so I look'd sharp for a Prize.

" 1718. Took one, with a great deal of Liquor on Board, so kept the Company hot, damned hot, then all Things went well again."

TEAGUE, ROBERT.

A Scotch pirate, one of Captain Gow's crew. On May 26th, 1725, the crew were tried in London and found guilty and sentenced to death, except Teague and two others who were acquitted.

TEMPLETON, JOHN.

One of Captain John Quelch's crew of the ship *Charles*. Tried for piracy at Boston in 1704, but, being discovered to be not yet 14 years of age and only a servant on board the pirate ship, was acquitted.

TEW, CAPTAIN THOMAS, or TOO.

A famous pirate, whose headquarters were at Madagascar. He was mentioned by name in King William III.'s Royal Warrant to Captain Kidd to go hunting for pirates, as a specially "wicked and ill-disposed person."

He sailed with Captain Dew from the Barbadoes with a Commission from the Governor to join with the Royal African Company in an attack on the French factory at Goori, at Gambia. Instead of going to West Africa, Tew and his crew turned pirates, and sailed to the Red Sea. Here he met with a great Indian ship, which he had the hardiness to attack, and soon took her, and each of his men received as his share £3,000, and with this booty they sailed to Madagascar. He was already held in high esteem by the pirates who resided in that favourite stronghold. At one time he joined Misson, the originator of "piracy-without-tears" at his garden city of Libertatia. A quarrel arose between Misson's French followers and Tew's English pirates. A duel was arranged between the two leaders, but by the tact of another pirate—an unfrocked Italian priest—all was settled amicably, Tew being appointed Admiral and the diplomatic ex-priest suitably chosen as Secretary of State to the little republic. Such a reputation for kindness had Tew that ships seldom resisted him, but on knowing who their assailant was they gave themselves up freely. Some of Tew's men started a daughter colony on their own account, and the Admiral sailed after them to try and persuade them to return to the fold at Libertatia. The men refused, and while Tew was arguing and trying to persuade them to change their minds, his ship was lost in a sudden storm. Tew was soon rescued by the ship *Bijoux* with Misson on board, who, with a few men, had escaped being massacred by the natives. Misson, giving Tew an equal share of his gold and diamonds, sailed away, while Tew managed to return to Rhode Island in New England, where he settled down for a while. To show the honesty of this man, being now affluent, he kept a promise to the friends in Bermuda who originally set him up with a ship, by sending them fourteen times the original cost of the sloop as their just share of the profits.

At last, Tew found the call of the sea and the lure of the " grand account " too great to resist, and he consented to take command of a pirate ship which was to go on a cruise in the Red Sea. Arrived there, Tew attacked a big ship belonging to the Great Mogul, and during the battle was mortally wounded.

His historian tells us " a shot carried away the rim of Tew's belly, who held his bowels with his hands for some space. When he dropped, it struck such terror to his men that they suffered themselves to be taken without further resistance." Thus fell fighting a fine sailor, a brave man, and a successful pirate, and one who cheated the gallows awaiting him at Execution Dock.

THOMAS, Captain, *alias* Stede Bonnet.

THOMAS, John.
   Of Jamaica.
   This Welsh pirate was one of Major Stede Bonnet's
crew of the *Royal James*. Hanged at Charleston,
South Carolina, in 1718.

THOMPSON, Captain.
   A renegade pirate who joined the Barbary corsairs,
becoming a Mohammedan. Commanded a pirate
vessel, and was taken prisoner off the coast of Ireland
by an Elizabethan ship. Hanged at Wapping.

THURBAR, Richard.
   Tried for piracy at Boston in 1704.

THURSTON, Captain. Buccaneer.
   Of Tortuga Island.
   Refused to accept the Royal offer of pardon of 1670,
when all commissions to privateer on the Spanish were
revoked. Thurston, with a mulatto, Diego, using
obsolete commissions issued by the late Governor of
Jamaica, Modyford, continued to prey upon Spanish
shipping, carrying their prizes to Tortuga.

THWAITES, Captain Joseph.
   Coxswain to Captain Hood, he was promoted in 1763
to be a midshipman in H.M.S. *Zealous,* cruising in
the Mediterranean. Putting into Algiers, Thwaites
was sent ashore by the captain to buy some sheep, but
did not return to the boat and, it being supposed he
had been assassinated, the ship sailed without him.
The fact was that young Thwaites, who spoke Turkish
and Greek, had accepted an invitation to enter the
Ottoman service. Embracing the Mohammedan religion, Thwaites was put in command of a forty-four
gun frigate.

His first engagement was with the flagship of the Tunisian Admiral, which he took and carried to Algiers. He soon brought in another prize, and so pleased the Dey that he presented him with a scimitar, the hilt of which was set with diamonds.

Thwaites, having soiled his hands with blood, now became the pirate indeed, taking vessels of any nation, and drowning all his prisoners by tying a double-headed shot round their necks and throwing them overboard.

He stopped at no atrocity—even children were killed, and one prisoner, an English lieutenant and an old shipmate of his, called Roberts, he murdered without a second thought. When Thwaites happened to be near Gibraltar, he would go ashore and through his agents, Messrs. Ross and Co., transmit large sums of money to his wife and children in England. But Thwaites had another home at Algiers fitted with every luxury, including three Armenian girls.

For several years this successful pirate plundered ships of all nations until such pressure was brought to bear on the Dey of Algiers that Thwaites thought it best to collect what valuables he could carry away and disappear.

Landing at Gibraltar in 1796, dressed in European clothes, he procured a passage to New York in an American frigate, the *Constitution*. Arriving in the United States, he purchased an estate not far from New York and built himself a handsome mansion, but a year later retribution came from an unlooked-for quarter, for he was bitten by a rattlesnake and died in the most horrible agonies both of mind and body.

TOMKINS, JOHN.
Of Gloucestershire.

Hanged at the age of 23 at Rhode Island in 1723. One of Charles Harris's crew.

TOPPING, Dennis.

He shipped on board the sloop *Buck* at Providence in 1718, in company with Anstis and other famous pirates. Was killed at the taking of a rich Portuguese ship off the coast of Brazil.

TOWNLEY, Captain. Buccaneer.

A buccaneer who in the year 1684 was one of the mixed English and French fleet blockading Panama. On this occasion, he commanded a ship with a crew of 180 men. By the next year the quarrels between the English had reached such a pitch that Townley and Swan left Davis and sailed in search of their French friends. In May, 1685, Townley was amongst the company that took and sacked Guayaquil. In January, 1686, Townley rescued the French pirate Grogniet and some 350 Frenchmen who, when attacking the town of Quibo, were surprised by a Spanish squadron, which burnt their vessels while the crews were on shore. Townley then sailed north with his French comrades and sacked Granada.

His next adventure was to take the town of Lavelia, near to Panama, where he found a rich cargo which the Viceroy had placed on shore because he was afraid to send it to sea when so many pirates were about.

In August of the same year, Townley's ship was attacked by three Spanish men-of-war. A furious fight took place, which ended by two of the Spanish ships being captured and the third burnt. In this action the gallant Townley was gravely wounded, and died shortly afterwards.

TRISTRIAN, Captain. French buccaneer.

In the year 1681 Dampier, with other malcontents, broke away from Captain Sharp and marched on foot across the Isthmus of Darien. After undergoing terrible hardships for twenty-two days, the party arrived on the Atlantic seaboard, to find Captain Tristrian with his ship lying in La Sounds Cay.

The buccaneers bought red, blue, and green beads, and knives, scissors, and looking-glasses from the French pirates to give to their faithful Indian guides as parting gifts.

TRYER, MATTHEW.

A Carolina pirate, accused and acquitted on a charge of having captured a sloop belonging to Samuel Salters, of Bermuda, in 1699.

TUCKER, ROBERT.
Of the Island of Jamaica.

One of Major Stede Bonnet's crew. Tried, condemned, and hanged at Charleston, South Carolina, on November 8th, 1718. The prisoners were not defended by counsel, because the members of the South Carolina Bar still deemed it " a base and vile thing to plead for money or reward." We understand that the barristers of South Carolina have since persuaded themselves to overcome this prejudice. The result was that, with the famous Judge Trott, a veritable terror to pirates, being President of the Court of Vice-Admiralty, the prisoners had short and ready justice, and all but four of the thirty-five pirates tried were found guilty.

TUCKERMAN, CAPTAIN.

Sailed with Captain Porter in the West Indies. Captain Johnson gives an account of the meeting between these two pirate novices and the great Captain Roberts at Hispaniola.

TURNLEY, Captain Richard.

A New Providence pirate who received the general pardon from Captain Woodes Rogers in 1718. When, a little later, the scandal of Captain Rackam's infatuation for Anne Bonny was causing such gossip among the two thousand ex-pirates who formed the population of the settlement, it was Turnley who brought news of the affair to the notice of the Governor. In revenge for this action, Rackam and his lady, one day hearing that Turnley had sailed to a neighbouring island to catch turtles, followed him. It happened that Turnley was on shore hunting wild pigs and so escaped, but Rackam sank his sloop and took his crew away with him as prisoners.

TYLE, Captain Ort Van.
A Dutchman from New York.

A successful pirate in the days of the Madagascan sea-rovers. For some time he sailed in company with Captain James, taking several prizes in the Indian Ocean.

Van Tyle had a plantation at Madagascar and used to put his prisoners to work there as slaves, one in particular being the notorious Welsh pirate, David Williams, who toiled with Van Tyles's other slaves for six months before making his escape to a friendly tribe in the neighbourhood.

UPTON, Boatswain John.
Born in 1679 of honest parents at Deptford.

Apprenticed to a waterman, he afterwards went to sea, serving on different men-of-war as a petty officer. Until July, 1723, when 40 years of age, Upton lived a perfectly honest life, but his wife dying, Upton found she had contracted various debts and that he was in danger of being arrested by the creditors. Leaving his four orphans, Upton hurried to Poole in Dorsetshire, and was taken on as boatswain in the *John and Elizabeth* (Captain Hooper), bound for Bonavista in Newfoundland. He seems to have continued to sail as an honest seaman until November 14th, 1725, when serving as boatswain in the *Perry* galley, on a voyage between Barbadoes and Bristol, the vessel was taken by a pirate, Cooper, in the *Night Rambler*. At his subsequent trial witnesses declared that Upton willingly joined the pirates, signed their articles, and was afterwards one of their most active and cruel men.

Upton kept a journal, which was his only witness for his defence, in which he described how he was forced to sign the pirates' articles under threats of instant death. If his journal is to be believed, Upton escaped from the pirates at the first opportunity, landing on the Mosquito coast. After being arrested by the Spaniards as a spy, he was sent from one prison to another in Central America, at last being put on board a galleon at Porto Bello, to be sent to Spain. Escaping, he got aboard a New York sloop and arrived at Jamaica in December, 1726. While at Port Royal he was pressed on board H.M.S. *Nottingham*, serving in her for more than two years as quartermaster, until one day he was accused of having been a pirate. Under this charge he was brought a prisoner to England in 1729, tried in London, and hanged, protesting his innocence to the last.

URUJ. See BARBAROSSA.

VALLANUEVA, CAPTAIN.
A Dominican.
Commanded in 1831 a small gaff-topsail schooner, the *General Morazan*, armed with a brass eight-

pounder and carrying a mixed crew of forty-four men, French, Italian, English, and creoles of St. Domingo.

VANCLEIN, CAPTAIN MOSES. Dutch filibuster.

Was serving with L'Ollonais's fleet off the coast of Yucatan when a mutiny broke out, of which Vanclein was the ringleader. He persuaded the malcontents to sail with him along the coast till they came to Costa Rica. There they landed and marched to the town of Veraguas, which they seized and pillaged. The pirates got little booty, only eight pounds of gold, it proving to be a poor place.

VANE, CAPTAIN CHARLES.

Famous for his piratical activities off the coast of North America, specially the Carolinas.

In 1718, when Woodes Rogers was sent by the English Government to break up the pirate stronghold in the Bahama Islands, all the pirates at New Providence Island surrendered to Rogers and received the King's pardon except Vane, who, after setting fire to a prize he had, slipped out of the bay as Rogers with his two men-of-war entered. Vane sailed to the coast of Carolina, as did other West Indian pirates who found their old haunts too warm for them.

Vane is first heard of as being actively engaged in stealing from the Spaniards the silver which they were salving from a wrecked galleon in the Gulf of Florida. Tiring of this, Vane stole a vessel and ranged up and down the coast from Florida to New York, taking ship after ship, until at last the Governor of South Carolina sent out a Colonel Rhet in an armed sloop to try and take him. On one occasion Vane met the famous Blackbeard, whom he saluted with his great guns loaded with shot. This compliment of one pirate chief to another was re-

turned in like kind, and then " mutual civilities "
followed for several days between the two pirate captains and their crews, these civilities taking the form
of a glorious debauch in a quiet creek on the coast.

Vane soon had a change of fortune, when, meeting
with a French man-of-war, he decided to decline an
engagement and to seek safety in flight, greatly to the
anger of his crew. For this he was obliged to stand
the test of the vote of the whole crew, who passed a
resolution against his honour and dignity, and
branded him a coward, deprived him of his command,
and packed him off with a few of his adherents in a
small sloop. Vane, not discouraged by this reverse
of fortune, rose again from the bottom rung of the
ladder to success, and quickly increased in strength
of ships and crew, until one day, being overcome by
a sudden tornado, he lost everything but his life,
being washed up on a small uninhabited island off the
Honduras coast. Here he managed to support life by
begging food from the fishermen who occasionally
came there in their canoes.

At last a ship put in for water, commanded by one
Captain Holford, who happened to be an old friend
of Vane's. Vane naturally was pleased at this piece
of good fortune, and asked his dear old friend to
take him off the island in his ship, to which Holford
replied : " Charles, I shan't trust you aboard my
ship, unless I carry you as a prisoner, for I shall have
you caballing with my men, knock me on the head,
and run away with my ship a-pirating." No promises
of good behaviour from Vane would prevail on his
friend to rescue him; in fact, Captain Holford's
parting remark was that he would be returning in a
month, and that if he then found Vane still on the
island he would carry him to Jamaica to be hanged.

Soon after Holford's departure another ship put
in for water, none of the crew of which knew Vane by

sight, and he was too crafty to let them find out the
notorious pirate he was. They consented to take off
the shipwrecked mariner, when, just as all seemed to
be going well, back came the ship of friend Holford.
Holford, who seems to have been a sociable kind of
man, was well acquainted with the captain who was
befriending Vane, and Holford was invited to dine
on board his ship. As the guest was passing along
the deck of his host's ship on his way to the great
cabin he chanced to glance down the open hold, and
there who should he see but his dear old friend Vane
hard at work ; for he had already won his new master's
good graces by being a " brisk hand." Holford at
once informed his host that he was entertaining a
notorious pirate, and with his consent clapped Vane
in irons, and removed him to his own ship, and when
he arrived in Jamaica handed his old friend to the
justices, who quickly tried, convicted, and hanged him.

VANHORN, Captain Nicholas. A Dutch filibuste..
Of Hispaniola.

Sailed from England in 1681 in command of the
Mary and Martha, alias the *St. Nicholas,* a merchant
ship. Vanhorn soon showed his hand by putting two
of his merchants ashore at Cadiz and stealing four
Spanish guns. Next he sailed to the Canary Islands,
and then to the Guinea coast, plundering ships and
stealing negroes, until November, 1682, when he
arrived at the city of San Domingo. In April, 1683,
he picked up some 300 buccaneers at Petit Goave, and
joined the filibuster Laurens in the Gulf of Honduras
with six other buccaneer captains, who were planning
an attack on the rich city of Vera Cruz. The fleet
arrived off the city in May, and the pirates, hearing
that the Spaniards were expecting the arrival of two
ships from Caracas, they crowded a landing party of
800 men into two ships, and, displaying Spanish

colours, stood in boldly for the city. The inhabitants, imagining these were the ships they were expecting, actually lit bonfires to pilot them into the harbour. Landing on May 17th two miles away, they soon found themselves masters of the town and forts, all the sentinels being asleep. For four days they plundered the churches, convents, and houses, and threatened to burn the cathedral, in which they had put all the prisoners, unless more booty was forthcoming. An Englishman found the Governor hiding in some hay in a loft, and he was ransomed for 70,000 pieces of eight. While this was taking place a Spanish fleet of fourteen ships had arrived from Cadiz, and anchored just outside the harbour, but would not venture to land nor to attack the buccaneer ships. The buccaneers, feeling it was time to depart, sailed right past the fleet without opposition to a cay not far off, and there divided the spoils; each of the 1,000 sailors getting 800 pieces of eight as his share, while Vanhorn's own share was 24,000 pieces of eight. This division of the spoil did not take place without some bickering, and the two leaders, Vanhorn and Laurens, came to blows, and Vanhorn was wounded in the wrist. Although the wound was little more than a scratch, he died of gangrene a fortnight later.

It is significant that Vanhorn had originally been sent out by the Governor of Hispaniola to hunt for pirates, but once out of sight of land and away from authority the temptation to get rich quickly was too great to resist, so that he joined the pirates in the expedition to sack Vera Cruz.

VEALE, Captain.

On July 1st, 1685, he arrived at New London in a sloop, but was compelled to hurry away, being recognized as a pirate by one of the crew of a ship he had previously taken in Virginia.

VEALE, THOMAS.

One of four New England pirates who in the middle of the seventeenth century rowed up the Saugus river and landed at a place called Lynn Woods. The boat contained, besides the pirates, a quantity of plunder and a beautiful young woman. They built a hut on Dungeon Rock, dug a well, and lived there until the woman died. Three of the pirates were captured, and ended their days on the gallows in England.

Thomas Veale escaped and went to live in a cave, where he is supposed to have hidden his booty, but he continued to work as a cordwainer. In the earthquake of 1658 the cave was blocked up by pieces of rock, and Veale was never seen again.

VERPRE, CAPTAIN.   French filibuster.

His ship *Le Postillion* carried a crew of twenty-five men and was armed with two guns.

VIGERON, CAPTAIN.   French filibuster.
Of San Domingo.

Commanded a bark, *La Louse,* thirty men and four guns.

VILLA RISE.

In the year 1621 this Moorish pirate commanded a small squadron of five vessels which took an English ship, the *George Bonaventure* (Captain John Rawlins, Plymouth), in the Straits of Gibraltar.   One of the finest deeds ever achieved by English sailors was the escape of Rawlins and some of his crew from the Moors at Alexandria in a stolen ship.

VAN VIN, MOSES.   Buccaneer.

One of L'Ollonais's officers. After burning Puerto Cavallo and torturing and murdering the inhabitants,

L'Ollonais marched away to attack the town of San Pedro with 300 of his crew, leaving van Vin as his lieutenant to govern the rest of his men during his absence.

VIRGIN, HENRY.
  Of Bristol.

One of Major Stede Bonnet's crew of the *Royal James*. Hanged for piracy at White Point, Charleston, South Carolina, on November 8th, 1718, and buried in the marsh below low-water mark.

VIVON, CAPTAIN M. LA. French filibuster.

Commanded the *Cour Valant* of La Rochelle. In December, 1668, his ship was seized by Captain Collier for having robbed an English ship of provisions.

WAFER, LIONEL. Surgeon, buccaneer, and author.
  Believed to have been born about the year 1660.

He could speak Gaelic and also Erse, which languages he had learnt during his childhood, which was spent partly in the Highlands of Scotland and partly in Ireland.

In 1677 he sailed as mate to the surgeon of the *Great Ann*, of London (Captain Zachary Browne), bound for Java.

Two years later, he again sailed as surgeon's mate on a voyage to the West Indies. He deserted his ship at Jamaica and set himself up as a surgeon at Port Royal, but one day meeting with two noted buccaneers, Captain Linch and Captain Cook, he agreed to sail with them as ship's surgeon.

Wafer's subsequent adventures are recounted by Basil Ringrose in his "Dangerous Voyage and Bold Assaults of Captain Bartholomew Sharp and Others," and by William Dampier in his "New Voyage Round

the World." After taking part in 1679 in the futile
expedition of the buccaneers to Panama, Wafer joined
the party of malcontents who left Captain Sharp and
returned on foot across the Isthmus of Darien. Wafer
was accidentally wounded in the knee by an explosion
of gunpowder on May 5th, 1681, which he recounts
in his narrative as follows : " I was sitting on the
ground near one of our Men, who was drying of Gunpowder in a Silver Plate : But not managing it as
he should, it blew up and scorch'd my knee to that
degree, that the bone was left bare, the Flesh being
torn away, and my Thigh burnt for a great way above
it. I applied to it immediately such Remedies as I
had in my knapsack : and being unwilling to be left
behind by my companions, I made hard shift to jog
on."

The whole story of these adventures is told by
Wafer in a book he wrote, and which was published
in London in 1699. It is called " A New Voyage and
Description of the Isthmus of America, giving an
Account of the Author's Abode there," and is illus-
trated by some quaint copperplates.

Wafer and his companions suffered extreme hardships as they struggled through the dense tropical
jungle during the wettest season of the year.

On one occasion when in danger of his life, Wafer
was spared by the Indians owing to his skill as a
phlebotomist, after he had been allowed to exhibit his
skill to an Indian chief called Lacentra, when he bled
one of his wives so successfully that the chief made
Wafer his inseparable companion, to the no little discomfort of the buccaneer, who wished to reach the
Atlantic and rejoin his companions who had left him
behind.

Wafer described the birds, animals, fishes, and
insects with considerable minuteness, although it is
obvious that he had no special training in, or great

gift for, natural history. Wafer eventually reached Philadelphia, where he availed himself of King James's general pardon to pirates.

WAKE, CAPTAIN THOMAS.

A notorious pirate, one of those particularly named in the Royal Warrant issued in 1695 to Captain Kidd, authorizing him to go in search of the American pirates.

WALDEN, JOHN, *alias* " MISS NANNEY."
Born in Somersetshire.

Taken in the *Blessing*, of Lymington, by Roberts in Newfoundland, he joined the pirates, and was later on hanged at the age of 24 in West Africa. Walden was one of Captain Roberts's most active men. On taking Captain Traher's ship, Walden carried a pole-axe with which he wrenched open locked doors and boxes. He was a bold and daring man, of violent temper, and was known amongst his shipmates by the nickname of Miss Nanney. He lost a leg during the attack on the *Swallow*. After the pirates took the *King Solomon,* Walden had to get up the anchor, but he cut the cable, explaining to the captain that the weather was too hot to go straining and crying " Yo Hope," and he could easily buy another anchor when he got to London.

WANSLEY, THOMAS.

A negro steward on the brig *Vineyard,* he mutinied and assisted to murder the captain and mate, afterwards becoming one of Captain Charles Gibbs's crew. Hanged at New York in February, 1831.

WANT, CAPTAIN.

A Carolina pirate who was referred to at the trial of Captain Avery's crew at London in 1696.

WARD.

One of the first English pirates to establish himself on the Barbary coast in North Africa. By the year 1613 some thirty others had their headquarters at the mouth of the Sebu River.

WARD, Captain.

As a poor English sailor he went to Barbary, turned Mohammedan, offered his services to the Moors, and became captain of a galley. He grew to be very rich, and "lived like a Bashaw in Barbary."

WARREN, William.

Joined Captain Pound's crew from Lovell's Island.

WATERS, John.
Of Devonshire.

Quartermaster to Captain Charles Harris. Tried and hanged at Newport, Rhode Island, on July 19th, 1734. Aged 35.

WATKINS, John.

An English soldier stationed at Fort Loyal, Falmouth, Maine. Deserted and sailed with the pirate Pound. Killed at Tarpaulin Cove in 1689.

WATLING, Captain John. Buccaneer.

When Bartholomew Sharp's crew mutinied on New Year's Day in 1681 on the *Most Holy Trinity*, they clapped their captain in irons and put him down below on the ballast, and elected an old pirate and a "stout seaman," John Watling, in his place. One of the reasons for the revolt was said to be the ungodliness of Captain Sharp.

Watling began his command by giving orders for

the strict keeping of the Sabbath Day, and on January
9th the buccaneers observed Sunday as a day apart,
the first for many months. One of the first acts of
this godly Captain Watling was to cruelly shoot an
old man, a prisoner, whom he suspected, quite
wrongly, of not telling the truth.

On January 30th Watling headed a surprise attack
on the town of Arica in North Chile, but it turned out
later that the Spaniards had three days' warning of
the intended attack, and had gathered together no less
than 2,000 defenders. A furious attack was made,
with great slaughter of the Spanish defenders and
considerable loss amongst the pirates. In one attack
Watling placed 100 of his prisoners in front of his
storming party, hoping this would prevent the enemy
firing at them. After taking the town, the buccaneers
were driven out owing to the arrival of a number of
Lima soldiers. During the retreat from the town
Watling was shot in the liver and died. Perhaps he
gave his name to Watling Island in the Bahama
Islands, the first spot of America that Christopher
Columbus ever saw, and a great resort of the buccaneers.

WATSON, HENRY.

One of Captain Lowther's crew in the *Happy
Delivery*. Hanged at St. Kitts on March 11th,
1722.

WATTS, EDWARD.
Born at Dunmore.

One of Captain Roberts's crew. Hanged in 1722 at
the age of 22.

WATTS, SAMUEL.
Of Lovell's Island.

One of Captain Pound's crew.

WATTS, William.
An Irishman.

Hanged, at the age of 23, along with the rest of Roberts's crew.

WAY, John.

Tried at Boston in 1704 for piracy with the rest of the crew of the *Charles* brigantine.

WEAVER, Captain Brigstock.
Of Hereford, England.

One of Captain Anstis's crew in the *Good Fortune* when he took the *Morning Star*. After the prize had been converted for Anstis's use, Weaver was given command of the *Good Fortune*. He proved himself to be a capable pirate captain, taking between fifty and sixty sailing ships in the West Indies and on the Banks of Newfoundland.

Here are particulars of a few of his prizes:

In August, 1722, he took a Dutch ship, and out of her got 100 pieces of holland, value £800, and 1,000 pieces of eight. On November 20th in the same year he plundered the *Dolphin*, of London (Captain William Haddock), of 300 pieces of eight and forty gallons of rum.

Out of the *Don Carlos* (Lot Neekins, master) he stole 400 ounces of silver, fifty gallons of rum, 1,000 pieces of eight, 100 pistols, and other valuable goods.

Out of the *Portland*, ten pipes of wine valued at £250.

This period of prosperity came to an end, for in May, 1723, Weaver, dressed in rags, was begging charity at the door of a Mr. Thomas Smith in Bristol, telling a plausible tale of how he had been taken and robbed by some wicked pirates, but had lately managed to escape from them. The kindly Mr.

Smith, together with a Captain Edwards, gave Weaver £10 and provided him with a lodging at the Griffin Inn. Being now dressed in good clothes, Weaver enjoyed walking about the streets of Bristol, until one day he met with a sea-captain who claimed former acquaintance and invited him into a neighbouring tavern to share a bottle of wine with him. Over this the captain reminded the pirate that he had been one of his victims, and that Weaver had once stolen from him a considerable quantity of liquor; but at the same time he had not forgotten that the pirate had used him very civilly, and that therefore, if he would give him four hogsheads of cider, nothing further would be said about the matter. Weaver would not, or could not, produce these, and was apprehended, brought to London, and there tried and sentenced to death, and hanged at Execution Dock.

WELLS, LIEUTENANT JOSEPH.

An officer on board Captain John Quelch's *Charles* galley. Attempted to escape at Gloucester, Massachusetts, in the *Larimore,* but was captured by Major Sewell and brought to Salem, and there secured in the town gaol until tried for piracy at Boston in June, 1704.

WEST, RICHARD.

One of Captain Lowther's crew. Hanged at St. Kitts in March, 1722.

WETHERLEY, TEE.

A Massachusetts pirate, with only one eye. Captured in 1699 with the pirate Joseph Bradish and put in prison. They escaped two months later. A reward of £200 was offered for the recapture of Wetherley, which was gained by a Kennekeck Indian called Essacambuit, who brought him back to prison. He was taken, in irons, to England in H.M.S. *Advice* in 1700, and tried and hanged in London.

WHETSTONE, Sir Thomas, or Whitstone.   Buc-
    caneer.

In 1663 he commanded a ship, a Spanish prize, armed with seven guns and carrying a crew of sixty men.   In August, 1666, Sir Thomas was with a small English garrison of some sixty men in the buccaneer stronghold of New Providence in the Bahama Islands. Suddenly a Spanish fleet arrived from Porto Bello, and after a siege of three days the garrison capitulated.   The three English captains were carried prisoners to Panama and there cast into a dungeon and bound in irons for seventeen months.

WHITE, Captain Thomas.   South Sea pirate.
    An Englishman.   Born at Plymouth.

As a young man he was taken prisoner by a French pirate off the coast of Guinea.   The French massacred their prisoners by painting targets on their chests and using them for rifle practice.   White alone was saved by an heroic Frenchman throwing himself in front of him and receiving the volley in his own body.   White sailed with the French pirates, who were wrecked on the coast of Madagascar.   White himself managed to escape, and found safety with a native, King Bavaw, but the French pirates were all massacred.   White not very long afterwards joined another pirate ship, commanded by a Captain Read, with whom he sailed, helping to take several prizes, amongst others a slave ship, the *Speaker*.   White soon found himself possessed of a considerable fortune, and settled down with his crew at a place called Methelage in Madagascar, marrying a native woman, and leading the peaceful life of a planter.   The call of piracy at length proving irresistible, he sailed before the mast with Captain Halsey, then returned to his native wife and home, shortly afterwards to die of fever.

In his will, he left legacies to various relatives and friends, and appointed three guardians for his son, all of different nationalities, with instructions that the boy should be taken to England to be educated, which was duly done.

White was buried with the full ceremonies of the Church of England, his sword and pistols being carried on his coffin, and three English and one French volley fired over his grave.

WHITE, James.

Hanged in Virginia in 1718 along with the rest of Captain Edward Teach's crew.

WHITE, Robert.

One of Captain George Lowther's crew. Hanged on March 22nd, 1722, at St. Kitts.

WHITE, William.

A Newfoundland fish-splitter. With John Phillips and three others, he stole a fishing-boat at St. Peter's Harbour in Newfoundland in August, 1723. The other four were made officers in the pirate craft, White having the distinction of being the only private man in the crew of five. He appears to have been a man lacking in ambition, as he never showed any desire to become even a petty officer amongst the pirates; in fact, we hear no more of William until June 2nd, 1724, when he was hanged at Boston and "dy'd very penitently, with the Assistance of two grave Divines that attended him."

WHITTING, William.

One of Captain Quelch's crew. In 1704 we read that he "lyes sick, like to dye, not yet examined" in the gaol at Marblehead, when awaiting trial for piracy.

WIFE, Francis.

An unwilling mutineer with Philip Roche in a French vessel sailing from Cork in 1721.

WILES, William.

One of John Quelch's crew of the brigantine *Charles*. Tried at Boston in 1704.

WILGRESS, Captain. Buccaneer.
Of Jamaica.

Sent by the Governor of Jamaica in 1670 to search for, and capture or sink, a Dutchman called Captain Yallahs, who had entered the Spanish service to cruise against the English logwood cutters. But Wilgress, instead of carrying out his orders, went a-buccaneering on his own account, chasing a Spanish vessel ashore, stealing logwood, and burning Spanish houses along the coast.

WILLIAMS, Captain John, *alias* " Yanky." Buccaneer.

In 1683, when the pirate Hamlin in his famous ship, *La Trompeuse*, was playing havoc with the English shipping around Jamaica, Governor Lynch offered Williams a free pardon, men, victuals, and naturalization, and £200 as well if he would catch the Frenchman.

WILLIAMS, Captain Morris. Buccaneer.

In November, 1664, he applied to Governor Modyford to be allowed to bring into Port Royal, Jamaica, a rich prize of logwood, indigo, and silver, and, in spite of the Governor's refusal, he brought the ship in. The goods were seized and sold in the interest of the Spanish owner. At this time the English Government was doing all it could to stamp out the pirates and buccaneers.

WILLIAMS, Captain Paul.

A Carolina pirate, who began as a wrecker with the pirate Bellamy in the West Indies. He later on took to piracy and ended a not too glorious career by being hanged at Eastman, Massachusetts. Williams was one of the pirates who accepted King George's offer of pardon at New Providence Island in 1718.

WILLIAMS, David.

This son of a Welsh farmer was a poor pirate but a born soldier. He was described by one who knew him as being morose, sour, unsociable, and ill-tempered, and that he "knew as little of the sea or of ships as he did of the Arts of Natural Philosophy." But it is recorded to his credit that he was not cruel. He started life in a merchant ship bound for India, and was accidentally left behind in Madagascar. Taken care of by friendly natives, he fought so well on the side of his benefactors in an inter-tribal battle that the King made him his intimate friend. A little later this tribe was wiped out and Williams taken prisoner. The King of this hostile tribe, knowing Williams to be a brave man, put him in charge of his army, for his success as a leader was known far and wide. He was next seized by a very powerful King, Dempaino, who made him Commander-in-Chief over his army of 6,000 men, and supplied him with slaves, clothes, and everything he could want. After several years as commander of Dempaino's army, a pirate ship, the *Mocha* (Captain Culliford), arrived on the coast, and Williams escaped in her and went for a cruise. He was afterwards captured by the Dutch pirate Ort Van Tyle of New York, and made to work as a slave on his plantation. After six months he escaped and sought safety with a Prince Rebaiharang, with whom he lived for a year. He next joined a Dutchman, Pro, who had a small settlement, to be again taken prisoner by an English frigate. In a skirmish between the crew and some natives, Williams and Pro managed to escape, and, procuring a boat, joined Captain White's pirates at Methalage, in Madagascar.

Williams now spent his time pirating, unsuccessfully, until one day in a sloop he attempted a raid on an Arab town at Boyn. This attempt proved a fiasco, and Williams was caught by the Arabs, cruelly tortured, and finally killed by a lance thrust. He was so loved and admired by the Madagascar natives that his friend and benefactor, King Dempaino, seized the Arab chief of Boyn and executed him in revenge for the death of Williams. Williams seems to have been as much beloved by the natives as he was hated by men of his own colour. As a pirate he was a failure, but as a soldier of fortune with the native tribes he was a great success.

WILLIAMS, John.

A Cornish pirate, who sailed from Jamaica with Captain Morrice, and was captured by the Dutch. Eventually he reached Boston, and sailed with Captain Roderigo in 1674 in the *Edward and Thomas*, a Boston vessel.

Tried for piracy, but acquitted.

WILLIAMS, Lieutenant James. Welsh pirate.

Sailed as a hand on board the *George* galley from Amsterdam in 1724. Conspiring with Gow to bring about a mutiny, he took an active part in murdering the captain, the chief mate, super cargo, and surgeon. Gow promoted him to be his mate. He was a violent, brutal man, and a bully. On one occasion, he accused Gow of cowardice, and snapped his pistol in Gow's face, but the weapon failed to go off, and two seamen stand-

ing by shot Wiliams, wounding him in the arm and
belly. The next day Gow sent away a crew of prisoners in a sloop he had taken and plundered, and
Williams, heavily manacled, was cast into the hold of
this vessel, with orders that he should be given up as
a pirate to the first English man-of-war they should
meet with. He was taken to Lisbon and there put on
board H.M.S. *Argyle,* and carried to London. When
Gow and his crew eventually arrived in irons at the
Marshalsea Prison, they found Williams already there
awaiting trial. Hanged at Newgate on June 11th,
1725, his body being hanged in chains at Blackwall.

WILLIAMS, WILLIAM.
" Habitation—nigh Plymouth."

One of Captain Roberts's crew. Deserted the
pirates at Sierra Leone, but was delivered up by the
negroes, and as a punishment received two lashes
from the whole ship's company. Hanged at the age
of 40.

WILLIS, ROBERT.

One of Captain George Lowther's crew. Tried for
piracy at St. Kitts in March, 1722, and acquitted.

WILSON, ALEXANDER.

One of the mutineers of the ship *Antonio*. Hanged
at Boston in 1672.

WILSON, GEORGE. Surgeon and pirate.

Originally he sailed as surgeon in a Liverpool ship,
the *Tarlton,* which was taken by the pirate Bartholomew Roberts. Wilson voluntarily joined the pirates.
One day, being accidentally left on shore, he had to
remain amongst the negroes at Sestos on the West

Coast of Africa for five months, until he was eventually rescued by a Captain Sharp, of the *Elizabeth*, who ransomed Wilson for the value of £3 5s. in goods. Wilson was again captured by Roberts, and served with him as surgeon. At his trial for piracy at Cape Coast Castle in 1722, witnesses proved that Wilson was " very alert and cheerful at meeting with Roberts, hailed him, told him he was glad to see him, and would come on board presently, borrowing a clean Shirt and Drawers " from the witness " for his better Appearance and Reception : signed the Articles willingly," and tried to persuade him, the witness, to sign also, as then they would each get £600 or £700 a man in the next voyage to Brazil.

When the election of senior surgeon took place, Wilson wanted to be appointed, as then he would receive a bigger share of the booty. Wilson became very intimate with Captain Roberts, and told him that if ever they were taken by one of the " Turnip-Man's ships "—*i.e.*, a man-of-war—they would blow up their ship and go to hell together. But the surgeon proved such a lazy ruffian, neglecting to dress the wounded crew, that Roberts threatened to cut his ears off.

At the trial Wilson was found guilty and condemned to be hanged, but his execution was withheld until the King's pleasure was known, because it was believed that owing to information given by Wilson a mutiny of the prisoners was prevented.

WILSON, JAMES.
    Of Dublin.

One of Major Stede Bonnet's crew in the *Royal James*. Hanged at Charleston, South Carolina, on November 8th, 1718, and buried in the marsh below low-water mark.

WILSON, JOHN.

Of New London County.

Tried for piracy in 1723 at Newport, Rhode Island, and acquitted.

WINTER, CAPTAIN CHRISTOPHER.

Of New Providence Island.

He took a sloop off the coast of Jamaica, the mate on board which was one Edward England, who, on Winter's persuasion, turned pirate and soon reached the summit of his new profession.

In 1718 Winter accepted the King's offer of pardon to all pirates who surrendered. Winter soon afterwards not only returned to piracy, but did even worse, for he surrendered to the Spanish Governor of Cuba, and turned Papist. From Cuba he carried on piracy, chiefly preying on English vessels, and made raids on the coast of Jamaica, stealing slaves, which he took away to Cuba. The Governor of Jamaica, Sir Nicholas Laws, sent Lieutenant Joseph Laws, in H.M.S. *Happy* snow, to demand the surrender of Winter and another renegade, Nicholas Brown, but nothing resulted but an exchange of acrimonious letters between the Lieutenant and the Governor of Cuba.

WINTER, JOHN.

One of Gow's crew in the *Revenge*. Hanged in 1725 at Wapping.

WINTER, WILLIAM, *alias* MUSTAPHA.

A renegade English sailor amongst the Algiers pirates. Taken prisoner in the *Exchange,* on which vessel he was carpenter.

WINTHROP.

One of Fly's crew. Took an active part in the mutiny aboard the *Elizabeth*. Winthrop it was who chopped off the hand of Captain Green, and in a fight with Jenkins, the mate, severed his shoulder with an axe and then threw the still living officer overboard. He was hanged at Boston on July 4th, 1726.

WITHERBORN, Captain Francis.

Captured, with his ship, by Major Beeston and brought to Jamaica. Tried for piracy at Port Royal, he was condemned to death, and sent a prisoner to England.

WOLLERVY, Captain William.

A New England pirate who sailed in company with a Captain Henley in 1683 off the Island of Elenthera. He burnt his vessel near Newport, Rhode Island, where he and his crew disappeared with their plunder.

WOOD, William.
Native of York.

One of Captain Roberts's crew. Hanged in April, 1722, at the age of 27.

WORLEY, Captain.

His reign was short, lasting but six months from start to finish. He was first heard of in September, 1718, when he set out, in company with eight other desperadoes, from New York in a small open boat "upon the account." They were provided with a few biscuits, a dried tongue, and a keg of water, half a dozen old muskets and some ammunition. They sailed down the coast for 150 miles, entered the river Delaware, and rowed up to Newcastle, and there seized a shallop. The news of this enterprise was quickly spread abroad, and roused the whole coast. Going down the river again, still in their open boat, they took another sloop belonging to a mulatto called Black Robbin. They changed into this sloop, and next day met with another sloop from Hull, which suited their purpose better. By now the country was much alarmed, and the Government sent out H.M.S. *Phœnix,* of twenty guns, to cruise in search of the pirates. In the meantime the latter sailed to the Bahama Islands and took another sloop and a brigantine. Worley now commanded a tidy craft of six guns and a crew of twenty-five men, and flew a black ensign with a white death's head upon it. So far all had gone well with the pirates, but one day, when cruising off the Cape of Virginia, Worley sighted two sloops as he thought making for the James River, but which were really armed vessels sent in search of him. Worley stood in to cut them off, little dreaming what they really were. The two sloops and the pirate ship all standing in together, Worley hoisted his black flag. This terrified the inhabitants of Jamestown, who thought that three pirates were about to attack them. Hurried preparations for defence were made, when all of a sudden the people on shore were surprised to see the supposed pirates fighting amongst themselves. No quarter was asked, and the pirates were all killed in hand-to-hand fighting except Captain Worley and one other pirate, who were captured alive but desperately wounded. The formalities were quickly got through for trying these two men, so that next day they were hanged before death from their wounds could save them from their just punishment. "Thus," writes Captain Johnson, "Worley's beginning was bold and desperate, his course short and prosperous, and his end bloody and disgraceful."

WORMALL, Daniel.

Master on the brigantine *Charles,* commanded by Captain John Quelch. Attempted to escape from Gloucester, Massachusetts, by sailing off in the *Larimore* galley, but was followed and caught by Major Sewell and taken to Salem. Here he was kept in the town gaol until sent to Boston to be tried for piracy in June, 1704.

YALLAHS, Captain, or Yellows. A Dutch buc-
    caneer.

In 1671 fled from Jamaica to Campeachy, there selling his frigate to the Spanish Governor for 7,000 pieces of eight. He entered the Spanish service to cruise against the English logwood cutters, at which business he was successful, taking more than a dozen of these vessels off the coast of Honduras.

YEATES, Captain.

In 1718 this Carolina pirate commanded a sloop which acted as tender to Captain Vane. When at Sullivan Island, Carolina, Yeates, finding himself master of a fine sloop armed with several guns and a crew of fifteen men, and with a valuable cargo of slaves aboard, slipped his anchor in the middle of the night and sailed away.

Yeates thought highly of himself as a pirate and had long resented the way Vane treated him as a subordinate, and was glad to get a chance of sailing on his own account. Yeates, having escaped, came to North Edisto River, some ten leagues off Charleston. There, sending hurried word to the Governor to ask for the Royal pardon, he surrendered himself, his crew, and two negro slaves. Yeates was pardoned, and his negroes were returned to Captain Thurston, from whom they had been stolen.

ZEKERMAN, ANDREW.

A Dutch pirate, one of Peter M'Kinlie's gang, who murdered Captain Glass and his family on board a ship sailing from the Canary Islands to England. Zekerman was the most brutal of the whole crew of mutineers.

He was hanged in chains near Dublin on December 19th, 1765.

SOME FAMOUS PIRATE SHIPS, WITH
THEIR CAPTAINS

Black Joke	Captain de Soto.
Bravo	,, Power.
Flying Horse	,, Rhoade.
Fortune	,, Bartholomew Roberts.
Royal Fortune	,, Bartholomew Roberts.
Good Fortune	,, Bartholomew Roberts.
Batchelor's Delight	,, Dampier.
Delight	,, Spriggs.
Flying King	,, Sample.
Night Rambler	,, Cooper.
Cour Valant	,, La Vivon.
Most Holy Trinity	,, Bartholomew Sharp.
Flying Dragon	,, Condent.
Sudden Death	,, Derdrake.
Scowerer	,, Evans.
Queen Ann's Revenge	,, Teach.
Happy Delivery	,, Lowther.
Snap Dragon	,, Goldsmith.
Revenge	Captains Cowley, Bonnet, Gow, Phillips, and others.
Bonne Homme Richard	Captain Paul Jones.
Blessing	,, Brown.
New York Revenge's Revenge	,, Cole.
Mayflower	,, Cox.
Childhood	,, Caraccioli.
Liberty	,, Tew.